Just for Men: A Practical Daily Devotional Guide for Men

By

Dr. David Nichols

PRESS

Preface

⟨∿⟩

For more than forty years I have endeavored to walk with God each day. His constant love and never-ending grace have been sufficient for me despite my own weaknesses and failures. God has been so good to me through every circumstance of life. I have been the recipient of His blessings when I knew that I was unworthy. He has been my strength through times of disappointment, physical illness, spiritual crises, temptation, failure, disillusionment and despair. Though I stumbled many times during those forty years, He has always been there to lift me up, dust me off and restore me to fellowship with His Holy Spirit.

I have had the privilege of regularly reading His Word, listening to Spirit-anointed messages from passionate ministers and learning about real life experiences, not only through my own, but from those of other Godly men who share their deepest hurts and struggles. This daily devotional is for every Christian man who has felt that no one cares or understands the dilemmas and crises he faces. Many Godly men continue to be burdened with the legalistic notion that they have to be "good" to be a Christian and to be accepted by their wives, friends and fellow believers. When they find themselves not meeting the expectations of others and those of their own, they become weary and ready to give up. It is the aim of each day's scriptures and commentary to offer daily encouragement by sharing stories from the Bible about ordinary men like themselves who failed miserably but were not discarded by God. Instead He took them where they were and used them mightily to accomplish His purpose.

God wants to do the same for you. God wants you to be proud of your masculinity. He wants to use your masculinity to be a courageous warrior fully clothed with His armor. He accepts no less than a man who is willing to surrender his own will and accept the purpose for which he was made. Every scripture and every commentary is written to encourage you in your daily walk with God and to help you understand that you can be a conqueror through total dependence on Him. It is my hope that as you awaken each morning and read the day's devotion that you will find yourself growing deeper in His love and grace. I pray that you will trust Him completely, more than in yourself. I believe that you will discover the real peace and joy you can have everyday as you walk in Him as a Godly man. May God richly bless you and inspire you to reach out and touch the lives of others each and every day.

David Nichols

January 1
A New Man for a New Year

"Cast away from you all the transgressions which you have committed, and get yourselves a new heart and a new spirit." Ezekiel 18:31
"Therefore, if anyone is in Christ, he is a new creation; old things have passed away; behold, all things have become new." I Corinthians 5:17

The first day of a new year conjures a feeling that you can shed your old self with all its flaws, failures and foolish decisions and replace it with a new and better man who will make good decisions and enhance your walk with God this year. In this Colossians scripture, Paul is addressing relatively new Christians reminding them that since Jesus rescued them from sin and eternal death, that they should no longer practice carnal, sinful behaviors, but become new Christ-like people evidenced by their holy conduct and conversation. As a Christian man, you can strive to become a "new man" this year in all areas of your life. There is truth to the "feeling" you have that you can have a new start with high expectations to live life to its fullest. As a renewed man in Christ you can make a difference in those with whom you come in contact. Ask God to renew your mind and spirit and to give you a deeper knowledge of Him so that your life will be a reflection of His. Then walk in the Spirit daily, knowing that you are a new creation in Christ.

January 2
A Commitment......Not a Resolution

"Meditate on these things; give yourself entirely to them, that your progress may be evident to all. Take heed to yourself and to the doctrine. Continue in them, for in doing this you will save both yourself and those who hear you." I Timothy 4: 15-16
"Therefore, brethren, stand fast and hold the traditions which you were taught, whether by word or our epistle." II Thessalonians 2:15

New Years resolutions are good intentions to do things better in the year ahead. They are fine and can result in positive changes in your life. Many well-intended resolutions seem to fade as the days, weeks and months go by and at the end of the year you either forgot your resolutions or realize you did not achieve them. However, you can successfully achieve your goals for this year if you replace those self-made resolutions with a Christ-based commitment. In our scripture for today, Paul is motivating a young man, Timothy, to set his mind and his efforts on *"these things."* Paul is encouraging Timothy to be an example *"in word, in conduct, in love, in spirit, in faith, in purity." (I Timothy 4:12)*

Ed McElroy of *USAir* stated: "Commitment gives us new power. No matter what comes to us – sickness, poverty or disaster – we never turn our eye from the goal." (1) During your prayer time today, ask God to show you an area in your life in which a genuine commitment to improve is needed and ask Him for perseverance to keep your eye on the goal.

January 3
The Right Time and Place

"Oh God, You are my God: Early will I seek you;" Psalm 63:1
"And when He had sent the multitude away, He went up on the mountain by Himself to pray." Matthew 14:23

Prayer is worship. Prayer is communion with our Heavenly Father. Prayer is the lifeblood for Christian discipleship. Prayer is powerful. Prayer changes circumstances and people.

Whether you call it your quiet time, your devotional time or your prayer time, it is essential for the man of God to find the right time and the right place to get alone with God every single day. It should not be viewed as optional or dispensable. There must be a commitment to a daily prayer time where there are no distractions or interferences. In the first of the two scripture passages we find David rising early in the morning to pray. In the second, Jesus removed all distractions and found a place of solitude. Every individual has a best time of day for prayer. It is important that if praying in the evening is the most opportune time for you, then that is when you should set aside adequate time and a place to be alone with God. I find that starting my day with time with God better prepares me to deal with life. If for the next 362 days, you read God's Word, pray, and use a devotional guide, you will experience spiritual growth, touch the lives of others, and find peace and strength through life's inevitable struggles.

January 4
His Amazing Grace

"By grace you have been saved through faith, and that not of yourselves; it is the gift of God." Ephesians 2:8
"My grace is sufficient for you, for My strength is made perfect in weakness." II Corinthians 12:9.
"You therefore, my son, be strong in the grace that is in Christ Jesus." II Timothy 2:1

Grace......God's goodness manifested to undeserving man. God's unmerited favor. As a child growing up in rural Alabama attending a small country church, I recall hearing the small congregation sing "Amazing Grace", often without instrumental accompaniment. I can hear the harmony, see the tears, and feel the fervor of their gratitude for God's grace. "Amazing grace, how sweet the sound that saved a wretch like me. I once was lost but now am found; was blind but now I see." (2) The grace of God is the fundamental basis for salvation through Jesus' death and resurrection. God's provision of grace changes you forever. It took me nearly 30 years to comprehend the significance, the depth and the assurance of God's grace. Though much is written and preached about grace, it is still difficult to comprehend God's marvelous "no matter what" grace toward His children. As you begin or end this day, be confident that His grace covers you and it is sufficient for all of your failures, your sin, your shortcomings, your struggles and your doubts.

January 5
When God Does Not Calm Your Storm

"Now when neither sun nor stars appeared for many days, and no small tempest beat on us, all hope that we would be saved was finally given up" **Acts27:20** *"But the centurion...commanded those who could swim should jump overboard first and get to land." Acts 27:43*
"The Lord has His way in the whirlwind and in the storm, and the clouds and dust of His feet." Nahum 1:3

The storms of life are inevitable, even for the Christian. You are not immune from crises and overwhelming circumstances in which there seem to be no way out. We know that Jesus calmed a storm when he and His disciples were out to sea simply by saying, "Peace Be Still" (Mark 4:39). But He does not always do that and you may not understand why He is just not there to say, "Peace, be still" for all to become calm. Yet, as a Christian your faith can keep you safe during the storm and you will be stronger and wiser when it passes. The words of a contemporary song, "Sometimes He Calms the Storm" (3), say it well: "Sometimes He calms the storm and other times He calms His child." Whatever storm you face now or in the future, remember that though the storm may be long and strong, Jesus is still the master of the sea and the pilot of your ship.

January 6
Behold and Appreciate His Creation

"And the men are shepherds, for their occupation has been to feed livestock; and they have brought their flocks, their herds, and all that they have" Genesis 46:32

"When I consider Your Heavens, the work of Your fingers, the moon and the stars, which you have ordained." Psalm 8:3

Some men enjoy being outdoors. It offers you a feeling of freedom. The Bible is full of accounts of men who worked outdoors. As in the story of Joseph and his brothers, our scripture describes their occupation. They spent most of their lives raising and living with sheep. They watched the stars and responded to impending weather. For you men who work, jog, camp with the family or bike outdoors there is something that connects you to God's nature. For Christian men, it offers opportunities to be alone with God, to behold His creation and to commune with Him. By beholding His handiwork, you experience another aspect of Him as the Creator of all things. You can gain perspective of just how small you are in such an immeasurable universe. Life's problems can seem less significant. Perhaps most importantly you will be renewed in mind, body, and spirit. Pray today that God will remind you to be in awe of His creation and to have a new appreciation for the skies, the sun, the moon, the stars and the rivers which flow through the valleys.

January 7
Making Choices

"And if seems evil to you to serve the Lord, choose for yourselves this day whom you will serve......But as for me and my house, we will serve the Lord."
Joshua 24:15

For over six years of my career I served as an associate dean of students at a Christian university. A significant part of my responsibilities included dealing with student misconduct. It was a wonderful experience since I usually had the opportunity to meet one-on-one with students. It gave me the opportunity to counsel young men and women. Whether the student conduct violation was plagiarism, assault, or alcohol possession/consumption, it always came down to the same issue - making choices. You make choices everyday, some routine and less significant than others. Yet, inevitably you have to face decisions which involve more serious matters such as your integrity, your faithfulness, your spiritual conduct, and a myriad of other decisions affecting not only you but your family. In today's scripture, Joshua had just reminded the Israelites about God's faithfulness despite their tendency to worship other gods. His decision was easy and firm because he had made his decision to serve the Lord long ago and nothing would change his mind. That's what I tried to instill in those college students. As a Godly man, a firm decision to do the right thing is essential long before the moment you face a temptation.

January 8
The Secular Culture's Assault on Masculinity

"Then the Spirit of the Lord came upon him; and the ropes that were on his arms... and his bonds broke loose from his hands. He found a jawbone of a donkey, reached out his hand and took it, and killed a thousand men with it." Judges 15:14-15
"...then he arose at midnight, took hold of the gate of the city ad the two gateposts, and pulled them up, bar and all and put them on his shoulders, and carried them to the top of the hill." Judges 16:3

The Bible is replete with real men of courage, strength and faith. David, a musician, poet and song writer, was a valiant warrior in battle. Daniel chose the lions' den rather than to cease praying to God. Moses chose to obey God rather than live in luxury and power. Paul chose to be beaten and stoned for preaching Christ. In today's scripture passages, one of the most physically strong men found in the Bible, Sampson, represents the ultimate in masculinity, though he ultimately yielded to sin. Today, you are bombarded with men on TV sitcoms, in the movies, and in the entertainment business who portray effeminate characteristics, attempting to make that image more acceptable. While physical size or strength is not necessary to be a real man, God's men were masculine and were spiritual leaders of their families. Reject the new tolerance and political correctness which may diminish what God made you to be. Ask God today to develop you into a man of courage, strength, and faith.

January 9
Man to Man... Support and Accountability

"Two are better than one, because they have good reward for their labor. For if they fall, one will lift up his companion..." Ecclesiastes 4:9-10
"Brethren, if a man is overtaken in any trespass, you who are spiritual restore such a one in a spirit of gentleness, considering yourself lest you also be tempted. Bear one another's burdens, and so fulfill the law of Christ." Galatians 6:1-2

It is your responsibility to uphold and encourage other Christian men. You will find difficulty in enduring the race, resisting temptation and getting up after falling without a Godly brother being there to help. Often you struggle with an ethical or morality issue. Sometimes a trusted "accountability partner" can help you to make right choices and to encourage you. Former University of Colorado football coach, Bill McCartney, speaking at Promise Keepers rally said, "We have not come to compete. We have come to complete one another." (4) If you see a fellow Christian moving toward engaging in sin or is already involved, pray for him and ask the Holy Spirit if you should intervene and pray with him. If you see a Christian brother experiencing difficulty, with the Holy Spirit's guidance, is there to listen, to encourage and to stand with him through his storm. Bob Barnes, in his book, **"15 Minutes Alone with God for Men"** prays: "Direct me to a group of men who will be good role models and who will hold me accountable to my promise." (5) Let this be your prayer to God today.

January 10
A Balanced Man

"And when He had removed him [Saul], He raised up for them David as king, to whom also he gave testimony and said, 'I have found David as king...a man after My own heart, who will do all my will'." Acts 13:14

"Look, I have seen a son of Jesse... who is skillful in playing [the harp], a mighty man of valor, a man of war, prudent in speech, and a handsome person; and the Lord is with him." I Samuel 16:18

It is important that you be temperate in all things and not be "overdone" or consumed with only one activity or life interest. By living a balanced life, you are more likely to be healthier, have more relationships and broaden your interests. Some men become so single-minded about their favorite activity, whether it is golf, body building, fishing, or even work, to the exclusion of family, friends, and a variety of experiences. David represents the most balanced man in the Bible. As a young man he was a shepherd boy, an accomplished harpist and a giant killer. He was a mighty warrior. He was a leader. He was a poet and songwriter. He was a devoted friend. He was a man of prayer. He worshiped God in dance. And most importantly, he was a man after God's own heart. If you find yourself giving too much time and effort to only one thing, ask God if you should step out of your box and discover the challenges of finding new interests. The Holy Spirit can broaden your horizons with new challenges and opportunities. And He'll always provide you with the ability and courage to accept them.

January 11
Needed: Real Men to Stand in the Gap

"So I sought for a man among them who would make a wall, and stand in the gap before Me on behalf of the land, that I should not destroy it; but I found no one." Ezekiel 22:30
"Watch, stand fast in the faith, be brave, and be strong. I Corinthians 16:13

At this particular time in today's scripture God's people in Jerusalem had rebelled against Him. Ezekiel was a prophet who was sent by God to warn the people of Israel that if they didn't turn from their sin, they would be destroyed and scattered. Israel's leaders, prophets, and priests had become wicked and there was no one to rise to the occasion and turn the people back to the Lord. God had looked for one righteous man to step up to the plate and to make an effort to lead the people back to Him. He found not one man to "stand in the gap." Our secular culture attempts to remove God from public life. People in America have become de-sensitized. Openly vulgar entertainment and a lack of moral values are tolerated. Godly men are needed. You are needed to "stand in the gap" in your home, in your community and in your workplace. You may face persecution and resistance, but it is important that every Christian man become Spirit-filled and bold to take a stand for Christ. As you pray today, ask God to give you holy boldness to stand up, speak out, and stand in the gap.

January 12
Sin's Inevitable Consequences

"Yet they did not obey or incline their ear, but everyone followed the dictates of his evil heart;"
Jeremiah 11:8
Therefore thus says the Lord: Behold, I will surely bring calamity on them which they will not be able to escape;" Jeremiah 11:11
"...you have sinned against the Lord; and be sure your sin will find you out." Numbers 32:23

In the Old Testament God punished people for their sin and disobedience. God sent consequences for sin. However, Jesus' crucifixion and resurrection cleared the debt and consequences of sin for those who become Christ's followers. As the Apostle Paul asked and answered, "Shall we continue in sin that grace may abound? Certainly not!" (Romans 6:1) God no longer punishes you for your sin because of Christ's sacrifice. God has already forgiven your sins on the cross. But the "fallout" from your sin and disobedience often can sometimes be much worse than if God still administered the consequences. Adultery, for example, will have long-lasting effects on your life and the lives of others. Even if you think no one knows and you got by with it, it impacts your relationship with your wife, your children, and takes it toll on your emotions knowing that you have been unfaithful to your wife and to God. Every sin has its consequence on you and others. Ask God today to remind you when you are faced with a choice to sin that is He is there to give you victory, thus, giving you peace of mind that your joy may be full.

January 13
Where is God When I Need Him?

"Now Martha said to Jesus, 'Lord, if you had been here, my brother would not have died'." John 11:21
"...and His mother said to Him, 'Son, why have You done this to us? Look, Your father and I have sought You anxiously." Luke 2:48

The entire eleventh chapter of John surrounds Jesus' raising his beloved friend, Lazarus, from the dead. Though Lazarus' sisters, Mary and Martha, sent for Jesus to come immediately to Bethany and pray for their ailing brother, he did not go immediately. He delayed going to Bethany for two days, during which time Lazarus died and was buried. Have you ever really needed Jesus to be there and He just didn't seem to show up? Chuck Norris, the six-time World Professional Middle Weight Karate Champion, did. (5) At seventeen years old, Chuck gave his heart to Christ at a Billy Graham crusade. After years of training and winning, he experienced a rotator cuff tear that wouldn't heal. For three years, he suffered with this ailment and felt that his career was over. Where was God when he needed him? He was there all along, but for some unknown reason waited three years to provide healing. Remember that God's timing is not always in our time zone. As you pray today, thank God for his constant presence through the indwelling of the Holy Spirit and ask Him for the assurance that He knows the right time to show up...and He will.

January 14
Dealing with Disappointment

"But the Lord said to my father David, 'Whereas it was in your heart to build a temple for My name, you did well that it was in your heart. Nevertheless you shall not build the temple, but your son whom will come from your body, he shall build the temple of my name.'" I Kings 8:18-19

"Then, when Mary came where Jesus was, and saw Him, she fell down at His feet, saying to Him, Lord, if You had been here, my brother would not have died." John 11:32

Disappointment has and will come your way. It could be a missed promotion, a lost job, your child's bad choices, or failure to reach a career goal. Sometimes disappointment comes in more devastating forms. You may face the disappointment of an unfaithful spouse or a personal disability. In today's first scripture, David had wanted to and had planned to build a temple for the Lord. However, God chose to deny David the opportunity to build His temple, rather appointing David's son Solomon for the job. Building the temple of the Lord in Jerusalem would have been the crowning accomplishment of David's life. He was disappointed, but he accepted God's decision with humility. The second scripture finds Mary disappointed that Jesus had not arrived sooner – before Lazarus died. Remember, when you experience disappointment, it may be God's way of protecting you, knowing that He has something better in His perfect timing. Thank God for His infinite wisdom. His Holy Spirit will be your comforter in times of disappointments. Ask Him to teach you how to respond to disappointments which may come your way.

January 15
Hunting: It's a Man Thing

"So the boys grew. And Esau was a skillful hunter, a man of the field; but Jacob was a mild man, dwelling in tents." Genesis 25:27

Historians tell us that for many men have an innate drive to get outdoors to hunt and to bring home food. They attribute this drive to part of a man's nature. Whether that is theory or science, millions of men are avid hunters. They take pride in their pick-up trucks with rifle/shotgun racks in the back window. You may spend countless hours in the woods hunting. If not, it doesn't make you any less of a man. Some guys are more into golf, tennis, or other less rugged sports. But if you're the kind of man with a yearning to get out and hunt from dawn to dusk, then you know that there is that opportunity to feel close to God. As you enjoy your hunting, consider ways to make Him part of your experience. Be in awe of God's creation of the nature's outdoors. Also, enjoy the fellowship of other Godly men, pray silently, meditate on Him, relax, and deepen your fellowship with the Holy Spirit. And, above all, listen closely when God speaks to you through His Holy Spirit. Perhaps God may provide the perfect opportunity to share your testimony with a fellow hunter of what Jesus means in your life.

January 16
Sickness, Disease and Disabilities

"For indeed he was sick almost unto death; but God had mercy on him…" Philippians 2:27
"Bless the Lord, O my soul, and forget not all His benefits: Who forgives all your iniquities, Who heals all your diseases…" Psalm 103:2-3
"And a certain man lame form his mother's womb was carried, whom they laid daily at the gate of the temple…" Acts 3:2

Since the beginning of time, sickness, disease, and disabilities have plagued mankind. Social status, eating right, wealth, exercise or living a Godly life do not make you immune from the human condition caused by the original sin of man. You should know that you will experience illness, or disease, or disability if you live long enough. Your family is not immune either. Can and does God still heal? Absolutely. Does He heal those for whom we pray? Sometimes. Since we do not know the mind of God, we do not understand His purpose or His plan for the future. We do know of thousands of people who have been healed as a result of prayer. Research studies clearly indicate that patients in hospitals who had people interceding to God on their behalf, recovered more quickly than those who had no one praying for them. Always follow God's Word and pray for the sick and believe He will heal. He still does. But when he chooses not to heal, it makes Him no less the Almighty God who hears our every prayer.

January 17
<u>Confronting Anxiety and Depression</u>

"Be anxious for nothing, but in everything by prayer and supplication, with thanksgiving, let your requests be made known to God;" Philippians 4:6
"Now when neither sun nor stars appeared for many days...all hope that we would be saved was finally given up." Acts 27:20

Based on medical research both anxiety and depression are increasing at an alarming rate. Billions of dollars are spent on therapy, medications, and the many misdiagnoses attributed to these conditions. According to Richard O'Connor, Ph.D., "approximately 20 million Americans will experience an episode of major depression in their lifetimes." (7) Men, especially have trouble admitting they are depressed or are suffering from the related symptoms of anxiety. In this high-tech, high-paced society men struggle daily with these symptoms. Often it feels like life is not even worth living. O'Connor says that men are five times more likely to commit suicide than women. Are you ill-tempered? Are you sometimes so unhappy with life and even feel like crying? Do you tend to avoid friendships and social activities? Understand this: God does not want you to be anxious or to be depressed or to worry. Talk honestly to God today and open your heart, asking Him to give you peace of mind and heart. Seek His guidance in getting help from those trained in helping you recover from depression and anxiety. You may need medication. But as a Christian man, seek help for yourself and your family.

January 18
A Peace That Surpasses Understanding

"...and the peace of God, which surpasses all understanding, will guard your hearts and minds through Christ Jesus." Philippians 4:8
"I will both lie down in peace, and sleep: For you alone, O Lord make me dwell in safety." Psalm 4:8

Peace is sought by every human on earth. The opposite of peace is fear and anxiety. As a man of God, you can grow in the Lord and you can have His peace to comfort you in those everyday frustrations and worries. You can have His peace that "surpasses all understanding." You can have His peace when you lose your job, when a close loved one dies, when one of your children is very ill, when you have failed Him and when you face death. David was a marked man, hunted down by King Saul to kill him. He faced enemies many times, his young son died because of his disobedience and his own sons betrayed him. Yet, in the fourth Psalm, he slept in peace knowing that God his Father would watch over him and to keep him safe. In human terms, it is difficult for a man whose life is in turmoil to have that deep peace that only God can give. This is a promise of God and is available to you if you will turn to God and ask for a much needed divine peace and for trust that He is ever present. His grace is sufficient for you in every circumstance.

January 19
The Covenant of Marriage

"Therefore a man shall leave his father and mother and be joined to his wife, and they shall become one flesh." Genesis 2:24
"Marriage is honorable among all, and the bed undefiled; but fornicators and adulterers God will judge." Hebrews 13:4

Marriages in America now have about a fifty percent chance of ending in divorce. Many marriages are entered into with no counseling or planning. Brief engagements based solely on physical attraction and romantic feelings often do not last long. Some couples live together first before deciding if marriage is right for them. The Bible refers to this as "fornication." Marriage is a covenant which, according to Webster, is a "solemn, binding agreement between two individuals..." Marriage is about love, sex, sharing and taking care of one another "until death do you part." Unfortunately, many couples marry with the idea that the romantic feelings and the sex should remain at the pre-marriage intensity. And when these begin to "cool", often one spouse will say something to the effect of "Well, I just don't love him/her as I once did." Divorce seems to be the option rather than working to keep their commitment. Of course, there are exceptional circumstances in which divorce may be acceptable. Seek Godly counsel together and try to be sure that she is committed to God, to you, and to family for a lifetime. And be committed to her "till death do your part."

January 20
A Man's Role in the Family

"But I want you to know that the head of every man is Christ, the head of every woman is man, and the head of Christ is God." I Corinthians 11:3
"Let the husband render to his wife the affection due her, and likewise also the wife to her husband." I Corinthians 7:3
"Husbands, love you wives, just as Christ loved the church and gave Himself for her." Ephesians 5:25

In this day of relativism, the feminist movement, homosexual marriages and sex changes, you and your family sometimes may feel like you are out of step with a changing culture. Even some church leadership and church denominational officials reject the scriptures found throughout the Bible that man is the head of the family. Often you may begin to doubt the truth in these Biblical teachings. However, the Word of God today is as relevant as it has been for thousands of years. Peter, speaking of the Apostle Paul's epistles, warns of those who "twist [the scriptures] to their own destruction, as they do also the rest of the scriptures." (II Peter 3:16) As head of the home, the husband should be the spiritual leader and teach and model a Christian lifestyle. As the head of the family, the scripture is clear that you should love your wife. Men, treat your wife with respect, affection, kindness and faithfulness both at home and in public. Demonstrate your love through your attitude and actions such as helping her with household chores.

January 21
Being a Father: Unconditional Love

"But the father said to his servants, 'Bring out the best robe and put it on him, and put a ring on his hand and sandals on his feet'... 'For this my son was dead and is alive again; he was lost and is found'." Luke 15: 22, 24

Unconditional love...That is what God has demonstrated to mankind by sending His Son to the cross. Unconditional love......that is the message of this parable in Luke in which Jesus describes a father's reaction when his wayward son leaves home, squanders his inheritance and returns home penniless and desperate. The father saw his son coming from a distance and ran to welcome him home, despite the son deserting his father and home. Unconditional love is that of a father in our church who, without hesitation, donated one of his kidneys to his son who otherwise would have died. As a Godly man, no matter what your sons or daughters do, where they go, how much they disrespect you or how deep in sin they go, you must have that unconditional love that God, your Father, has for you when you sin, when you fail or when you turn your back on Him. Sometimes "tough love" may be appropriate, but the key word is "love" no matter what. It may be very difficult to accept a wayward adult child back and to forgive and to tell him/her they still have your unconditional love. But you can do no less than God has done for you.

January 22
Stepping in Your Footsteps: A Son

"Now the days of David drew near that he should die, saying: 'I go the way of the earth; be strong, therefore, and prove yourself a man. And keep the charge of he Lord your God: to walk in His ways, to keep His statutes, His commandments, His judgments, and His testimonies...that you will prosper in all that you do and wherever you turn:'" I Kings 2: 1-3

Just as David admonished his son Solomon, it is your responsibility to teach your son how to live a Godly life and how to value justice and righteousness. This is a tremendous responsibility. It is one you cannot shirk. For whether you accept this responsibility or refuse it, what you say, what you do, how you treat your wife, how you treat your fellowman and what you believe are the footsteps he will follow. As a child, I recall my Dad taking me rabbit hunting. Whether it was snow, mud or grass, I tried to place my footsteps in his. And as I become older, I recognize the influence my Dad had on me in so many ways. Your son is watching and listening whether or not you realize it. The words of the old hymn "Footsteps of Jesus" are so true today: "Footprints of Jesus that make the pathway glow; we will follow the steps of Jesus where-e'er they go." Set a Godly example and share with your son that the first priority of life is to follow Jesus. Let him see you pray, read your Bible and listen to you voice your faith in God.

January 23
Her Protector and Role Model: Your Daughter

"And behold, one of the rulers of the synagogue came, Jairus by name, and when he saw Him, he fell at His feet and begged Him earnestly, saying 'My little daughter lies at the point of death. Come and lay Your hands on her, that she may be healed, and she will live'." Mark 5: 22-23

If you have a daughter, you have the Godly responsibility as the head of the family to love her, to protect her, to be her Christian male role model and to let your know that you will always be there for her no matter what. Your daughter needs a father who is gentle with her and who adores her. She needs to know that you think she is beautiful and that you are proud of her. She will see men in the community, at church and at her friends' homes whom she will compare to you. She will watch your every action and listen to your every word. Though Jairus was a ruler in the synagogue he came humbly to Jesus on behalf of his daughter. That day, his position, his pride or the act of begging were of no importance to him because he loved his "little daughter" and was willing to do whatever it took to have Jesus pray for her and for her to become well. He loved his daughter with all his heart. As you pray today, ask God to make you the Godly father that you should be for your daughter. You should always be her most important man in the world.

January 24
God's Purpose for Your Life

"It's in Christ that we find out who we are and what we are living for. Long before we first heard of Christ...He had His eye on us, had designs for us for glorious living, part of the overall purpose He is working out in everything and everyone." **Ephesians 1:11, The Message**
"Who has saved us and called us with a holy calling, not according to our works, but according to His own purpose and grace..." II Timothy 1:9

Let's get this straight right up front. You were created for God's pleasure and He has a purpose for you. In other words, it is not about you or your plans. It is, however, to your advantage to discover His plans and His purpose for your life. In his book, "The Purpose Driven Life", Rick Warren puts in this way: "Bringing enjoyment to God, living for His pleasure, is the first purpose of your life. When you fully understand this truth, you will never again have a problem with feeling insignificant." (8) Many Christian men trudge through life not knowing why God created them or what His purpose is for them. Do you feel that you are able just to keep your head above water, do a devotional, go to church, and try to be good? God created you to become like Christ, to serve a special purpose, and to fulfill His mission for you. As you pray, ask God to open your spiritual eyes and your heart to His special purpose for you. He will.

January 25
Men and Pornography

"For this is the will of God, your sanctification: that you should abstain from sexual immorality; not in passion of lust, like the Gentiles who do not know God." I Thessalonians 4: 3, 5
"...having eyes full of adultery and that cannot cease from sin, enticing unstable souls..." II Peter 2:14

Christian men to include the clergy are not immune from that part of the male instinct which attracts them to sexuality and, sometimes illicit, illegal forms of sexual material. While some men struggle more than others, many are tempted at one time or another to pornographic material and/or movies. Some become addicted to the extent that it becomes harmful to their mental health, to their finances and, most importantly, to their families. On a "Focus on the Family"-related internet site, "Focus on Social Issues", Daniel L. Weiss states: "Whether or not one becomes addicted, virtually no one is immune to the mental, emotional, spiritual, and even physical effects of viewing pornography." He also puts pornography production in America at between $10 billion and $14 billion annually. This is an area of a Godly man's life that is a prime target of the devil. Men who travel overnight in their business are vulnerable to adult movies and magazines. Pray every day that the Holy Spirit will strengthen your resolve not to go near any pornography. As Paul wrote to the Thessalonians, "Abstain from every form of evil." (I Thessalonians 5:22) Ask God for the resolve not to take the first look.

January 26
The Fervent Prayer of a Righteous Man

"The effective, fervent prayer of a righteous man avails much." James 5:16

"Now while Ezra was praying, and while he was confessing,weeping, and bowing down before the house of God, a very large assembly of men, women and the children gathered to him from Israel; for the people wept very bitterly." Ezra 10:1

Most men know that prayer is a fundamental part of worshiping God and communicating needs to Him. However, many men underestimate the power of prayer and the effects of prayer. Ezra was praying to God for the people of Israel who were marrying pagan women in disobedience to God. While Ezra was praying, a group of Israelites came to him and committed to return to the true God and His commandments. In their book, ***Touch Points for Men***, Rhonda O'Brien and Jonathan Gray (9) describe prayer and its value:

1. "Prayer is an act of humble worship in which we seek God with all our hearts;
2. Prayer often begins with a confession;
3. Prayer is an expression of an intimate relationship with our heavenly Father;
4. Through prayer we praise our mighty God; and
5. Sometimes like Paul, we will find that God answers prayer by giving us not what we asked for but something better."

Ask God to help you pray more earnestly, believing for specific needs of your church, your unsaved friends, your family and other needs. Become an intercessor for others.

Pray in faith expecting God to do "abundantly above all that we [you] can ask or think."

January 27
It's "Hoops" Season: Follow the Rules of the Game

'And also if anyone competes in athletics, he is not crowned unless he competes according to the rules." II Timothy 2:5
"...the blessing, if you obey the commandments of the Lord your God which I command you today." Deuteronomy 11:27

It's that time of year that high school, university, and professional basketball players are in the early to mid part of their seasons. If you're a basketball fan, you know that winning teams are those teams which practice, condition their bodies, sharpen their skills and review the rules. If a player doesn't play by the rules, he can contribute to losing the game as well as affecting his personal self esteem and confidence. In the Godly man's game of life there are also rules, boundaries, and consequences. Breaking life's rules by being disobedient to God and/or practicing sin is out of bounds and there are consequences for you as well as those around you. Pray today, that in life as in sports you will stay conditioned and become well acquainted with His written word so as to avoid committing a foul. God expects you to be obedient and walk in the Spirit. And know this; it is a hard life to live for the Christian man who lives in disobedience. Ask God to help you be a star player on His team through listening to and obeying Him in all things.

January 28
Every Man's Struggle with Lust

"But I say unto you that whoever looks at a woman to lust for her has already committed adultery with her in his heart." Matthew 5:28
"But each one is tempted when he is drawn away by his own lust and enticed." James 1:14

Sexual lust is one of a Godly man's most difficult struggles. It is a subject seldom preached from the pulpits of our churches or discussed in Sunday school classes. Perhaps some men feel that they are unique among men having to deal with it. No illicit affair ever started without that first step of lust. It is important that men admit it and deal with this temptation. Bill Perkins says: "I've discovered that every man has his own personal battle with lust – nobody escapes its appeal. Nobody." (10) Jesus addressed it, David had a man killed because over it, and the New Testament writers confronted immorality within the ranks of the early Christian church. It is almost a constant battle that rages within some men. You are tempted at work, in the supermarket, driving down the highway, at social events and even at church. The good news is that God cares and wants you to win in this continuous struggle. I Corinthians 10:13 says. "…but God is faithful, who will not allow you to be tempted beyond what you are able, but with the temptation will also make the way to escape, that you may be able to bear it."

January 29
<u>The Love and Friendship of a Lifetime</u>

"The Lord said 'It is not good for the man to be alone'." Genesis 2:18
"Let your fountain be blessed, and rejoice with the wife of your youth. As a loving deer and a graceful doe, let her breasts satisfy you at all times; and always be enraptured with her love." Proverbs 5:19
"Live joyfully with the wife whom you love all the days of your vain life..." Ecclesiastes 9:9

What beautiful scriptures to describe the essence of a healthy marriage! Certainly, the best of marriages have problems and issues. But the deepening love and the intimate, growing friendship between a husband and his wife surpass any of the difficulties of marriage. Thirty five years ago God blessed me with the most wonderful gift a man could have. As unworthy as I am, He presented me with the most beautiful, the most devoted, the best friend, and the best mother for our children I could ever have imagined. Sure, we've had our share of "issues". But despite my struggles as a Christian man, her love and her devotion have kept us together thus far. Maybe you're struggling in your marriage relationship. Maybe you think the "grass is greener in other pastures". With very few exceptional circumstances, you should hold fast to your wife. Let God reveal to you what a privilege and joy it is to love your wife. It is God's will and purpose for you to renew that love, joy, and friendship with the girl you asked to be your wife "for better or for worse."

January 30
<u>A Man of Integrity</u>

"These are the things that you shall do: Speak each man truth to his neighbor; Give judgment in your gates for truth, justice, and peace." Zechariah 8:16
"The righteous man walks in his integrity; His children are blessed after him." Proverbs 20:7

Revelations of embezzlement resulting in the collapse of major corporations, cheating scandals in professional sports and immoral and illegal behavior of our elected officials cause one to wonder if there is any integrity left in our traditional institutions. How do we know if the guys in the white hats are still the good guys? My Dad grew up on a farm where he plowed the fields with a mule and quit school in the seventh grade. At seventeen he got a job working in the ore mines where he worked for twenty-nine years until they closed down. Our new car was re-possessed. Then he worked eighteen more years in a cement plant where he retired and died a year later. He never had much money, social status, and never bought another new car. But he had something that he passed on to me – integrity. John C. Maxwell writes: "Anyone can say that he has integrity, but action is the real indicator of character. Your character determines who you are. Who you are determines what you see. What you see is what you do." (11) Christian man, it is your responsibility to be a man of integrity. You represent Jesus and His church.

January 31
<u>Getting Revenge</u>

"Vengeance is Mine, and recompense; Their foot shall slip in due time." Deuteronomy 32:35
"If you are reproached [insulted] for the name of Christ, blessed are you, for the Spirit of glory and of God rests upon you." I Peter 4:14
"But I tell you not to resist an evil person. But whoever slaps you on your right cheek, turn the other over to him." Matthew 5:39

Revenge is a natural inclination of the carnal man. However, the Bible is very clear that we are to leave vengeance to God. This may run counter to your masculine nature. However, no matter how angry, how full of rage or wronged you've been, revenge belongs to God. That separates the believer from the non-believer. As a husband and father, whose wife or child has been offended, it can be difficult not to exact revenge of the wrongdoer. However, civil and criminal laws do not permit one to take revenge on someone who wrongs you. Now, revenge and justice are different. If you suffer for being a Christian that is religious persecution which the scriptures say you are to endure. Otherwise, there are avenues and processes that are available to you to see that justice and punishment is accomplished for the wrong-doer. Pray today that, though you may feel the need and right to get revenge that God will give you the inner strength to let Him handle it, and trust that He will. Jesus says to love your enemies.

REFERENCES FOR JANUARY

1. John C. Maxwell, "The 21 Indispensable Qualities of a Leader" (Nashville, Tennessee, Thomas Nelson Publishers, 1999) 18
2. John Newton, "A Homecoming Celebration" Compiled and arranged by Tim Fettke" (Gaither Music Company, 2004) 97-98
3. Kevin Stokes and Tony Wood, "Sometimes He Calms the Storm", (BMG Songs and Careers-BMG Publishing Company, Inc.) 1995
4. John C. Maxwell, "Teamwork Makes the Dream Work" (J. Countryman, a division of Thomas Nelson, Inc., Nashville, Tennessee) 2002
5. John Barnes, "15 Minutes Alone with God for Men" (Harvest House Publisher, Eugene Oregon) 1995 p.63
6. Chuck Norris, "Chuck Norris: Against the Odds, My Story" (Broadman and Holman Publishing, Nashville, Tennessee) 2004
7. Richard O'Connor, "Undoing Depression" (Berkley Books, New York) 1997
8. Rick Warren, "The Purpose Driven Life" (Zondervan, Grand Rapids, Michigan) 2002
9. Rhonda O'Brian and Jonathan Gray, (Tyndale House Publishers, Wheaton Illinois) 1996 p.199-201
10. Bill Perkins, "When Good Men are Tempted" (Zondervan, Publishing House, Grand Rapids, Michigan) 1992 p.9
11. John C. Maxwell, "The 21 Indispensable Qualities of a Leader" (Thomas Nelson Publishers, Nashville, Tennessee) 1999 p.4

February 1
"Jesus Loves All the Children of the World—Red and Yellow, Black and White"

"There is neither Jew nor Greek, there is neither slave nor free, there is neither male nor female; for you are all one in Christ Jesus." Galatians 3:28

"And he [Peter] arose and went. And behold, a man of Ethiopia, a eunuch ...had come from Jerusalem to worship, was returning. And he [the eunuch] answered and said 'I believe that Jesus Christ is the Son of God.'" And both Peter and the Eunuch went down into the water, and he baptized him." Acts 8:27, 37, 38

February is Black History month. It is celebrated across the America to commemorate the history and struggles of the African-American. Over three hundred years ago many black Africans were taken from their native land and brought to America as slaves. Though slavery was outlawed during the late nineteenth century, significant efforts gain equal treatment and equal rights were not begun until a freedom movement led by Dr. Martin Luther King, Jr. His leadership eventually led to changes in federal and state laws. God's love and grace never acknowledged differences in race or ethnicity. Our scriptures for today show that the Kingdom of God is for all people in all the earth. In the Bible the Jews considered the Gentiles [you and me] as not worthy of knowing God. The Jewish priests despised the very presence a Gentile. There are sects, groups and individuals who have difficulty accepting the fact that Jesus died for all. Ask God to search your heart and remove any prejudice toward individuals of different races and love them as your brothers and sisters in Christ. And never hinder or limit sharing the gospel with all peoples.

February 2
<u>Your Rock in Times of Storms</u>

"When my heart is overwhelmed; Lead me to the rock that is higher than I" Psalm 61:2
"...I will liken him to a wise man who built his house on the rock: and the rain descended, the floods came, and the winds blew and the beat on the house; and it did not fall, for it was founded on the rock." Matthew 7:24-25

Storms of life will come; that is a fact. As a believer, you have a strong, unmovable rock to which you can go and to which you can cling. That rock is Jesus. You may face storms of financial failure, marital problems, job loss, temptation, depression, disease and disability, death, war or a host of other major crises which you may consider storms. There will be times when you have no one which to turn or your family and friends can offer no real help. But remember, if you are God's man, your life is founded upon Christ the rock, the foundation on which you are secure until the storms passes by. The lyrics to a song which George Beverly Shea often sang at Billy Graham's crusades are so encouraging: "That rock is Jesus, the only one; be very sure, be very sure, your anchor holds and grips the solid rock." That is the same rock to which David referred in Psalm 18:3: "The Lord is my rock and my fortress and my deliverer;" Ask God today to keep your feet planted on the rock of Christ that is higher and stronger than any storm that you go through or any problem that you face.

February 3
Rest in the Lord

"Come to me, all you who labor and are heavy laden, and I will give you rest." Mathew: 11:28
"Rest in the Lord, and wait patiently for Him."
Psalm 37:7

Men tend not to get enough rest for optimal health. Many men work long hours, go to bed late, get up early and do it all again. Other men's hours are set, but the kind of work they do may be stressful mentally and physically. As a former police officer sometimes assigned to the night shift, I found that I never got enough rest and sleep during daytime hours. Eventually, I developed health problems. According to an article in "Men's Health" magazine, if you're working with weights to increase muscle size and strength you should incrementally increase the weight and repetitions. This requires enough rest. (1) God wants you to rest to renew your physical and spiritual strength. Jesus frequently retreated to places of solitude for prayer and rest. You will be healthier physically, emotionally, and spiritually when your body gets sufficient rest. As you pray, ask God to help you get more rest to better enjoy your family and to more effectively serve Him.

February 4
Use Your Sword

"For the word of God is living and powerful, and sharper than any two-edged sword..." Hebrews 4:12

"And take the helmet of salvation, and the sword of the Spirit, which is the word of God." Ephesians 6:17

A sword is used in warfare or a duel with an opponent. It was a sword that killed King Saul, swords were the primary weapons used in wars throughout the Old Testament. It was with a sword that Peter cut off the ear of one of the soldiers who came to take Jesus. In today's scripture the writers use the sword to represent the word of God. As a real sword is used for war, the sword of the Spirit is used in your spiritual warfare that you fight daily. In the sixth chapter of Ephesians, Paul tells the Christians at Ephesus to put on the whole spiritual armor of God. All of the pieces of armor he lists are defensive ones except "the sword of the Spirit which is the word of God". The sword is included because God knows that as a Christian soldier you will face the enemy every day and you will need the word of God. Daily planned Bible reading, along with devotional books are important for you to learn the word of God. The sword of the word of God is sharp and powerful and will be useful to you in claiming spiritual victories.

February 5
Coping with Adversity

"And a great and effective door has opened to me, and there are many adversaries." I Corinthians 16:9
"We are hard-pressed on every side, yet not crushed; we are perplexed, but not in despair, persecuted, but not forsaken; struck down, but not destroyed." II Corinthians 4:9

As a Christian you will face adversity and opposition if you serve the Lord and obey Him. Whatever you do for the kingdom of God the devil will be against you and try to defeat you. This is particularly discouraging when adversity often comes from fellow brothers and sisters in Christ. That's what Nehemiah experienced as he obeyed God in rebuilding the walls of Jerusalem which had been torn down some seventy years earlier. As he and the people built they were ridiculed, threatened, and scoffed at by religious critics. Charles R. Swindoll writes: "Nehemiah was faced with opposition – those sidewalk supervisors who would have had him discontinue building the Jerusalem wall. He did two significant things in response to the criticism: He prayed and he persisted." (2) Bill Perkins writes: "The identity of a warrior isn't destroyed by adversity, it's strengthened." (3) Read God's word, seek Him in prayer and begin to follow His purpose for your life. Ask God to strengthen you from it and then do as Nehemiah – pray and persist.

February 6
Trust God in All Things

"Yes, we had the sentence of death in ourselves, that we should not trust in ourselves but in God who raises the dead, who delivered us from so great a death, and does deliver us; in who we trust that He will still deliver us." II Corinthians 1:9-10
"He will not be afraid of evil tidings; His heart is steadfast, trusting in the Lord." Psalm 112:7

Trusting God…really trusting God is one of the most difficult commandments men face because "being in control" is part of our masculinity. To completely trust God means to let go of your control (or attempt to control) the circumstances. It means that you are to stop worrying needlessly. It means that you place the person and/or the circumstances into God's control and believe that He can solve the problem, meet the need or change the person without your help. That's a tough task, but it's time that you have peace of mind. As difficult as it is, trust Him totally with every area of your life. Despite the problem, despite the person, despite the seemingly overwhelming circumstances facing you today, say to God: "God I have been unable to resolve this thing. I come to You now in faith and give it up and put it in Your hands. Strengthen my faith in You and help be believe beyond a doubt that you will handle this." God can be trusted in His own time and in His own way to "work all things for good".

February 7
Controlling Your Anger

"Cease from anger and forsake wrath..." Psalm 37:8
"Be angry, and do not sin; do not let the sun go down on your wrath..." Ephesians 4:26

It is okay to be angry. In fact, in some circumstances you should be angry. Temper and anger are part of your masculinity. As a man, you are expected to rise to the occasion in defense of your wife and family. God became angry with the children of Israel for their disobedience many times. Moses was angry when he came down from the mountain where God had given him the Ten Commandments, and he saw the people of God worshiping idols. Jesus surely must have been angry when he made rope whip and drove the money changers from the temple of God. Peter got angry enough to cut of an ear of one of the soldiers who came to take Jesus. However, anger must be God-controlled. In other words there is a right time and a right place and a right reason to be angry, but never allow your anger to become sin. Guard your tongue and your actions. As a Godly man, you must be a Christian role model. If you have a problem with anger, seek out a Christian counselor. Ask God to help your listen to the Holy Spirit and, through wisdom, control your anger.

February 8
Stay Focused

*"But He gives more grace. Therefore He says:
'God "I press toward the goal for the prize of the
upward call of God in Christ Jesus." Philippians
3:14
"You will keep him in perfect peace whose mind
is stayed on you." Isaiah 26:3*

You have so much expected of you; family, career, church,
community service, your children's activities and responsibilities you have which often consume your attention and
time. You know that you are a Christian man and you know
that God's grace is sufficient. But sometime you become so
entangled with our earthly commitments, though worthy,
you lose focus of God's purpose of you staying prepared for
spiritual challenges. As a warrior, you must put on the armor
of God and focus on the battle that is being waged everyday
for your soul. As an athlete, if you are to win the game or
the race, you must stay focused on the goal of winning and
reaching the finish line. Read today's scriptures again. Are
you "pressing toward the goal"? Are your thoughts really
staying on Godly things? Now would be a good time to re-
focus your life on Christ by seeking Him in sincere prayer.
Ask Him to renew your strength.

February 9
<u>Growing In Grace</u>

"But grow in the Grace and knowledge of our Lord and Savior Jesus Christ..." II Peter 3:18
"You therefore my son, be strong in the grace that is in Christ Jesus." II Timothy 2:1

As a man of God you have been once and for all freed from the curse of sin in Jesus through God's grace. Placing theological interpretations and expositions aside, Webster defines grace as: "unmerited divine assistance given man for his regeneration or sanctification." The Apostle Paul says that we have all sinned, but we are justified "...by His grace through the redemption that is in Christ Jesus" (Romans 3:24) He really nailed it down in Romans 5:20: Moreover the law entered that the offense might abound. But where sin abounded, grace abounded much more." Therefore you do not have to "work" for salvation, but rest in His sufficient grace. God does want you to grow, or mature, in grace. Paul, admonishes young Timothy to be "nourished in faith and good doctrine", not to neglect his God-given gift and meditate on living a Godly life. James writes to the early Christians who are struggling with temptation, "but He gives more grace." Peter charges Christians to become steadfast in this grace. As you pray today, thank God for His abundant grace and ask Him that you grow you in grace so that you will become a mature warrior for Him.

February 10
Dealing with Discouragement

"Look, the Lord your God has set the land before you; go up and possess it, as the Lord God of your fathers has spoken to you; do not fear or be discouraged." Deuteronomy 1:21
"Nevertheless God, who comforts the down-casts, comforted us by the coming of Titus." II Corinthians 7:6

You have experienced discouragement and will experience it again. A synonym for discouragement is "to dishearten". Discouragement can come out of nowhere when you least expect it. You can experience discouragement over major life crises or over minor unfulfilled expectations. It can range from not getting a promotion at work to the betrayal by a close friend to losing your house by a fire. Discouragement can be crippling spiritually if you do not turn to God and seek His comfort and strength. That's an advantage you have as a Christian man. You have the Holy Spirit within you to speak encouraging and hopeful words to you. There is a gospel song that offers encouragement for those times you become discouraged. The lyrics of "Hide Thou Me" say: *"Sometimes I feel discouraged and think my work's in vain; I'm tempted oft to murmur and complain. But then I think of Jesus and all He's done for me. Then I cry to the Rock of Ages, 'Hide thou me'."* (4) As you pray today, ask God to give you His peace and His trust that will sustain you through any discouragement.

February 11
The Significance of a Man's Work

"Whatever you do, whether in word or deed, do it all in name of Jesus." Colossians 3:17
"So I sent messengers to them, saying, 'I am doing a great work, so that I cannot come down. Why should the work cease while I leave it and go down to you?'" Nehemiah 6:3

My Dad told me several times: "Son, work is honorable. Respect any man who works..." Work is a significant part of every man's life whether he it brings him pleasure or if it is drudgery. There is no where in the scriptures where God instructs man to stop working, even if he retires. Paul both preached and was a tentmaker to support his ministry. He had little patience for those who did not work. He told the Thessalonians, "If anyone will not work, neither shall he eat." The Bible is replete with men who worked. It was expected and honored so that a man provide for his family and give offerings to God. Eugene H. Peterson writes: "Dignity is inherent in work. A major and essential task of the Christian is to recover work as a vocation – as holy work. Every Christian takes holy orders." (5) Don't become obsessed with your work and career, but work you should. Pray today that your work will be as unto the Lord and part of His purpose for a spiritually fulfilled life. Take pride in your work and look for ways to make it a ministry. Remember, "Work is honorable."

February 12
<u>Overcoming Fear</u>

"For God has not given us a spirit of fear, but of power and of love and of a sound mind." II Timothy 1:7

"Yes, though I walk through the valley of the shadow of death, I will fear no evil, for You are with me; Your rod and Your staff, they comfort me." Psalm 23:4

There are two types of fear: 1.There is the fear of the Lord which you should possess as a Christian. 2. There is the fear that comes from Satan's efforts to cause you not to trust God. Stuart Briscoe says this about the fear of the Lord: "When we fear the Lord, our overriding desire is to honor his majesty and respect his authority while appropriating his grace, reveling in his love, basking in his forgiveness, and seeing only to please him." (6) Many men today suffer with unholy fear…fear of losing your salvation, fear of growing old, fear of dying, fear of a person and fear of not coping with life. If you are dealing with fear, know that God wants you to have peace in your mind and heart. Most of your spiritual battles take place in your mind. Fear comes from not trusting God. Fear can be crippling. Let today be the beginning of seeking God to remove your fear and give you "that peace that surpasses understanding." Read Isaiah 41:10: "Fear not, for I am with you, be not dismayed for I am your God."

February 13
The Real Measure of Success

"And He said to them, 'for one's life does not consist in the abundance of the things he possesses'." Luke 12:15
"Beloved, I pray that you may prosper in all things and be in good health, just as your soul prospers." III John: 2

Often men, in particular, measure their success or that of other men by money, wealth, and power. These are not the things with which the Bible measures the success of a man. There are many wealthy entrepreneurs in America. Sam Walton, for example, started Wal-Mart as a small store in 1945. By the year 2000 he had expanded his business to 3,000 stores with over $150 billion in revenues. (7) At his death in 1996, David Packard of "Hewlett and Packard" left a personal estate worth $5.6 billion. (8) While both of these men may have been good men, did their massive wealth they left behind, make them successful? In Ecclesiastes 5:10 Solomon says: "He who loves silver will not be satisfied with silver; nor he who loves abundance, with increase. This is also vanity." At the end of your life, your success will be measured in how you walked with God and served others in His name. The best epitaph you can have engraved on your headstone is what God said of Joseph after he had been betrayed by his brothers and was a slave in Egypt: "The Lord was with Joseph, and he was a successful man;" (Genesis 39:2).

February 14
Love is......

"In this is love, not that we loved God, but that He loved us and sent His Son to be the propitiation for our sins." I John 4:10
"For this is the love of God, that we keep His commandments." I John 5:3

God's love transcends human understanding. Today is the celebration of Valentine's Day, a day for you to give candy, flowers and cards to your special lady. The modern-day Valentine's Day love comes from the Greek word *eros*, relating to sensual or romantic desire. God's love in the Greek is *agape*, meaning Christ-like love. Love is described in the thirteenth chapter of I Corinthians. Love is placed above faith: "and though I have faith that could move mountains, but have not love, I am nothing." (I Corinthians 13:2) God loved you enough to send His son to die for your sins. God wants you to return His love with all your heart, your mind and your strength. His love should compel you to share His love in every aspect of your life. Your thoughts, your attitudes, your service to others and your faith all should be motivated by your deep abiding love for God. Ask God to increase your love for Him so that love's attributes are seen your life. The words of a song say it all: "I love you, I love you; that's what Calvary said; I love you, I love you, I love you - written in red." (9)

February 15
Staying Physically Fit and Healthy

"Therefore I run thus: not with uncertainty. Thus I fight: not as one who beats the air. I discipline my body and bring it into subjection, lest, when I have preached to others, I myself should become disqualified." I Corinthians 9:26-27

In the scriptures for today, Paul emphasizes keeping physically fit. It is his intention and expectation not to become physically disabled so as to lose or diminish his work for Christ. Perhaps you have never thought of physical fitness as important to your spiritual life. But the Godly man should include physical fitness along with his emotional and spiritual fitness so that he will be able to be his best in serving the Lord's work for many years. Getting and staying physically fit also serve to enhance your self-esteem, your energy to work and play and your mood – which affects everyone around you. In addition to a healthy, balanced diet, there are two general kinds of physical training you should do strength training and endurance exercise. This means lifting weights moderately and walking or jogging regularly to improve your cardio-vascular system. Your physical condition and appearance speaks volumes of about you. As a man of God you should model discipline of body and spirit. While God does not want you to become obsessed with physical fitness, he does want you to follow Paul's admonition to discipline your body as you should your mind and spirit.

February 16
Give God That Which Belongs to God

"You shall truly tithe all the increase of your grain that the field produced year by year."
Deuteronomy 14:22
"For you pay tithe and anise and cumin, and have neglected the weightier matters of the law: justice and mercy and faith. These you ought to have done, without leaving the others undone."
Matthew 23:23

The Bible is clear that Christians are to give one-tenth of their income to God. Additionally, we are to give offerings to our local church and/or to missionary needs. It is part of worship. In Malachi 3:10, God warned the people of Judah that they had not been faithful in giving to God that which was His. He said: "Will a man rob God? Yet you have robbed Me! But you say, 'In what way have we robbed You?' In tithes and offerings." Paying tithes and offerings is an issue some Christians question. While it is not a requirement of your salvation, by your disobedience to God's word you are missing a blessing beyond what you can imagine. I have heard many testimonies of couples who, when they started tithing, found that their financial problems disappeared and they began to prosper. This has been my family's experience. It is called the Biblical economy and it doesn't make sense to most secular financial advisors. But you cannot out give God. The way to financial prosperity is to give in obedience to His command. If you've never tithed seek God on this spiritual matter.

February 17
God's Promised Blessings

"Blessed be the Lord, who daily loads us with benefits." Psalm 68:19
"For I know the thoughts that I think toward you, says the Lord, thoughts of peace and not of evil, to you a future and a hope." Jeremiah 29:11

Let's cut to the chase today. God's word is absolutely full of His promises to bless those who follow Him in obedience. Books are written just on His blessings. He promises to bless you. Now, it is up to you to receive His blessings. Start thanking Him for what He has promised you in His word. Begin today by reading the promises in the scriptures above. As you spend time in prayer and reading your Bible, study the many blessings and promises He has made. Then thank Him for all those He is already given you; Your home, your wife and family, your health, your job, your church, your friends, your salvation, His grace, His peace, and many more blessings. In terms of material blessings, in comparison to most of the world, Americans are rich. But His spiritual blessings far exceed those material things that you have. As you pray, begin to claim His blessings and receive them with gratitude. The twenty-third verse of the third chapter of Lamentation nails it all down: "Great is Your faithfulness;"

February 18
The Habit of Worry

"Then He said to His disciples, 'Therefore I say to you, do not worry about your life..." Luke 12:22
"Do not fret, it only causes harm." Psalm 37:8
"Be anxious for nothing, but in everything by prayer and supplication, with thanksgiving, let your requests be known unto God." Philippians 4:6"

Worry, like depression, is often seen as a women's condition, but not a "real man's" problem. But men worry too. As the head of the family, you're considered the "bread winner" even if your wife works. You're probably responsible for the house maintenance, the yard, the automobiles, the finances and any major crisis. Then there are work issues, relationship problems and even church issues. The Bible, from cover to cover, speaks with clarity about worry. DON'T! It is useless. You worry, not about the present but about what might happen in the future whether tomorrow, next week or next year. The psalmist says worry only causes harm. It can lead to anxiety and affect your health. Max Lucado writes: "He promises a lamp unto our feet, not a crystal ball into the future. We do not need to know what will happen tomorrow. We only need to know he leads us and 'we will find grace to help us when we need it'." (10) (Heb.4:16 NLT). If you worry, ask God's to transfer any future thoughts of concern to Him and trust His omniscient power and "know that all things work together for good." (Romans 8:28)

February 19
Believe, Confess, and Repent

"If you confess with your mouth the Lord Jesus and believe in your heart that God has raised Him from the dead, you will be saved." Romans 10:9
"I have not come to call the righteous, but sinners, to repentance." Luke 5:32

Men, there are a few basic tenets about accepting Jesus as Lord which you should understand and embrace. An unsaved person must recognize that Jesus died for his sin and he is in need of a Savior who paid the price for that sin. As the Holy Spirit speaks to his heart, he must first believe that Jesus is the only way to eternal life. Then he must confess that he is a sinner, accept Jesus as Lord, which includes repenting or turning from his sinful lifestyle. Simple, yet many reject Jesus. There is the notion that it only requires believing that He is the Son of God. However, James, writing to the early church says "You believe that there is one God. You do well. Even the demons believe – and tremble!" (James 2:19) A majority of Americans believe in God, but many do not know Him as Savior. Don't accept that just believing who Jesus is and joining a church without a spiritual re-birth will make Jesus Lord and Savior of anyone's life. Believe, confess, and repent...it is that simple. It will change a heart, mind, and conduct. Live out your salvation as a witness to others.

February 20
<u>Hope: More Than a Wish</u>

"For we are saved in this hope, but hope that is seen is not hope; for why does one still hope for what he sees? But if we hope for what we do not see, we eagerly wait for it with perseverance." Romans: 8: 24, 25

"This hope we have as an anchor of the soul, both sure ad steadfast, and which enters the presence behind the veil, where the forerunner has entered for us, even Jesus…" Hebrews 6:19-20

Often Christians think of hope as a wish or as a desire. It's often used in the context of: "I hope is doesn't rain tomorrow." That is not the hope that God gives. His hope is interwoven in trust, faith, and grace. Our hope is a for sure thing. Our hope is in the promise of God. In the book, "Touch Points for Men", several observations are made about hope: 1. "The Lord himself is the source of hope because he determines our future. 2. God has proven his power over everything, and by this power he keeps his promises. 3. Hope it trusting God to act in his good timing." (10) As a Godly man you don't need to wish God will work all things out for your good. You don't have to wish He will forgive or wish He'll pick you up when you fall. His hope in you is a "given" you can count. Hope for the future is just a matter of waiting patiently for God to fulfill His promises.

February 21
Waiting on God

"But those who wait on the Lord shall renew their strength; they shall mount up with wings like eagles, that shall run and not be weary, they shall walk and not faint." Isaiah 40: 31
"Rest in the Lord, and wait patiently for Him."
Psalm 37:7

Waiting is, for some, is a grueling, annoying thing. It seems men dislike waiting more than women do. Waiting is very stressful for a lot of men. In particular: Waiting in the doctor's or dentist's office, waiting in traffic, waiting in the grocery store line and waiting for the family to get ready for church on Sunday mornings. Then there are more serious areas of life that we find waiting so difficult. Waiting on God to answer a prayer about a job, waiting for God to heal your wife and or waiting to reach that spiritual victory over some sin are times that seem unachievable. David was anointed by Samuel to become King of Israel, but he had to wait some twenty years before Saul would be killed and David would be crowned King. To make things worse, during many of these years of waiting, Saul was chasing David to kill him. The great coach of the Florida State Seminole football team, Bobby Bowden coached for over forty years before achieving an undefeated season. Pray today that God will grant you patience in prayerful waiting on Him to come through. He will...just wait and see!

February 22
A Man after God's Own Heart

"The Lord has sought for Himself a man after His own heart, and the Lord has commanded him to be commander over His people..." I Samuel 13:14

David was described as a man after God's own heart. What set David apart from other Godly men in the Bible to earn him such a distinguished attribution? Certainly there were other men who loved God and walked close to Him. "And Enoch walked with God; ("Genesis 5:24) "Noah walked with God." (Genesis 6:9) The Apostle Paul said, "What things were gain to me, these I have counted loss for Christ." (Philippians 3:7) Eugene Peterson says this about David: "The single most characteristic thing about David is God. David believed in God, thought about God, imagined God, addressed God, prayed to God. The largest part of David's existence wasn't David but God." (11) Becoming a man after God's heart is not something that requires work. David, Jesus' disciples, Paul and the prophets all had one thing in common...they knew God intimately. They were not supermen or heavenly beings, but men like you. But their thoughts, their prayers and their lives were focused on God. As you pray today, tell God of your desire to know Him intimately and to let your life become immersed in Him.

February 23
Encourage Someone Today

"But exhort {encourage} one another daily, while it is called 'Today', lest any of you may be hardened through the deceitfulness of sin".
Hebrews 3:13
"Likewise, exhort [encourage] the young men to be sober-minded." Titus 2:6

One of the easiest and most rewarding acts you can do today and every day is to encourage someone. Whether or not you have been gifted with the gift of encouragement, you should be aware what a tremendous impact you have on the person whom you encourage by a compliment, by an expression of affirmation or by a smile with a "Have a blessed day." Often when you go through a check-out line in a store you have the opportunity to encourage the clerk whose weariness and frustration is obvious. "Each day provides countless opportunities to encourage others and to praise their good works. When we do, we not only spread seeds of joy and happiness, but we also follow the commandments of God's Holy Word." (12) At your workplace look for those occasions to compliment the work of a co-worker or one of your employees. Notice those who do menial tasks such as empty trash cans, clean floors, or maintain the landscape and tell them how much you appreciate their dependability and how important they are. You will find that you, too, will be encouraged knowing that you are obeying God and making someone smile.

February 24
Fishing: It's a Man's Thing

"And when He had stopped speaking, He said to Simon, 'Launch out into the deep and let down your nets for a catch'." Luke 5:4
"So they gave Him a piece of a broiled fish and some honeycomb. And He took it and ate in their presence." Luke 24:42-43

Fish was a staple for thousands of years. Villages tended to develop near water, both fresh and salt water. Fishing as an industry thrives to meet the demand for fish in markets and restaurants. Fishing has become a big time sport with expensive boats, high tech sonar and sophisticated electronic contour maps. According to the Sporting Goods Manufacturers Association, fishing goods accounted for $1.03 billion in the outdoor sporting industry sales. (13) As a boy, some of my first experiences with my Dad were fishing. We'd take our fishing poles, tackle box, earth worms and minnows and, of course, lunch. Fishing can provide opportunities for the Godly man to grow spiritually as he meditates on God's promises and has intimate conversations with God. It can also be a meaningful time to spend with your son or daughter passing along your Christian values. If you enjoy fishing, look at it as not just about you, but a time for spiritual growth and sharing Jesus with others.

February 25
Sharing Jesus with Other Men

"Then He said to them, 'Follow me, and I will make you fishers of men'." Matthew 4:19
"But you shall receive power when the Holy Spirit has come upon you; and you shall be witnesses to Me..." Acts 1:8

Men enjoy getting with a best friend or group of friends and talking football, baseball, hunting and other "men things." Men usually feel comfortable having lunch with a colleague or a close friend and talking about marital issues, financial problems or work-related topics. But one of the most difficult things for some Godly men to do is share the gospel. There's a fear of their reaction. You may feel like you're not equipped to explain the plan of salvation if they ask questions. You may not want to suddenly broach the subject by asking "do you know Jesus as your personal Savior?" Despite the reluctance of laymen to witness as Jesus commanded, it is something that you should do to fulfill His great commission. Perhaps you often wonder what God's will for your life is and what you can do to be obedient. It's the "elephant in the living room" thing. Sharing Jesus with others is God's will for you. Ask God to give you boldness which will enable you to give your testimony to a friend. Ask Him to make you aware each day of situations in which you can share His blessings with others.

February 26
A Warrior's Armor: Wear It

"Therefore take up the whole armor of God that you may be able to withstand in the evil day, and having done all, to stand." Ephesians 6:13
All you men of valor shall cross over armed before your brethren, the children of Israel." Deuteronomy 3:18

In the sixth chapter of Ephesians Paul deals directly with the spiritual armor men must wear to fight against the onslaught of temptation, sin, and adversity. He says "be strong in the Lord." He makes it clear that the enemy is not "flesh and blood" but spiritual in nature. He instructs you to put on the belt of truth, the breastplate of righteousness, the gospel of peace, the shield of faith, the helmet of salvation, and the sword of the Spirit which is the Word of God. But perhaps the most significant motivational advice he gives follows when he says "praying always." You face the enemy of your soul every day of your life. It may come in the form of criticism, temptation, financial loss, illness or discouragement. Satan is real and he is evil. He wants to devour you. You are a warrior of God. God will give you the strength and courage to win every battle. Begin to see yourself as a spiritual warrior who stays armed to include the ammunition of prayer.

February 27
Coping with Rejection

"The Son of Man must suffer many things, and be rejected by the elders and chief priests and scribes, and be killed, and be raised the third day." Luke 9:22
"Then they cried out with a loud voice, stopped their ears, and ran at him with one accord; and they cast him out of the city and stoned him." Acts 7: 57-58

Rejection may be one of the most devastating experiences men encounter. No one is immune from being turned down, turned away, not being chosen or being left out. It can be the most difficult wound to heal. Rejection can hurt to the bone, it can be cruel and it can take years to recover. The Bible is full of Godly men who were rejected. The prophet Jeremiah's message was soundly rejected and he was scorned and ridiculed. David was rejected by King Saul who sought to take his life. Joseph was rejected by his own bothers and abandoned. Stephen's message of the gospel was rejected by the Jewish leaders who stoned him to death. The Apostle Paul was rejected many times and suffered physical abuse and ultimately death. Rejection for you may be God's way of protecting you from some future regrets or circumstance. Instead of self deprecation and questioning your worth, let God use the rejection to make you rely on Him as to who you are in Christ. If you're feeling the pain of rejection, just remember your Savior accepted rejection and willingly died on the cross. His grace is sufficient for you and you matter to Him.

February 28
Some Days I Barely Get By

"From the Jews five times I received forty stripes minus one. Three times I was beaten with rods; once I was stoned; three times I was shipwrecked; a night a day I have been in the deep; in journeys often, in perils of water, in perils of robbers, in perils of my own countrymen...in weariness and toil, in sleeplessness often, in hunger and thirst, in fastings often, in cold ad nakedness – besides the other things, what comes upon me daily: my deep concern for all the churches." II Corinthians 11: 24-28

Ever had days like the Apostle Paul? Many men experience days in which you feel as if you can go no further with the burdens of family, bills, work, children, heath problems, vehicle breakdowns, stress in your marriage and then your spiritual walk with God may be lacking or mundane. There is a country music song with lyrics which say: "Some days I barely get by; I want to give up, lay down and die." You would think that's exactly how Paul felt. But he continued with joy and praise and encouraged others in the Lord. Most men's bad days pale in comparison to Paul's. Yet, Paul continued to preach Jesus and the Cross with unbelievable spiritual passion. Be reminded today that God told Paul and He tells you today: "My grace is sufficient for you..." (II Corinthians 12:9) Despite how you feel and what your circumstances you face, God's love and care are sufficient.

REFERENCES FOR FEBRUARY

1. Anonymous author, "Multiply Your Muscles by Two", Men's Health (MaryAnn Bekkedahl, Publisher) December 2003, p.19-20
2. Charles R. Swindoll, "Hand Me Another Brick" (W. Publishing Group, A Division of Thomas Nelson Inc., Nashville, Tennessee) 1998 p.59
3. Bill Perkins, "Six Battles Everyman Must Win" (Tyndale House Publisher, Wheaten, Illinois) 2004 p. 46
4. L.R. Tolbert and Thoro Harris, (Singspiration Music)
5. Eugene Peterson, "Leap Over a Wall" (Harper San Francisco) 1997 p.32
6. Stuart Briscoe, "Vital Truths to Shape You Life" (Tyndale House Publishers, Inc., Wheaton, Illinois) 2002 p.56
7. Jim Collins, "Good to Great" (HarperCollins Publishers) 2001 p. 191
8. Ibid p.193
9. Gordon Jensen, "Written In Red" (Word Music) 1984
10. Max Lucado, "Traveling Light" (W Publishing Group, A Division of Thomas Nelson Inc.) 2001 p.52
11. Peterson, p. 206
12. Prayers of a Righteous Man, Second Editions, (Brighton Books, Nashville, Tennessee) 2002, p. 46
13. "BASSMASTER" Magazine, January 2005, p. 46

March 1
<u>What about Hypocrites?</u>

"And when you pray, you shall not be like the hypocrites. For they love to pray standing in the synagogues and on the corners of the streets, that they may be seen by men. Assuredly, I say to you, they have their reward." Matthew 6:5
"Or how can you say to your brother, 'Brother, let me remove the speck that is your eye' when you have a plank that is in your own eye? Hypocrite!" Luke 6:42

The age old complaint by unbelievers and believers alike is "what about those hypocrites at church?" A hypocrite is one who pretends that he/she has some quality or spiritual attribute. Webster's dictionary uses the word "actor." Some hypocrites are not Christians and claim to be. Then there are those who are Christians pretending to be spiritually sincere sometime, but like the chameleon, change colors with whomever they're around. No one respects a hypocrite. But God is not pleased when you criticize the faults of others, even hypocrites. Before worrying about that fault of your Christian brother, deal with the failures and sin in your life. Paul wrote to the Romans; "But why do you judge your brother? For we shall all stand before the judgment seat of Christ." (Roman 14:10) As you pray, ask God to help you take your eyes off the hypocrisy of others and to help you to be an authentic Christian at all times and in all places.

March 2
Think on Good Things

"Finally, brethren, whatever things are true, whatever things are noble, whatever
things are just, whatever things are pure, whatever things are lovely, whatever things are of good report, if there is any virtue and if there is anything praise-worthy meditate on these things."
Philippians 4:8
"...casting down arguments and every high thing that exalts itself against the knowledge of God, bringing every thought into captivity to the obedience of Christ." I Corinthians 10:5

Controlling the mind is one of the greatest barriers to enjoying the joy of the Lord and becoming a contagiously positive person. Throughout the Bible the thoughts of man result in how he lives his life, how he influences others, and how he relates to God. In II Corinthians 10:5, Paul explains to the early Christians that the way to fight this spiritual battle is by "bringing every thought into captivity to the obedience of Christ." Often we indulge in negative thoughts and focus on our problems to the extent that we find ourselves in the depths of discouragement and unhappiness. There is good news however. We can, through prayer and obedience, practice thinking on positive things. Thomas Kinkade wrote: "Meditating on the world, on the beauty of God's creation and joyful sounds of singing will help us to rediscover our cups of joy. If we redirect our focus to these things and contemplate them, we will be drinking from the cup of joy and be reminded how wonderful it is to be alive." (1) Ask God to remind you to think on all the good things around you, your family, your parents and His goodness and grace.

March 3
<u>Sexually Immorality</u>

"For this is the will of God, your sanctification: that you should abstain from sexual immorality; that each of you should know how to possess his own vessel in sanctification and honor." I Thessalonians 4:3- 4

Immorality, as Webster defines it is "unchastely" and "...being immoral." Moral, the antonym of immoral, means "ethical, virtuous, righteous, noble which conform to a standard of what is right and good." The scriptures clearly and explicitly condemn sexual immorality. Your standard is the Word of God. The record of sexual immorality goes all the back to the sixth chapter of Genesis where sexual immorality became so rampant that God was sorry that he made man. Now, in the twenty first century sexual immorality has exploded into a multi-billion dollar industry. It has become increasingly acceptable in our society. Sexual immorality can be fornication (sexual acts between two unmarried people), adultery, homosexuality and other perversions. One false notion among many teenagers and young adults is that oral sex is not immoral. You are bombarded daily by sex in every form of media. You are in spiritual warfare. You must "abstain from sexual immorality" and stay sanctified through the help of the Holy Spirit. Sex within marriage can be a wonderful, loving experience. Men, stand in the gap on sexual purity and pass it own to your children.

March 4
We All Stumble

"For we all stumble in many things." James 3:2
"Oh that my ways were directed to keep your statutes!" Psalm 119:5

The reality is that you cannot live a perfect Christian life. It is believed by some non-believers and some misled believers that Christians do not sin if they do good. Some churches and religions who preach the legalistic doctrine that one can live without sinning; don't understand God's grace through the cross. As a Christian man, you will stumble as Apostle James and the Psalmist David recognized. A poem written by Greg Aismakoupoulos entitled "The Long Haul", says: *"Heroes don't quit. They are marathon runners who won't walk away from what they agreed to do. They complete what they start, though their feet may stumble."* (2) Endurance is essential for every Christian man. If every time you stumble and fall you give in to discouragement and defeat, God will not be able to use you for the purpose He has designed for your life. No matter what you do, God's grace is sufficient! Though there are consequences, He has already paid the price of sin on the cross. When you stumble get up, confess and repent of your failure. Then ask God to restore you spiritually as you pray and study His word, and seek a Godly man to encourage you.

March 5
<u>Resisting Evil Today</u>

"Be sober, be vigilant; because your adversary, the devil walks about like a roaring lion, seeking whom he may devour. Resist him, steadfast in the faith, knowing that the same sufferings are experienced by your brotherhood in the world." I Peter 5: 8-9

"No temptation has overtaken you except such as is common to man; but God is faithful, who will not allow you to be tempted beyond what you are able, but with the temptation will also make a way to escape..." I Corinthians 10:13

Every Godly man is constantly being targeted by the evil schemes of the devil. Satan never lets up in his attempts to make evil attractive and beneficial. You know the strategies. He attacks your thoughts with fantasies of beautiful women. He tries to make cheating or stealing at work a fair way to get what you deserve. He subtly and continuously draws your attention to anything that will take your thoughts off of God, i.e. golf, gambling, fishing, your career, etc. He knows that if he can break your regular communion with God and Christian brothers, you will become weak, discouraged, and unfit for the Master's purpose in your life. Be consistent in prayer, in Bible study and in fellowship with Christian men. Then choose everyday before your day begins to who you will be faithful. In the book "Being God's Man in the Face of Temptation" the authors say it well: "How we choose to respond in the midst of excruciating inner impulses will either leave us spiritually bankrupt or will move us a step closer to a Christ-like heart and character." (3) Remember that you are empowered with the Holy Spirit who helps you discern and resist sin.

March 6
God's Standard of Conduct: Holiness

"I beseech you therefore brethren, by the mercies of God, that you present your bodies a living sacrifice, holy, acceptable to God..." Romans 12:1
"Just as He chose us in Him before the foundation of the world, that we should be holy and without blame before Him in love..." Ephesians 1:4

No one can be holy except through Christ's death on the cross which took your sins and nailed them there, thus pardoning you of all sin and making you holy in His sight. Yet, since your body is carnal (in the flesh) you will struggle in the battle between the flesh and the Spirit. Let your conduct and character reflect the holiness of God. You can do no less. God demands that we "cleanse ourselves from everything that can defile our body or spirit." (II Corinthians 7:1) "Holiness is purity, cleanness, and separation from everything that defiles the body and the spirit." (4) In your every role, whether husband, father, brother, son, co-worker, employee, friend, or leader, God's standard for your life is holiness in both inner-sanctification and outward conduct. Your holy walk with God will produce spiritual fruit in your life. Holiness should be demonstrated in every aspect of your life. Remember, Christ's blood has already made you holy. Keep your human, carnal spirit and your earthly body holy in conversation and conduct. A Godly man's holy conduct will influence the lives of everyone with whom he comes into contact.

March 7
The Crisis of Despair

"We do not want you to be uninformed, brothers, about the hardship we suffered in the province of Asia. We were under great pressure, far beyond our ability to endure, so that we despaired even of life."
II Corinthians 1:8 **NIV**

Webster defines despair as: "to lose all hope or confidence." Hope is that which keeps Christians afloat even when circumstances are bleak. You may be facing or have faced circumstances in your life in which you could not "feel" hope. When you "lose all hope" you are in a crisis. You may have been in a fierce battle during wartime, gone through a divorce and lost your wife and your children, faced the death of a child, lost your job, bankrupted, faced that dreaded disease of cancer, or were trapped in some addiction. In today's scripture verse we find the Apostle Paul in despair "even of life." Yet, in the two verses which follow, he comes to the conclusion that "we should not trust in ourselves, but in God who raises the dead, who delivered us from so great a death, and does deliver us;" (verses 9 & 10) During one of life's crises you may feel that there is no hope and feel abandoned. There is no hope if we depend on ourselves or others to rescue us. It is God who, through His immeasurable love and grace, will deliver you and restore your hope in Him. Praise the Lord for His amazing grace in time of despair and never lose hope in Christ.

March 8
Winning Requires Teamwork

"Then he divided the three hundred men into three companies, and he put a trumpet into every man's hand, with empty pitchers, and torches inside the pitchers." Judges 7:16

Winning is a word seldom used within the context of your Christian walk. It is often acknowledged that Godly men are warriors and must "put on the armor of God." Words like overcoming, enduring and resisting the enemy do not fully convey the concept of winning. But the Bible is full of victories over the power of the devil and against evil people. One of the most exciting stories includes the verse in today's scripture. The Midianites along with several other armies were camped in the Valley of Jezreel. They were waiting there to assault and destroy the people of Israel. Gideon started out with a volunteer army of thirty-two thousand. But God told him that was too many. After several "screening" processes, God whittled them down to three hundred courageous men. Against all odds, but obeying God's unique orders, these men led by Gideon destroyed tens of thousands of the enemy. That was a win! God wants us to win everyday over every spiritual battle and temptation. The key to winning these daily spiritual battles is teamwork. No one can live out this Christian walk alone. Fellowship with Godly men, your wife, and Christians is essential to winning. Find a faithful prayer partner. "Two are stronger than one." (Ecclesiastes 4:9)

March 9
<u>Knowing and Using Your Gifts</u>

"Having then gifts differing according to the grace that is given to us, let us use them:" Romans 12:6
"Therefore I remind you to stir up the gift of God which is in you through the laying on of my hands." II Timothy 1:6

God, through the work of the Holy Spirit, gifts His disciples with special gifts and talents for the purpose of serving God and His kingdom here on earth. The Apostle Paul discusses spiritual gifts in both Romans and I Corinthians. The gifts he mentions include prophesy, ministry, encouragement, leadership, teaching mercy, the word of wisdom, the word of knowledge, faith, healing, discernment, different kinds of tongues, and the interpretation of tongues. Notice that all of these gifts are for serving and edifying others, not you. You probably have several gifts which God has given for you to use. Rick Warren says: "You have a dozen of hidden abilities and gifts you don't know you've got because you've never tried them out." (5) We find our gifts by serving when God opens doors and by volunteering for service in the church and for missions work. Warren goes on to say: "Whatever gifts you have been given can be enlarged and developed through practice." (6) Ask God to use the gifts He has given you and ask him for opportunities to serve when asked. You can discover gifts and you can develop them so that you will touch others for Jesus Christ.

March 10
A Man of Passion

"But none of these things move me; nor do I count my life dear to myself, so that I may finish my race with joy, and the ministry which I received from the Lord Jesus, to testify to the gospel of the grace of God." Acts 20:24
"But His word was like fire shut up in my bones; I was weary with holding it back, and I could not." Jeremiah 20:9

God wants you to be a man with spiritual passion. If you lack enthusiasm seek God for a renewed spirit of passion in serving Him. This means praying fervently to be a Godly man who has a heart to encourage and to minister to others. It means being avid in your desire to share your testimony. Despite the obstacles, the beatings, the rejections, the Apostle Paul had passion to complete his mission to win Christ and tell the world about the grace of God. Jeremiah was ridiculed for telling the people to turn to God. He became discouraged. However, this prophet of God could not give up. He had a passion for God - "like fire shut up in my bones:" He continued to preach with passion. In a speech to the House of Commons during World War II, Winston Churchill proclaimed: "We shall go on to the end,... we shall fight with growing confidence and growing strength ...whatever the cost may be... we shall never surrender." (7) Not only was Churchill a passionate leader, he instilled passion in the people of England and in people around the free world. Godly men need to be passionate for God.

March 11
Once Dead, But God...

"But God, who is rich in mercy, because of His great love with which He loved us, even when we were dead in trespasses, made us alive together with Christ (by grace you have been saved)" Ephesians 2:4-5

Aside from philosophical and scholarly debate about the fall of man and God's omnipotence, the simple truth about salvation is that God, from the beginning of time had a plan. After the fall of man in the Garden of Eden, God strove with people to worship him, to obey Him and to commune with Him. But man, even God's chosen people Israel, could not measure up because of their inherent sin nature. They sinned, repented, and sinned more. God's only solution was to send His son, Jesus, to be the sacrifice for sin. On a rugged cross He paid the ultimate price that was required to raise man from spiritual death and to make him alive spiritually. Today you, as a Godly man, don't have to worry about your salvation from now throughout eternity. You are alive "together with Christ." Max Lucado, in his book, "No Wonder They Call Him Savior", says: "There it is. Almost too simple. Jesus was killed, buried and resurrected. Surprised? The part that matters is the cross. No more and no less. The cross." (8) "Once dead...but God made us alive together with Christ..." Rejoice this day and rest in His love and in His abiding grace.

March 12
<u>Self Pity</u>

"But he himself went a day's journey into the wilderness, and came and sat down under a broom [juniper] tree. And he prayed that he might die, and said, 'It is enough! Now, Lord, take my life, for I am no better than my fathers!'" I Kings 19:4

Today's scripture follows one of the most fascinating, incredible victories of God found in the Bible. Because of the sins of the people of Israel, Elijah the prophet told King Ahab there would be a drought for three and one-half years throughout the land. Ahab, who recognized Baal as the god of Israel, blamed Elijah for the drought. Elijah said to the people: "How long will you falter between two opinions? If the Lord is God, follow Him; but if Baal, follow him." Then Elijah's challenged the 450 prophets of Baal to a contest on Mount Carmel. Could Baal burn their sacrificial bull or could God set fire to Elijah's bull? Baal's prophets cried to Baal all day but no fire came. Elijah called on God and immediately the sacrifice was consumed with fire. What a victory! But in response to Jezebel's death threat, Elijah ran to the wilderness and sat under a broom tree in self pity. This once-courageous prophet asked God to take his life. How often do you find yourself allowing self-pity to rob your joy, peace and trust in Christ? Self-pity is "about me." Arise, face another day and win another victory. God is your strength.

March 13
Beyond Your Imagination!

"Now to him who is able to do exceedingly abundantly above all that we ask or think according to the power that works in us..." Ephesians 3:20
Such knowledge is too wonderful for me; It is high, I cannot attain it. Psalm 139:6

God is a big God who loves you and wants to bless you. So many people just can't get it in their heads that God of the world and the universe is interested in every intricate part of their lives. In fact, God knew you before you were created. In verse sixteen of Psalm 139, David so poetically describes how God knew him before he was born and knew about the days of his life. He writes: "Your eyes saw my substance being yet unformed. And in Your book they all were written, the days fashioned for me, when as yet there were none of them." If God knows you that well and He has paid the price for your sin, He certainly is able to do more for you than you can ask or imagine in your finite mind. You face the enemy of your soul every day and you suffer the condition of humanity. But God has so much He wants to do for you as you follow Him and discover His purpose for you. Don't limit what God wants to do in your life. Believe in His great love for you and surrender to Him.

March 14
Running from God

"Arise and go to Nineveh, that great city, and cry out against it: for their wickedness has come up before me. But Jonah arose to flee to Tarshish from the presence of the Lord." Jonah 1:2-3

Jonah ran from God instead of obeying Him. God told him to go to Nineveh to turn the wicked people back to God. You know the story about Jonah and the whale and how Jonah eventually obeyed God, his turn-around and how his staying the course of God's purpose resulted in great revival in Nineveh. This story teaches us several lessons. When you know the Holy Spirit has spoken to you to accomplish a certain thing, despite your reluctance and fear, it is best to obey Him immediately rather than procrastinating, hoping that someone else will go. Another lesson is related to staying power and commitment. Jonah was not committed to God. He did not have a close relationship with God, thus he was unwilling to obey His Lord. It was all about Jonah. Stu Weber in his book, "The Heart of a Tender Warrior" (9) says it well: "A man was made for a purpose beyond himself. When we give ourselves irrevocably to the ultimate Tender Warrior, we find the vision, purpose, and direction to sustain us for a lifetime." Today as you pray seek a deeper relationship with Him and pray for a willing heart to yield your will to His.

March 15
March Madness

"Everyone who competes in the games goes into strict training. They do it to get a crown that will not last; but we do it to get a crown that will last forever." I Corinthians 9:25

It's "March Madness" time and whether you're a basketball fan or not, you cannot escape all the "hoopla" that comes with "March Madness". Of over 300 teams competing in of the National Collegiate Athletic Association's Division (NCAA) I universities, 65 will be selected for the "March Madness" tournament. Myles Brand, President of the NCAA, had this to say: "There are no losers because every team in these tournaments has earned the right to play for the title of National Collegiate Champion." (10) The intensity of millions of fans serves to complement the culmination of discipline and devotion by the players for an entire year. It should remind you that life, at best, seems as a fleeting moment. Whatever stage of life you're in, your daily spiritual discipline and devotion to Christ is important for you grow wiser, become stronger and stay spiritually fit. In doing so, you will be able to encourage others. And at the end of your season, you will attain the crown of victory to treasure throughout eternity. Pray for more intensity in your prayer life and in your daily living.

March 16
When You Would Do Good

"For the good that I will to do, I do not do; but the evil I will not to do, that I practice" Romans 7:19

"Oh that my ways were directed to keep Your statutes!" Psalm 119:5

Do you ever get frustrated that you can't seem to always think and do right? Does it seem that other Christian men seem to live is such harmony with God and never struggle with temptation? Or have you ever experienced going along for days feeling so filled with the Spirit you'd think, "Man, I finally have the victory…" only to fail miserably the next day? Well, join the Christian men's club! If the Apostle Paul couldn't achieve perfection and David longed to keep God's word but never got it right, who are you to think you can live on clouds of ease and fly like an eagle above making mistakes, sinning, and falling short of God's purpose. Though you have been set free from sin's consequence of eternal death, you're human. You still have that old nature which you must constantly battle so that God can use you for His purpose. Just stay the course, committing your life anew each day to His will. Now, read Paul's answer to his own dilemma: "What a wretched man I am! Who will deliver me from this body of death? I thank God— through Jesus Christ our Lord!" Romans 7:24-25

March 17
Love My Enemies?

"But I say unto you, love your enemies, bless those who curse you, do good to those who hate you, and pray for those who spitefully use you and persecute you" Matthew 5:44
"And they stoned Stephen as he was calling on God and saying 'Lord Jesus, received my spirit.' Then he knelt down and cried out with a loud voice, 'Lord, do not charge them this sin.'" Acts: 7:59-60

Your enemies may be those who intentionally harm you or are your adversaries for any number of reasons. You have two choices how you handle your enemies. You can hold a grudge and "get even." If you choose to, you'll probably hate them and will refuse to forgive and definitely not forget. Sometimes it's a man's pride thing that you don't want to be seen as less than a man who courageously extracts justice. Your second choice is clear enough in today's scriptures. Love them, bless them, be good to them and pray for them. "Fat chance", you say? But hating another person will make you miserable and diminish your relationship with God. Max Lucado says: "The key to forgiving others is to quit focusing on what they did to you and start focusing on what God did for you."(11) Just ask yourself what if God will not forgive you though you hurt Him by sinning hundreds of times? Ask Him today to help you forgive and love your enemies. Share His marvelous grace.

March 18
Seasons of a Man's Life: Spring

"Most assuredly, I say to you, when you were younger, you girded yourself and walked where you wished; but when you are old, you will stretch out your hands, and another will gird you and carry you where you do not wish" John 21:18
"O God, You have taught me from my youth; And to this day I declare Your wondrous works." Psalm 71:17

Spring is the season of new life and a time of beginning. During spring new foliage bursts forth. It is vibrant and resilient. Spring brings hope and awe of God's creation. There are parallels to the first season of a man's life. It begins with the miracle of his birth and grows in strength and stature. It is a time of opportunities, at time of learning, a time of preparation and a time of maturation. This season usually comes to a close during a man's mid-to-late twenties or thereabout. It is an important time for a man to establish strong relationships with family, friends, and God. It is a time to enjoy his childhood, his youth and early manhood...it passes so quickly. Whether you are in the springtime of your life or watching your son grow, it is the time to form and to develop that masculine part of a man and the understanding of that role. Be there for your son or some young man who needs a role model on how to become a Godly man for the rest of his life. Spring grows a personality and values that will last a lifetime.

March 19
Daily Sanctification

"Now may the God of peace Himself sanctify you completely." (I Thessalonians 5:23)
"By that will we have been sanctified through the offering of the body of Jesus Christ once for all." Hebrew 10:10

The work of sanctification is one of the least preached topics and one of the most misunderstood tenets of Christianity today. You hear much about salvation through Christ and the work of the Holy Spirit in daily living, but little about the role of sanctification in your spiritual walk. Yet, it is so important to your spiritual journey. It is Christ in you. Henry and Tom Blackaby define it this way: "Sanctification is the process by which you are made holy. This begins at conversion when you are justified through Christ and lasts throughout your life as the Holy Spirit continues to work." (12) Sanctification is accomplished by the Holy Spirit and by your obedience to and your cooperation with the Holy Spirit. It's not easy to resist worldly thoughts and conduct. Sanctification is an on-going process that you must renew everyday. Oswald Chambers says: "...sanctification is that all the perfections of Jesus are at my disposal, and slowly and surely I begin to live a life of ineffable order and sanity and holiness." (13) As a Godly man, you should understand that, though God sanctified you through the Holy Spirit, it is a daily growing process to become more like Jesus.

March 20
Rejoice In this Day

"This is the day the Lord has made; We will rejoice and be glad in it." Psalm 188:24
"Rejoice in the Lord always. Again I will say, rejoice!" Philippians 4:4

You may be reading this during a serious illness, or following a recent death of a loved one or in the midst of discouragement and despair. You may be lonely. You may have just been rejected or lost your job. On the other hand, you may have awakened this morning full of vim and vigor and singing "Skipidy-do-dah" all the way to work. In the sixteenth chapter of Acts Paul and Silas were beaten and thrown into prison for preaching the gospel of Christ. "But at midnight Paul and Silas were praying and singing hymns to God, and the prisoners were listening to them." (Acts 16:25) What a time to rejoice! Despite the conditions you are in, whether joy and happiness, or down and out and ready to throw in the towel, you are to rejoice in this day! He has given you eternal life which should make this life, in its best or worst moments, pale in comparison to what God has prepared for you in a new heaven and a new earth. No matter what your circumstances make it a practice to arise each morning and rejoice in the day the Lord has made.

March 21
Courage against the Odds

"Moreover David said, "The Lord who delivered me from the paw of the lion and from the paw of the bear, He will deliver me from the hand of this Philistine.' And Saul said to David, 'Go and the Lord be with you.'" I Samuel 17:37

Most of you are familiar with the story of David and Goliath. Young David "stepped up to the plate" when all the soldiers of Israel's army were afraid of this giant of a man who cursed God and mocked the Israelite army. This story cannot be viewed in isolation from the rest of David's life. David was anointed to be the King of Israel when the time was right. From his youth David knew and trusted God. He had courage and that courage was part of what made him a man after God's own heart. Courage does not necessarily mean to be physically strong or to be a "real man". Real courage is demonstrated when all the odds of succeeding or overcoming are against you and, by trusting God as your strength, you stand strong for what is right. Sometimes being a man of courage is lonely. Taking an unwavering stand for righteousness at work, in your community, or even at church is courage. Nehemiah, David, Daniel, Stephen, and Peter were Godly examples of men with courage against the odds. Ask God to mold you into a Godly man of courage. Seek Him for wisdom to complement your courage.

March 22
Listen to God Today

"Therefore Eli said to Samuel, 'Go, lie down; and it shall be, if He calls you, that you must say,' 'Speak Lord your servant hears.'" I Samuel 3:9

So many people struggle with listening. This is a frequent issue in marriages, it causes communications breakdowns in the workplace and many good sermons are missed. Listening to God is a prerequisite to obeying God. God does speak to you. One way is through His written inspired Word. Another way God speaks to you is through His Holy Spirit. As you grow in spiritual maturity and develop an intimate relationship with God, the Holy Spirit will speak to your heart. You will know that it is Him and not just a passing thought. Listen and obey. Several years ago on a beautiful fall day, I was watching my favorite football team on television, when the Holy Spirit spoke to me to go pray for my son. He was on the way back from a hunting trip. Fortunately, I obeyed and prayed with a burdened heart at 12:15 pm...the exact time on the police report on the auto accident that could have taken my son's life. He came through unscathed. Learn to be sensitive to and to listen to the Holy Spirit's promptings. Then obey and trust in Him for the rest.

March 23
Be a Man Willing to Obey

"But Peter said and the other apostles answered and said: We ought to obey God rather than men."
Acts 5:29

Yesterday's devotion revealed how to develop a close relationship with Jesus and have a spiritual ear attentive to the Holy Spirit. When He speaks it may be to encourage you. But He also speaks to lead you to obey Him to touch the lives of others. As a Godly man, you should always be willing to obey, whether it is the written Word or whether it is a move of the Holy Spirit. Obedience should become a part of your spiritual character. Wrap it in your love and devotion to the Lord. This is not a situational decision-making style, but a solid, once-and-for all commitment of mind and heart that you will always obey when the Holy Spirit speaks. Henry and Tom Blackaby write: "Do you realize what happens when you obey God? Your obedience to the slightest word from God sets in motion the activity of God. He comes along side you and opens to you, your family and your church His mighty acts."(14) Because great men of the Bible listened to God and obeyed Him, great things followed that changed the lives of individuals and nations. Walk in the Spirit daily and don't fear to obey when He speaks.

March 24
A Man's Words Reveal His Heart

"Let the word of my mouth and the meditation of my heart be acceptable in Your sight, O Lord, my strength and my Redeemer." Psalms 19:14
"Out of the abundance of the heart his mouth speaks." Luke 6:45

Men's words belie their professed values and character. Be around a man for a significant amount of time and you will eventually know what is in his heart.

A man's words will almost always blatantly or by inference reveal his true character. Some say that you can tell what a man's priorities are by looking at his checkbook register. You can tell the content of a man's heart by his conversation. You probably work with other men, who serve as Christian role models at church. However, when at work you hear them profane or their conversations gravitate to impure subjects. Words, especially those of a professing believer, can have a tremendous impact on those who hear them. They can cause new Christians to be disillusioned. They can bring disrepute to genuine Christians and the church. James expresses this well: "Out of the same mouth proceed blessing and cursing. My brethren, these things ought not to be so." (James 3:10) You can do little about what others say. However, it should be your daily prayer that God will remind you that your words reveal the contents of your heart. They can help or hurt others.

March 25
Your Weakness Can Make You Strong

"Joseph is a fruitful bough, a fruitful bough by a well; His branches run over the wall." Genesis 49:22
"It is good that I have been afflicted, that I may learn Your statutes." Acts 119:71

James Dobson relates a story told by Dr. Tony Campolo. As a speaker at a summer camp for teenagers Dr. Campolo noticed a boy named Jerry who had cerebral palsy. The other teens were unkind to Jerry and kept their distance. He had great difficulty speaking and walking. On the last day of camp the students each stood on a platform and gave their testimonies. To everyone's amazement, Jerry struggled to get up the steps onto the platform. Finally at the podium he said: "I looovvveee Jeeeessssuuusss aaannndddd Jeeesssuuusss looovvveeesss meeeeee." Teenagers filed to the front with tear-filled eyes to commit their hearts to Jesus. (15) You may have your own shortcomings or weaknesses to overcome. You may ask where God is or why He's not making things okay. He has a purpose for everything that happens in your life. No theologian, Bible scholar or minister knows why God allows some to be prosperous with few troubles and others to struggle. My Christian brother, God can take your weakness and turn it into something wonderful. Whatever your circumstances, turn to Him, trust Him and rely on His grace. He loves you and, whether or not you understand, all things work for good.

March 26
<u>Get Out of the Boat</u>

"So He said, 'Come.' And when Peter had come down out of the boat, he walked on the water on the way to go to Jesus." Matthew 14:29

Today's scripture is familiar story. Usually, the emphasis of this miraculous event is on Peter walking on water. That was the easy part. Believing it was Jesus and taking one foot out of the boat is one of the Bible's most exemplary demonstrations of faith. Remember the boat was being "tossed by the waves", the wind was blowing, it was dark and out of nowhere comes a man walking on water! Yet, despite these dire circumstances, when Peter heard Jesus' voice, he got out of the boat. Perhaps you've heard His call and have an opportunity to step out. Maybe it is a mission trip to a remote area of a foreign county. Could it be to teach a Sunday school class or lead a men's Bible study? Or maybe it's spending more time in prayer and fasting to draw nearer to Jesus. Some men get petrified when Jesus calls to get out of the boat and walk by faith into unfamiliar waters. So, why did Peter get out of the boat? It was love, devotion and faith. Pray today that your love and devotion for Jesus will deepen and you'll have courage to get out of the boat.

March 27
Hiding Sin

"But Samuel said, 'What then is this bleating of the sheep in my ears and the lowing of the oxen which I hear?'" I Samuel 15:14

In today's scripture King Saul of Israel, was directed by God through the prophet Samuel to kill Amalek and all of his people in retribution for Amalek's attack on Israel. Saul was instructed not to spare any person or animals. However, he spared the best of the sheep and oxen for his own use. Following the battle, God told Samuel what Saul had done and approached Saul. Saul denied his sin. But Samuel told Saul the Lord had rejected him as Israel's king. You cannot hide your sin from God. Usually your sin will be exposed. Men who commit adultery may rationalize why they do and rely on God for understanding. While He understands your carnal flesh, He will not condone your sin. He knows that sooner or later there will be consequences. And most likely your sin will be revealed. Men commit corporate fraud believing they can hide it. But their names appear in media crime reports. Moses, warning the Israelites said: "...take note, you have sinned against the Lord; and be sure your sin will find you out." (Numbers 32:23) The penalty for you sin has been paid. But that doesn't remove consequence of sin. Search your heart. Renew your love for Him.

March 28
God's Perfect Knowledge of You

"O Lord, You have searched me and known me, You know my sitting down and my rising up; You understand my thought afar off, You comprehend my path and my lying down, and are acquainted with all my ways." Psalm 139:1-3

It is an awesome thought to know that there is nothing about you – your thoughts, your masculine nature, your problems, your fears – that God hasn't always known. You may struggle with who you are or with your relationships. God knows. He knew you while you were being formed in your mother's womb and He loved you then. As a man of God, you can never escape His presence. You are one of a kind. God made you to be a man and he understands the nature of a man. John Eldredge says it is not important to him to write about how to be a nicer guy. Rather, he focuses on "the recovery and release of a man's heart, his passions, his true nature which he has been given by God."(16) Just knowing that God knows about your innate longings to be a warrior, to have a need to win, to like the outdoors and to be drawn to the beauty of a woman is exciting. And most importantly, God knows your need for a relationship with Him. He knows that deep inside, you must learn that your strength and courage come from Him. Love and honor Him.

March 29
A Godly Man's Loyalty

"The Lord grant mercy to the household of Onesiphorus, for he oft refreshed me, and not ashamed of my bonds. The Lord grant to him that he may find mercy from the Lord in that Day—and you know very well how many times he ministered to me at Ephesus." I Timothy 1:16, 18

Loyalty, according to Webster is: "Unswerving allegiance." Loyalty is a value that seems to have been lost its importance among men. As a Godly man it is especially important to build a bond of friendship with a fellow Christian man that will weather the test of time and of uncommon circumstances. It is a rare friend who remains loyal to you despite your problems and failures. John Churton Collins once said: "In prosperity our friends know us; in adversity we know our friends." (17) Cultivate a friendship with a brother in Christ that is founded on honesty, openness, understanding, and loyalty. Love is an essential condition for loyalty and it is okay to say you love a Godly friend. Stories of loyalty between men often come from experiences in war and in law enforcement where men depend on their partner for preservation of life. Godly loyalty is most important because you need a friend to be there when all looks bleak and you're in despair. It is the love of Christ that binds you together with a friend. Pray that God will bless you with a Godly friend.

March 30
Your Wife's Battle with Cancer

"So husbands ought to love their own wives as their own bodies;" (Ephesians 5:28)
"The Lord is my rock and my fortress and my deliverer; My God, my strength, in whom I will trust." Psalm 18:2

Your wife should be your most prized possession. She is your best friend, your stongest supporter, your lover, the mother of you children and your counselor. You are to be her Godly warrior, her shoulder to lean on, her comforter, her helpmate, her lover, and her best friend. There are the good times and the tough times. One of the most frequent times of crisis is when your wife is diagnosed with cancer. It happens much too often to ignore. The American Cancer Society estimates that there are approximately 25,000 new cases of ovarian cancer diagnosed each year and an estimated 215,000 new cases of cancer diagnosed. If your wife is or has been diagnosed with cancer, it's important to remember that God says that a man will be "…joined to his wife, and they shall become one flesh."(Genesis 2:24) Part of your body and your life is ill and both parts need to be as one throughout the duration of her illness. Your faithfulness in prayer and devotion to God during this time will provide incredible strength to her and to you. You should assure her everyday that you are there for her. And remind her that God loves her.

March 31
Godly Influence: Your Impact on Others

"Let your light so shine before men, that they may see your good works and glorify your Father in heaven." Matthew 5:16
"Let no man despise your youth, but be an example to the believers in word, in conduct, in love, in spirit, in faith, impurity." I Timothy 4:12

You will influence those around you and those with whom you come into contact. Every word you speak, every attitude you display and every action you take will impact someone's mind, someone's decision and perhaps someone's life. This is especially true with your children and other family members. You will impact those with whom you work day in and day out. You will influence another Christian brother or a young man who needs guidance. Some Godly men underestimate their influence on others. Ray Boltz's song "Thank You" (18) shares the story of a man who, dreaming he was in Heaven, is reminded of times he influenced others' lives. It tells of those whose lives were touched in some way because of his Godly character and conduct. As I age I realize those whose influence on me made a difference in my life. The influence of my father, a minister and several Godly men has made a real difference in my life. Ask God today to help you be a Godly influence with those around you. It will become part of your legacy.

REFERENCES FOR MARCH

1. Thomas Kinkade, "Beside Still Waters" (Thomas Nelson, Inc., Nashville, Tennessee) 2000 p. 139
2. "Heroic Faith: How to live a life of extreme devotion." (W. Publishing Co., a division of Thomas Nelson, Inc., Nashville, Tennessee) 2002 p. 78
3. Stephen Arterburn, Kenny Luck, and Todd Wendorff, "Being God's Man...in the Face of Temptation." (Waterbrook Press, Colorado Springs, Colorado) 2003 p.2
4. Rhonda O'Brien and Jonathan Gray, "Touch Points for Men" (Tyndale House Publishers Inc., Wheaton, Illinois) 1996 p.126
5. Rick Warren, "The Purpose Driven Life" (Zondervan, Grand Rapids Michigan) 2002 p.251
6. Ibid p. 254
7. James C. Humes, "The Wit & Wisdom of Winston Churchill" (HarperCollins Publishers, Inc.) New York, New York) 1995 p.119-120
8. Max Lacado, "No Wonder They Call Him The Savior" (Multnomah Publishers, Inc,) 1986 p. 13
9. Stu Weber, "The Heart of a Tender Warrion" (Multnomah Publishers, Inc. Sisters, Oregon) 2002 p. 90
10. Myles Brand, (NCAA March Madness Magazine, Host Communications Printing and Publishing, Lexington, Kentucky) March 2005, Inside cover
11. Max Lucado, "In the Grip of Grace" (Word Publishing, Dallas, Texas) 1996 p.156
12. Tom and Henry Blackaby, "The Man God Uses" (Broadman & Holman Publishers, Nashville, Tennessee) 1999 p. 76.
13. Oswald Chambers, "My Utmost for His Highest" (Discovery House Publishers, Grand Rapids, Michigan) 1963 p. 205

14. Henry and Tom Blackaby "The Man God Uses" (Broadman & Holman Publishers, Nashville, Tennessee) 1999 p.50
15. James Dobson, "When God Doesn't Make Sense" (Tyndale House Publishers, Wheaton, Illinois) 1993 p. 173-175
16. John Eldredge, 'Wild at Heart" (Thomas Nelson Publisher, Nashville, Tennessee) 2001 p.18
17. Chriswell Freeman, "The Gift of Friendship" (Delaney Street Press, Nashville, Tennessee) 2000 p.43
18. Ray Bolz, "Thank You" (Gaither Music Company) in "Contemporary Christian Corporation Guitar Chord Songbook," p. 210-211

April 1
A Fool

"The fool has said in his heart, 'There is no God'." Psalm 14:1
"The way of the fool is right in is own eyes..." Proverbs 12:15
"A fool multiplies words." Ecclesiastes 10:14

The first day of April has traditionally known as April Fool's Day. This is the only day of the year that one can acceptably trick, fib, or pull a joke on someone for a laugh at their expense. The Bible treats the word "fool" much more seriously. To be a fool is to lack wisdom and faith in God. Some fools talk incessantly with little substance. Webster defines the word fool as "a person lacking in judgment or prudence." However one describes a fool, it is not a characteristic of a Godly man. Keep your relationship with Jesus renewed and stronger on a daily basis. Seek Him for wisdom and ask Him to guide your every word. James 1:5 says: "If any on you lacks wisdom, let him ask of God, who gives to all liberally..." David, whose life and heart were all about God, asked Him to, "Let the words of my mouth and the meditation of my heart be acceptable in Your sight..." (Psalm 10:14) Guard your heart, your mind, and your words for the glory of God so that He is magnified.

April 2
Conditioning for the Race

"...let us lay aside every weight, and the sin which so easily ensnares us, and let us run with endurance the race that is set before us." Hebrews 12:1

The Apostle Paul used frequent references to competitive sports. He referred to boxing, running and fighting throughout his writings. Having been a Roman citizen and official, it is likely that he attended sporting events in the coliseum in Rome. He often used running as an analogy to encourage Christians in their spiritual race. Paul knew to reach maturity in Christ and fulfill God's purpose in your life requires daily spiritual and physical discipline. God's man must stay conditioned to stay in the race. During my youthful days, I believed that if I prayed enough and was Spirit-filled, I would have "arrived" and could "coast" effort-free. Though you may sometimes wish you could relax and live victoriously, that is not in God's plan. To have a close relationship with Jesus and to be a fruitful disciple means surrendering every area of you life to Him. It means daily time spent in prayer and Bible study. It means sharing Jesus with others. It means fellowship and accountability with other Godly men. This is spiritual conditioning and will make you stronger and more effective in your spiritual race toward becoming all He wants you to be.

April 3
Stay the Course

"But none of these things move me; nor do I count my life dear to myself, so that I may finish my race with joy and the ministry..." Acts 20:24
"I have fought a good fight, I have finished the race, I have kept the faith." II Timothy 4:7

In the 1992 Summer Olympics in Barcelona, a young runner, Derek Redman, was there with one goal in mind - to cross the finish line and win a medal. He had trained long and hard for this 400 meter event. The starting shot was fired and Derek, like a fleeting gazelle, was the front runner. Within 172 meters of the finish line, he felt a sharp pain in his leg...a hamstring tear. He fell on the track wincing with pain. But within seconds he pulled himself upright pushing away paramedics and began to hop on one leg toward the finish line. His father, Jim Redman, fought through the crowd of 65,000 to get to his son. He said: "I'm here son. We'll finish together." As he put his arm around Derek's waist and Derek wrapped his arm around his dad's shoulders they crossed the finish line. (1) You must have assurance that you will stay the course. Along the way you can expect barriers of discouragement and temptation. You'll feel like quitting. You may stumble. But when you can't go on, your Heavenly Father lift you up and say: "I'm here my son. We'll finish together."

April 4
Had It Not Been for the Cross

"looking unto Jesus, the author and finisher of our faith, who for the joy set before Him endured the cross, despising the shame, and has sat down at the right hand of the throne of God." Hebrews 12:2

The cross is the internationally recognized symbol of Christianity. As believers and Godly men, everything we believe, who we are, and everything we say or do is based on the cross. It represents the greatest event in the history of mankind. Because of the cross, millions have been imprisoned, ridiculed and martyred. Because of the cross millions have found peace and eternal life. It was the cross on which the Son of God paid the price of freedom from sin's enslavement. Today some churches with the intent not to offend with traditional "barriers", have removed the cross from prominence. Oswald Chambers so eloquently says: "The Cross of Jesus is the revelation of God's judgment on sin. Never tolerate the idea of martyrdom about the Cross of Jesus Christ. The cross was a superb triumph in which the foundations of hell were shaken. There is nothing more certain in time or eternity than what Jesus Christ did on the cross:" (1) Thank God for what He did for you on the cross and read an old hymn refrain, "At the Cross": "At the cross, at the cross where I first saw the light and the burden of my heart rolled away."

April 5
The Risen Christ, Our Hope

"...that Christ died for our sins according to the scriptures, and that He was buried, and that He rose again the third day according to the scriptures," I Corinthians 15:4-5

"Mary Magdalene came and told the disciples that she had seen the Lord, and that He had spoken to her." John 20:8

This event of Jesus' resurrection confirms and fulfills Old Testament references. More importantly, it is a life-changing message of hope. Those who saw Him and touched His wound (Thomas) were eye witnesses that Jesus was indeed alive. There was no doubt – only rejoicing and hope. It illuminated all that Jesus had foretold His disciples. It prepared them to believe His promises of the Holy Spirit's arrival and His second coming as He ascended into Heaven. The heart of Mary Magdalene was filled with, joy, fear and hope. In Matthew's account of this event, both Mary Magdalene and another Mary "ran to bring His disciples word." (Matthew 28:8) It was Mary Magdalene who first told His disciples that she had seen the Lord. A Bill and Gloria Gaither song recorded by Sandi Patti is "I've Just Seen Jesus". Its lyrics so beautifully describe Mary Magdalene's message. (2) This was the first proclamation of hope to the disillusioned disciples and hope that dwells in the hearts of Christians everywhere. As you pray, allow the Holy Spirit to renew in your heart the hope of His second return.

April 6
<u>Because He Lives</u>

"Therefore He is also able to save to the utmost those who come to God through Him, since He always lives to make intersession for them."
Hebrews 7:25
"For though He was crucified in weakness, yet He lives by the power of God." II Corinthians 13:4

Jesus' death on the cross, His resurrection and the fact that He is sitting at the right hand of God making intercession for us gives us such a privilege and a reason for living. He serves as our advocate to the Father. The fact that He lives should be a daily prayer of gratitude, knowing that because He lives you can face today and whatever tomorrow holds. Hebrews 4:15-16 says: "...but we have one, Jesus, who has been tempted just as we are – yet was without sin. Let us come boldly to the thrown of grace with confidence, so that we may receive mercy and find grace to help us in our time of need." He lives and you have the Comforter, the Holy Spirit, living within you to bring you through every storm of life, every disappointment, every hurt, every failure and every battle with your "self." Because He lives, you have hope that transcends that which you cannot see or understand. Because He lives, you will also live forever in His presence and in His love. This should be your joy and strength for today and everyday.

April 7
<u>A Promised Fulfilled: The Day of Pentecost</u>

"Behold, I send the Promise of My Father upon you; but tarry in the city of Jerusalem until you are endued with power from on high." Luke 24:49
"When the Day of Pentecost had fully come, they were all with one accord in one place." And they were all filled with the Holy Spirit..." Acts 2:1, 4

Following Christ's resurrection, the promised indwelling of the Holy Spirit is the next significant event in Christianity. God the Holy Spirit, a part of the Trinity along with the God the Father and God the Son, always made His presence known throughout the Bible. But Jesus explained to His disciples in John 14:16: "But you know Him, for He is with you and shall be in you." Following His ascension the disciples waited for the fulfillment of Jesus promise. He kept His promise and thousands received the Spirit. The filling of the Holy Spirit changed forever the lives of those on that day and through the Spirit, they changed the world. The Holy Spirit still changes lives today. Believers receive the Holy Spirit at conversion and can be baptized and continually filled with the Spirit. Men, seek God daily earnestly asking him for a fresh renewal of the baptism and filling of the Holy Spirit. You have within you the same power that Jesus poured out on the early disciples when you allow the Holy Spirit to have control of your mind, your heart and your body.

April 8
<u>**The Holy Spirit in Your Life**</u>

"Now hope does not disappoint, because the love of God has been poured out in our hearts by the Holy Spirit who was given to us." Romans 5:5
"Or do you not know that your body is the temple of the Holy Spirit who is in you, whom you have from God, and you are not your own?" I Corinthians 6:19

The work of the Holy Spirit in your life may be one of the most neglected topics of men's Bible studies and sermons. Except for the cross and the price Christ paid for your sin, the work of the Holy Spirit should be the most essential part of your relationship with Jesus. You must deepen your relationship with Him and allow Him to guide you, comfort you, strengthen you, and sanctify you. Jesus is your advocate to the Father and you are to commune with Him. Jesus told His disciples that He would send another Comforter to be "in" them. A late nineteenth century evangelist, Smith Wigglesworth, wrote: "If you will allow the Holy Spirit to have full control, you will find you are living in the Spirit. You will discover that your opportunities will be God's opportunities. Then the Holy Spirit will give you the exact words to speak, anointed words that will meet the need of the moment." (4) Seek to become more familiar with role of the Holy Spirit. Keep your mind and heart open to the moving of the Holy Spirit in your life so that you will "walk in the Spirit".

April 9
<u>These Things will be dissolved...The Brevity of Life</u>

"Therefore, since all these things will be dissolved, what manner of persons ought you to be in holy conduct and Godliness, looking for and hastening the coming of the day of God, because of which the heavens will be dissolved, being on fire, and the elements will melt with fervent heat." II Peter 3:11-12

It is not good to dwell on the negative. But it is good to know what is most important in life since this world and all that is in it is temporary. Knowing that the earth will be dissolved by fire should cause you no fear, but it should remind you how to live every single day of your life. It should cause you to place things in their proper perspectives and live accordingly. The earth may still be orbiting the sun when you pass from this life into eternal life. But no matter which occurs first, you should stay focused on the truth that everything around you is temporary. Life passes so quickly. David offers in Psalm 144:4 a bit of reality: "Man is like a breath; His days are like a passing shadow." James expressed it this way: "For what is your life? It is even a vapor that appears for a little time and vanishes away." (James 4:14) Allow these words to inspire you to be a Godly man, a better father and husband, an enthusiastic witness for Christ and an encourager to others. Look at every day as an opportunity to fulfill His purpose.

April 10
Growing Older

"I have been young, and now I am old; Yet I have not seen the righteous forsaken, nor his descendants begging bread." Psalm 37:25
"The glory of young men is their strength, and the splendor of old men is their gray head." Proverbs 20:29

You are growing older. If you are young, in your twenties or thirties, you probably feel invincible. You can't imagine yourself as ever getting old. In most instances, young men are focused on masculinity, strength and appearance. As you move into your forties and fifties, you may refuse to accept the limitations at the levels of a few years earlier. Yet, it is inevitable. Charles Gains writes in Men's Health: "Just as there's a time in a man's life for the full and unapologetic enjoyment of physical strength and beauty, there is a time to leave those things behind and journey toward completeness." (5) God is more interested in your spiritual conditioning than your physical attributes. Understanding the significance of spiritual maturity will help you accept the aging process as an opportunity to become wiser and to shift your focus toward others. Aging is not synonymous with quitting or retirement from God's purpose. Chuck Norris writes: "I take the time each day to read the Bible and pray and exercise spiritually. Besides, I don't see anywhere in the Bible anything about retiring." (6) Pray that God will help you age into a more complete, wise Godly man.

April 11
A Time for Cultivation and Growth

"Therefore, my brethren, you also have become dead to the law through the body of Christ...to Him who was raised from the dead, that we should bear fruit to God." Romans 7:4
"...but grow in the grace and knowledge of our Lord and Savior Jesus Christ." II Peter 3:18

By this time in the year, crops of vegetables and fruits trees should be in their various stages of cultivation and growth. Most of them were planted weeks ago. The farmer or gardener carefully cultivates by removing weeds, watering, keeping the soil fertile and protecting the crops from pestilence. Some vegetables and fruits are beginning to grow, yet not ready for harvesting. This is a critical time for cultivation for the growth and yield of healthy, nutritious food. Perhaps during this spring season is a good time for you to examine your spiritual condition and cultivate your heart and relationship with Christ for your continued healthy growth in Christ. Spiritual cultivation of your heart should include devoted time in prayer with God the Holy Spirit and as David did, pray "Search me of God and know my heart; Try me, and know my anxieties..." (Psalm 139:23) Be still and listen to what God has to say. Go to His word for sustenance and nutrients that will grow you in wisdom, faith and a deeper love for God. This season of prayer and Bible study will grow you into a stronger, healthier Godly man manifesting the fruit of the Spirit evident and encouraging to others.

April 12
Baseball: "Get in the Game"

"You therefore, beloved, since you know this beforehand, beware lest you also fall from your own steadfastness, being led away with the error of the wicked." II Peter 3:17 "Therefore let him who thinks he stands take heed lest he fall." I Corinthians 10:12

Growing up, I played baseball in little league, in the junior high league, and on the high school varsity team. I remember so well, our veteran coach who coached all of those leagues in our small community, frequently reminding the players to "get in the game." He meant that we weren't focusing on the runner on base, a curve ball, a bunt or keeping our eyes on the ball. Your walk with God is sort of like this. Stay focused. You need to be aware that your adversary, the devil, will throw you a curve ball or steal a base on you because you are not keeping your mind on your daily spiritual walk. You need to "get in the game" and beware that "your adversary the devil walks about like a roaring lion, seeking whom he may devour." (I Peter 5:8) If you let your mind wander on things which draw you away from your commitment and Christian responsibility and allow your daily devotion and commitment to God to fade, you become vulnerable to Satan's attacks which cause you to stumble. So "get in the game" and be alert as you grow in joy, peace and praise daily.

April 13
A Man of Compassion

"But a certain Samaritan, as he journeyed, came where he was. And when he saw him, he had compassion. So he went to him and bandaged his wounds, pouring on oil and wine; and he set him on his animal, brought him to an inn, and took care of him." Luke 10:33-34

In December of 1972, my 65 year old father lay in his bed at home dying with terminal cancer. My mother, who bore most of the burden for his care, was worn and discouraged. About a week before my Dad died, we asked his nearby family physician to come by for a cursory check. He never came. In desperation, we called the prestigious surgeon who performed the exploratory surgery and asked if he would come. It was about an hour's drive from the city to my folks' little frame house located at the end of an unpaved street. To our amazement, he made the trip, walked to my Dad's bedside, rendered some minor care and shared words of comfort to my Dad and our family. He was truly a man of compassion! This renowned surgeon's portrait is prominently displayed in the hospital as memoriam to his many years of caring for others. What a legacy he left! You also have the capacity to demonstrate Christ's love through your compassion for those less fortunate and in need. Those you may ignore - the elderly, the poor, the sick, the lonely – need Christ's love and compassion demonstrated through you.

April 14
Abandoned to Jesus

"Teach me to do your will, for you are my God;
Your Spirit is good. Psalm 143:10
"Also I heard the voice of the Lord, saying:
'Whom will I send and who will go for Us?'" Then
I said, 'Here I am! Send me'." Isaiah 6:8

The word "abandon" is a synonym for "surrender". It is not one of the more popular topics on which Christians discuss. Webster defines abandon as: "to give up to the control or influence of another person or agent." Abandonment is probably not the "thought of the day" you have in mind. But abandonment to the will and person of Jesus Christ to the extent that every action, thought and selfish desire becomes lost in Him will change you from the mundane to a passionate, sanctified man of God. In the words of an old hymn: "Humbly at His feet I bow, worldly pleasures all forsaken, take me, Jesus, take me now. I surrender all" (7) "To give up", to "surrender all" is what Jesus calls you to do. Oswald Chambers says: "In our abandonment we give ourselves over to God just as God gave Himself for us, without any calculations." (8) Are you ready to become surrendered to Jesus? Or is there an area of your life haven't let go? Seek God prayerfully asking Him to give you the willingness to give your all to Him.

April 15
Reaching Your Goals

"I press for the goal for the prize of the upward call of God in Christ Jesus." Philippians 3:14

In the game of baseball, hitting the ball and getting on base is good but is meaningless unless you touch all the bases and reach home plate. All men have goals. Spiritual goals should be foremost in your life as you give yourself to the will of God. The goals of gaining spiritual wisdom, sharing Jesus with more people, being an encourager or pulling down a stronghold in your life are important to you as a Godly man. But you should have goals in every part of your life. "Goals give us strength and hope. Goals give us purpose and direction." (9) As a young man you probably had goals. Maybe they included earning a degree, becoming a certified craftsman, getting married, becoming a professional athlete, and/or pursuing a ministry. As you accomplished those goals, you found that you continued to have goals to reach to become a contributor to your work or to provide opportunities for your children. While yielding to God should be your most important goal, continually set goals for your life that will enhance your life and that of others. Ask God today, that your goals will be pleasing to Him.

April 16
<u>Spring Brings New Life</u>

"For lo, the winter is past, the rain is over and gone. The flowers appear on the earth; the time for singing has come, and the voice of the turtledove is heard in the land. The fig tree puts for her green figs, and the vines with their tender grapes give a good smell." Song of Solomon 2:11-13

Everyone has their favorite season of the year. Perhaps there is a correlation between personalities and the seasons' characteristics. But of the four seasons, spring time brings new life to flowers, fruit trees, birds and little animals. The sun is warm and there is a fresh fragrance in the air. Everything around you turns a beautiful shade of light green often with brilliant colored blossoms, perhaps as it was when God created it with beauty and splendor. You need spring times in your spiritual life. You need those moments and periods of time when your winter of trials and discouragement is passed and the Holy Spirit breathes upon you afresh with His joy, hope and anticipation. You need to bask in His goodness and blessings, remembering the day He washed away your sin and gave you a new birth that was fresh and exciting as a beautiful spring day. Ask God for a spring time spiritual renewal today that will invigorate your heart and mind for Him. Anticipate with great expectation this newness of life that never grows old, but is as fresh as the day you came to know Him as your Savior and Lord.

April 17
<u>Making Your Marriage Last</u>

"Husbands, love your wives just as Christ loved the church and gave Himself for her." Ephesians 5:25
"Therefore a man shall leave his father and mother and be joined to his wife, and they shall become one flesh." Genesis 2:24

Marriage is the fundamental building block within any society. It is within marriage where children are to be nurtured in a Christian home. Marriage is ordained by God. However, recent studies on marriage and divorce in America commonly report 50% of first time marriages end in divorce. Divorce is an easy option for those who become unhappy or unfulfilled. In our culture marriage has lost its sacredness. Couples increasingly are "living together" before making a decision about marriage. A God-blessed marriage was always God's plan for a man and a woman to consummate their love. "But did He not make them one? And why one? He was seeks Godly offspring." (Malachi 2:15) Stuart Briscoe says: "But when two people are one "in spirit", it means something far beyond having sex. It means caring for a person rather than just enjoying a body, relating to someone of intrinsic worth whose fears and aspirations, whose loves and dislikes, whose beliefs and principles become part of your life." (10) If you are married or plan to marry, cherish your wife and keep your commitment … "till death do us part." The key to making your marriage last is *selflessness*.

April 18
Yesterday's Wrong is Today's Right...The New Tolerance

"And many will follow their destructive ways, because of whom the way of truth will be blasphemed. By covetousness they will exploit you with deceptive words..." II Peter 2:2-3

Do you remember reciting the pledge of allegiance to the flag and having prayer every morning in elementary school? How about the hit songs when you were in high school? Did you ever hear the "F-word" and lyrics demeaning women with despicable names? If you're over forty, you probably never imagined that these things would someday become part of the American fabric. To make matters worse, anyone who doesn't accept them are considered intolerant. As a Godly man, and perhaps a father, you should understand the "new tolerance." First, the old tolerance is the Biblically based concept of Christian love for all mankind even for those who don't believe Christ's teachings. The new tolerance believes there are no absolutes, everyone's own values are "right" for them and everyone should embrace them. Josh McDowell and Bob Hostetler write: "Jesus taught love, but never at the expense of truth." (11) God's word is absolute and is the foundation of righteous values, justice, and truth. Pray today that the Holy Spirit will make you keenly aware of the deceptiveness of the new tolerance.

April 19
Acknowledge the Ordinary and Unnoticed

"Now David said, 'Is there anyone who is left of the house of Saul, that I might show him kindness for Jonathan's sake' II Samuel 9:1
"'There is still a son of Jonathan who is lame in his feet.'" II Samuel 9:3
"So Mephibosheth dwelt in Jerusalem, for he ate at the kin's table." II Samuel 9:13

There are thousands of people with whom you come into contact but never really "see". They are "invisible people". They are people like cashiers, housekeepers, cooks, disabled, homeless, elderly and others who you may encounter but seldom acknowledge. In God's eyes we are all equal and He loves the alcoholic laying on a park bench just as much as He loves you. In today's scriptures David asked if anyone of Saul's family was still left. He respected Saul as the King of Israel and developed a bond of friendship with Saul's son, Jonathan. David's found there was one, Mephibosheth, Jonathan's crippled son. He was somewhere out of the way, unnoticed and forgotten. David called for him and gave him the status of a son and cared for him for the remainder of his life. Your role model is Jesus who stopped everywhere He went and healed the outcasts and touched the lives of "invisible" people. Begin today becoming more aware of these people. A genuine smile, a "Have a blessed day", or an encouraging word may be the only one they receive that day. Do it in the name of Jesus and you'll both receive a blessing.

April 20
Suffering Can Build Character

"But may the God of all grace, who called us to His eternal glory by Christ Jesus, after you have suffered a while, perfect, establish, strengthen, and settle you." I Peter 5:10
"Before I was afflicted I went astray, but now I keep Your word." Psalm 119:67

Suffering may come in different ways. You may suffer from an illness. You may suffer from deep emotional wounds. You may suffer from a career-related setback. Or you may suffer a spiritual battle and/or failure. Suffering in some form comes to everyone -Christian and a non-believer. Even Jesus who took on the form of a man suffered. He suffered temptation, He suffered ridicule, He suffered betrayal, He suffered public humiliation and ultimately, He suffered the excruciating pain of the cross. Suffering as a Godly man has its purpose. It is important that you patiently accept suffering, knowing that God is in control. God allow suffering to build your character and draw you closer to God. You may suffer for their faith, because it's part of the human condition or because of circumstances out of your control. But you may bring suffering on yourself by disobedience, by an unhealthy lifestyle or by making wrong choices. Suffering lung cancer or heart disease may result from years of smoking. When you experience suffering look for God's purpose in it and allow Him to grow you to deeper depths and higher heights in Him.

April 21
Dealing with Criticism

"I am in derision daily; everyone mocks me.
Jeremiah 20:7
"But it so happened, when Sanballat heard that
we were rebuilding the wall, that he was furious
and very indignant, and mocked the Jews. And he
spoke before his brethren and the army of Samaria,
and said, 'What are these feeble Jews doing?'"
Nehemiah 4:1-2

Speaking of God, Jesus said in Matthew 5:45: "...for He makes the sun rise on the evil and the good and sends rain on the just and the unjust." As a Christian you are not immune from criticism. As a Godly man you will experience criticism for two reasons. You may be criticized for your work performance, for your appearance, for your high temper, etc. Such criticism may have nothing to do with being a Christian and may, in fact, have some merit. The second reason for being criticized is because you are a believer in Jesus Christ. Often Christians make non-believers uncomfortable. As a high school student I was criticized and ostracized because I carried a pocket Bible to school and read it during the library. Many men who are openly committed to Christ will suffer criticism for their faith. Ask God today to help you endure criticism as Christ did. Rejoice when you are persecuted for being a Godly man. Often, when these critics face life's crises, they'll come to you for prayer!

April 22
Take Time to Say "I'm Proud of You"

"Likewise, exhort {encourage} the young men to be sober-minded. In all things showing yourself to be a pattern of good works..." Titus 2:6-7

Recently, my cousin who had been like brother as we grew up together, died from cirrhosis of the liver at fifty-five years old. For most of his adult life he was an alcoholic, a failure as an employer, a husband and a father. Several months before his death, he surrendered his heart to Jesus and the change was obvious. During a visit from his thirty year old son, my cousin told him that he loved him. That was the first time in his thirty years he had heard his dad say "I love you." This is an all too familiar story. Often there is no father in the home to encourage boys. Millions of boys grow up to become young men and never hear anyone say "I love you" or I'm proud of you." This was the message that Paul gave to young Titus. As a Godly man and a role model, ask God to make you aware of opportunities every day to tell a boy or young man that you are proud of him. It may be the first time he will have heard those words. It may well change his life forever.

April 23
Be Filled with the Holy Spirit

"If we live in the Spirit, let us also walk in the Spirit." Galatians 5:25
"And do not be drunk with wine...but be filled with the Spirit." Ephesians 5:18

There is much misunderstanding about the Holy Spirit. Many Christian men simply don't know how the Holy Spirit fits in with God and Jesus. The Trinity has always existed as God the Father, God the Son and God the Holy Spirit. You receive the Holy Spirit at the same moment you are saved. Jesus told His disciples that he would send the Holy Spirit to take His place, to comfort them, to guide them and to help them fulfill God's purpose for their your lives and fulfill the Great Commission to spread the Gospel. Each day as you begin your day, ask the Holy Spirit to fill you with His presence. He will produce the fruit of the Spirit which Paul listed in Galatians 5:22-23. Seek to stay filled so that you can stand against all the weapons of Satan and be a victorious warrior. Charles Stanley says: "Every day ask the Holy Spirit to fill you anew with His love, His peace, His truth. Every day, ask the Holy Spirit to fill you to overflowing with His compassion for others." (12) You will experience joy unspeakable and a peace which passes all understanding.

April 24
<u>When God Answers "No"</u>

"But the Lord said to my father David, 'Whereas it was in your heart to build the temple for My name, you did well that it was in your heart. Nevertheless, you shall not build the temple, but your son who will come from your body, he shall build the temple for My name'." II Chronicles 6:8-9

Sometimes you may be confused as to when God does and does not answer your prayers as you asked. Throughout the Bible God healed the sick, raised the dead and delivered men from death. We read of healings which took place as the disciples prayed for the sick. On the other hand, Paul had a "thorn in the flesh" which, after much prayer, God did not remove. Often we pray for God to intervene in our circumstances and things seem to get worse. I have witnessed my prayers answered for which I had prayed for years. Your faith in God can waiver if you don't understand one thing: God is sovereign and He knows what is best despite your questions and doubt when He says "no". He knows the future and works His purpose in men's lives for what He knows is best. James Dobson says this about your confusion when God doesn't seem to come through: "…let me offer this word of encouragement: the Father has not lost track of your circumstances, even though they seem to be swirling out of control. He is there. Someday His purposes will be known and you will have eternity to talk it over." (13)

April 25
Who Will Fill Their Shoes?

"And David said to his son Solomon, 'Be strong and of good courage, and do it; do not fear nor be dismayed, for the Lord God – my God – will be with you'." I Chronicles 28:20

"Then Moses called Joshua and said to him in the sight of all Israel, 'Be strong and of good courage, for you must go with this people to the land which the Lord has sworn to their fathers to give them, and you shall cause them to inherit it'." Deuteronomy 31:7

For you country music lovers, perhaps you will recall one of George Jones' greatest hits entitled "Who's Gonna Fill Their Shoes?" The gist of the song is that, as the old-time classic country music singers who filled the Grand Ole Opry fade away, who will take their places? Country music is still popular and some of the original genre of classic country music still lingers. In today's scriptures, you read about similar situations where legends and traditions are passed on to others who carry on God's message. Today those who have spread the gospel through preaching, teaching and singing, are passing on to their final destination to worship God for eternity. Sometime you may wonder who could fill the shoes of those like Billy Graham? Who will fill the shoes of that faithful Sunday school teacher or the faithful pastor? God is bringing up men who will stand in the gap and carry on His work. He uses Godly men like you. Be sensitive to the Holy Spirit and be willing to step into their shoes. When God asks, "Whom shall I send, and who will go for us", answer with Isaiah: "Here am I Lord, send me." (Isaiah 6:8)

April 26
The Struggle Men Have with Church

"And some of them were persuaded; and a great multitude of the devout Greeks, and not a few women, joined Paul and Silas." Acts 17:4

In many of today's churches women make up the majority of congregations and Sunday school classes. Does it seem that there are more seminars on women's issues than those for men? Women were frequently mentioned as followers and supporters of the disciples and of the Apostle Paul. Throughout the New Testament their presence and influence is apparent despite the fact they were relegated to roles such as serving and praying. Today, the feminine influence is more dominant than during those early years of the church. In his book, "Why Men Hate Going to Church", David Murrow writes: "Although males have not completely abandoned the church, *manly* men have all but disappeared. Today, a good Christian is often associated with meekness, sensitivity, passivity, and sweetness. This standard of Christian behavior is very tough on men…" (14) Perhaps you feel hypocritical trying to pretend the church is reaching you. Don't be "turned off" with church. Christ, our perfect role model was a masculine man. Get involved with worship services, accept invitations to teach and lead. Ask the Holy Spirit to lead you to take a more active role in reaching other men's needs through the church.

April 27
Church: A Place of Fellowship and Renewal

"When I thought how to understand this, it was too painful for me – until I went into the sanctuary of God; then I understood their end." Psalm 73:16
"So continuing daily with one accord in the temple...with gladness and simplicity of heart, praising God and having favor with all the people." And the Lord added to the church daily those who were being saved." Acts 2:46-47

Yesterday's theme centered on how some men find the church irrelevant, too feminine-minded and lacking in meeting their real masculine needs. Though some churches are not all they should be in addressing men's issues, the church remains an essential God-ordained institution for sustaining men and women in their spiritual warfare and in their Christ-like growth. Rick Warren points out five reasons you need to be actively involved in a local church: "(1) A church family identifies you as a genuine believer; (2) A church family moves you out of your self-centered isolation; (3) A church family helps you develop spiritual muscle; (4) The Body of Christ needs you; and (5) You will share in Christ's mission in the world." (15) As a Godly man, whether you are a truck driver, a construction worker, an executive, a police officer, a soldier, a physician, a salesman or a retiree, you need to be an example to other men and especially to young men. The church is where God's family worships Him, serves one another and grows spiritually to share the gospel with those who have not had that life-changing encounter with Jesus Christ.

April 28
Conditioning for the Fight

"Fight the good fight of faith, lay hold on eternal life, to which were also called and have confessed the good confession in the presence of many witnesses." I Timothy 6:6
"Therefore I run thus: not as with uncertainty. Thus I fight: not as one who beats the air. But I discipline my body and bring it into subjection, lest, when I have preached to others, I myself should become disqualified." I Corinthians 9:26-27

As a warrior in a daily spiritual warfare, you must stay prepared for Satan's manipulating tactics in forms of temptation, discouragement, betrayal, loss, illness, criticism and other evil schemes. Though you should be confident in Christ's gift of salvation, you must strive to be victorious in order to fulfill God's purpose for your life. If someone told you that being a Godly man day in and day out would be easy, they misled you. You will face battles in which your faith and love for God will be tested. You're in a fight in which losing is not an option. As Winston Churchill said, "To say we did our best is not good enough. We must do what is necessary." To remain strong in battle requires that you stay spiritually conditioned. Daily prayer will prepare you before your day begins. Consistent study of God's word will give you sustenance when Satan comes against you. Surrendering self to the Holy Spirit is necessary since most of your battles are fought on the battlefield of your mind. Remember, you are not God. You must unreservedly trust God and rely on Him to go before you.

April 29
At the End of the Day: A Clear Conscience

*"Let us draw near with a true heart in full assur-
ance of faith, having our hearts sprinkled from an
evil conscience..." Hebrews 10:22*
*"Then Paul, looking earnestly at the council,
said, 'Men and brethren, I have lived in all good
conscience before God until this day.'" Acts 23:1*

Is cheating to get ahead or engaging in an adulterous
affair or being untruthful at the expense of another worth the
feeling you'll have when you come in at the end of the day
and face your wife and children? Does stealing on the job or
profaning all day around the guys at work or giving a vulgar
hand gesture to another driver make you feel good toward
God as you lay your head on your pillow at night? Do the
things you do when no one is looking give you peace in your
heart toward God? A clear conscience is very important. It
allays guilt, builds a positive self-esteem and diminishes
the fear of be found out. A good conscience has no remorse
over wrong doing or regrets of evil thoughts and deeds. As a
Godly man, pray today that your life reflects Jesus in every
thought, word and action. Join the Apostle Paul in saying,
"I have lived in all good conscience..." You will have the
peace of God ruling your heart and the joy of the Lord as
your strength. Godly living will birth a good conscience.

April 30
Protecting Your Children

"Only take heed to yourself, and diligently keep yourself, lest you forget the things your eyes have seen, and lest they depart from your heart all days of your life. And teach them to your children and your grandchildren." Deuteronomy 4:9

Do you remember when Ricky and Lucy slept in separate beds? Remember when profanity was not permitted on television or radio? For many of you younger men, some of these well-defined lines between good and evil have gradually blurred during your lifetime. In 1973, the American Psychiatric Association removed homosexuality from the Diagnostic and Statistical Manual of Mental Disorders (16) If you believe it is a sin as the Bible teaches, you are labeled as an intolerant homophobic. Today, tolerance means accepting all others' beliefs and lifestyles. In their book, "The New Tolerance", Josh McDowell and Bob Hostetler write: "It is possible not only to understand but also to expose and counter the insidious agenda of the new tolerance. It is possible not only to keep your children from being 'assimilated' but also to instill within them a 'more excellent way', a way to accept others for who they are without compromising the truth." (17) There is only one Way and one Truth - Jesus Christ. It is your responsibility to protect your children from the steady onslaught of violence, indecent behavior and Godless music and movies. Pray fervently everyday for your family and keep yourself unspotted from the world.

REFERENCES FOR APRIL

1. Rick Weiberg, "ESPN 24: 94 Derek and dad finish Olympic 400 together" (ESPN. Com.) 2005
2. Oswald Chambers, "My Utmost for His Highest" (Discovery House Publishers, Grand Rapids, MI.) 1963 p.96
3. Bryce Inman (compiled and edited), "The Very Best of Sandi Patti" (Word Music) p. 144. (Words and Music by Bill and Gloria Gaither, Gaither Music Company, 1984)
4. Wayne Warner (Compiled & edited), "The Anointing of His Spirit" (Servant Publications, Ann Harbor, Michigan) 1994 p.153
5. Charles Gaines, "How to Grow Up" (Men's Health, Rondale Publishing, Emmaus, PA) Winter 2004, p.52
6. Chuck Norris, "Against All Odds, My Story" (Broadmad & Holman Publishers, Nashville, Tennessee) 2004 p. 245
7. Judson W. VanDeVenter and Windfield Weeden", "The Hymnal for Worship & Celebration" (Word Music, Waco Texas) 1936, "I Surrender All" p. 366
8. Chambers, Ibid.p.73
9. Rhonda O'Brien and Jonathan Gray, "Touch Points for Men" (Tyndale House Publishers, Inc., Wheaton, Illinois) 1998 p.116
10. Stuart Briscoe, "Vital Truths to Shape Your Life" (Tyndale House Publishers, Wheaton, Illinois) 2001 p.77
11. Josh McDowell and Bob Hostetler, "The New Tolerance" (Tyndale House Publishers, Inc., Wheaton, Illinois) 1998 p.98
12. Charles F. Stanley, "Living in the Power of the Holy Spirit" (Nelson Books a Division of Thomas Nelson, Inc. Nashville, Tennessee) 2005 p. 97

13. James Dobson, "When God Doesn't Make Sense" (Tyndale House Publishers, Inc.) 1993, p. 120
14. David Murrow, "Why Men Hate Going to Church" (Nelson Books, A Division of Thomas Nelson Publishers, Nashville, Tennessee) 2005 p. 6, 24
15. Rick Warren, "The Purpose Driven Life" (Zondervan, Grand Rapids, Michigan) 2002 p. 133-135
16. "And They Say All This Joy is Dangerous?" – A poster. (Focus on the Family, Colorado Springs, Colorado) 2000
17. Josh McDowell & Bob Hostetler, "The New Tolerance" (Tyndale House Publishers, Inc. Wheaton, Illinois) 1998 p.27-28

May 1
How Big Is Your God?

"Where can I go from Your Spirit? Or where can I flee for Your presence? If I ascend into heaven, You are there; If I make my bed in hell, behold you are there." Psalm 139: 7-8

"Now to Him who is able to do exceedingly abundantly above all that we ask or think according to the power that works in us." Ephesians 3:20

God is often relegated to the "great One in the sky", "the man upstairs" or the one who resides in the church where you go to worship Him. Some Godly men who are truly saved, pray daily and committed to Christ still don't fathom the omnipotence, the magnitude or the fact that God has always been and always will be the great "I AM". God is so much more than many Christians accept. It is men, in general, who seem less likely to seek God for everything in their lives and release their problems to Him. Perhaps it is that masculine nature that is reluctant to admit that you are incapable of handling your problems and admitting your weaknesses. Max Lucado writes: "...you need a God who can place 100 billion stars in our galaxy and 100 galaxies in our universe. You need a God who can shape two fists of flesh into 75 to 100 billion nerve cells, each with as many as 10,000 other nerve cells, place it in a skull and call it a brain".(1) Re-read today's scriptures. Ponder your God's attributes, His greatness, and His everlasting love for you.

May 2
A Safe Path for Your Journey

"You enlarged my path under me, so my feet did not slip." Psalm 18:36
"And {the Lord} set my feet upon a rock, and established my steps." Psalm 40:2
"He leads me in the paths of righteous." Psalm 23:2

David had to hide for years in the wilderness to avoid King Saul's dogged efforts to kill him. In the wilderness David found refuge in caves found in the mountains. Getting there meant scaling the rugged mountain terrain with its narrow slippery trails. It is probable that he and his loyal band of men had considerable difficulty engaging these dangerous paths moving their animals and supplies. No doubt there were incidents where his men or animals slid off the path and down the rocky slopes. Having had these real life experiences, David used metaphors in songs and poems relating God's providential care to providing safe paths on which to walk. You will face the realities of treacherous storms and the enemy's attempts to destroy you. But, like David, be assured that that God will rescue you by providing safe, wide paths. How eloquently he describes how God will make our paths firm as a rock and how He will lead us in righteousness. God will keep you from falling and give you strength and peace as you walk in Him. Trust Him to be your rock and guide you in right decisions.

May 3
<u>Struggling with Envy</u>

"For where envy and self-seeking exist, confu-
sion and every evil thing are there." James 3:16
"Let us walk properly...not in lewdness and lust
and envy." Romans 13:13

Do you ever wish you had the home, the boat, the car, the success, the money or the wife of a neighbor or a friend? Few of you can say you have never once wanted what someone else has. The old excuse, "I don't want what he has, I just want one like it" is a feeble effort to say you are not envious. Never feel just a bit of "painful or resentful awareness of an advantage enjoyed by another joined with a desire to possess the same advantage"? - Webster (2). Envy is a spirit of the devil which, if not dealt with will drain you spiritually and cause "confusion and every evil thing." Sometimes you may be unaware of your envy. It may be hidden just beneath your spiritual conscience. As you go to the Lord in prayer today, ask for the Holy Spirit to do what David asked: "Search me, O God, and know my heart...and see if there be any wicked way in me, and lead me in the way everlasting." (Psalm 139:23-24) If He reveals any envy in your heart, ask God to remove it so that through sanctification by the Holy Spirit you can live a victorious Godly life.

May 4
The Significance of Young Men

*"O God, You have taught me form my youth;
and to this day I declare Your wondrous works."
Psalm 71:17
"And when the Philistine looked down and saw
David, he disdained him; for he was only a youth,
ruddy and good-looking." I Samuel 17:42*

Few men in the Bible have their lives chronicled in relative detail from their youth to their death as does David. The Holy scriptures paint a portrait of the stages of his growth, victories and failures. We first see David as the youngest of eight brothers and tending sheep and the great prophet Samuel anointed him to become King of Israel. David would someday replace King Saul who had lost favor with the Lord because of his disobedience. The story of David serves to focus on the significance of young men. During David's late teens he was described as "skillful in playing [the harp], a mighty man of valor, a man of war, prudent in speech, and a handsome person; and the Lord is with him." (I Samuel 16:18) His seventeen year wait to become King was not easy. He struggled to survive. But David knew that he was anointed of God. Through patience and encouragement from others, David became the greatest King of Israel at thirty years old. Your Godly influence on the life of a boy or young man can make a difference in his life for God. Tell him God has a purpose for him.

May 5
Holy Boldness

"...and for me, that utterance may be given to me, that I may open my mouth boldly to make known the mystery of the gospel, for which I am an ambassador in chains; that in it I may speak boldly, as I ought to speak." Ephesians 6: 18-19

Moses faced Pharaoh and demanded, "Let my people go!" In defiance of King Darius's decree that no one could worship any god, Daniel went home and began to pray to God and he was thrown into a den of lions to be eaten alive only to be found the next morning alive and well. Gideon started with an army of 32,000, but following God's directions, trimmed it down to 300 men with which he defeated the formidable army of the Midianites. Following the Day of Pentecost when the disciples received the promise of the baptism in the Holy Spirit, it was Peter who stood boldly to speak to a large crowd to proclaim this fulfillment of prophesy. Stephen withstood evil men and was stoned to death. The Apostle Paul preached Jesus with boldness through beatings, imprisonment and death. These were real men. Their obedience to God's call was more important to them than the things of this world. They were available and willing when God called. Seek to be filled daily with Holy boldness and become willing to accept God's call and purpose. The Holy Spirit will give you incredible boldness and confidence through the power of God to change lives around you.

May 6
Coping with Betrayal

"And the Lord turned and looked at Peter. Then Peter remembered the word of the Lord, how He had said to him, 'Before the rooster crows, you will deny Me three times." Luke 22:61

Jesus had every reason to be hurt when Peter betrayed him by his denial of being associated with his Lord. Just a few hours earlier Jesus was betrayed by Judas with a kiss. Judas, like Peter, was one of the twelve who Jesus called to follow Him during His ministry. David was a victim of betrayal. When his son Absalom revolted and took over David's thrown, it was David's trusted and longtime friend Ahithophel who betrayed him and conspired with Absalom. Eugene Peterson writes, "No single piece of information could have been more devastating [For David]." (3) Have you ever felt betrayed by a close friend, a spouse, a business partner or a Christian "role model"? Most of you have experienced the pain and suffering of betrayal. It is leaves you with bitterness. As difficult as it may be, God wants you to turn to Him in prayer and ask Him for a forgiving spirit. Be open the Holy Spirit comfort and guidance when you feel betrayed. He will heal your hurt and he will restore the "peace that passes all understanding".

May 7
<u>Words of Wisdom</u>

"If any of you lacks wisdom, let him ask God, who give to all liberally...and it will be given him."
James 1:5
   "Get wisdom! Get understanding! Do not forsake her [wisdom], and she shall preserve you; love her, and she will keep you. Wisdom is the principal thing; Therefore get wisdom. And you all your getting, get understanding." Proverbs 4:5-7

Wise is defined as "Having or showing good sense; the ability to understand what happens and decide on the right action." (4) Solomon asked God for wisdom. God granted his prayer. The third chapter of I Kings describes an intriguing story of two women who came to Solomon with a dilemma. Two women living in the same house each gave birth to a baby boy three days apart. One woman's baby died during the night and she secretly exchanged her dead baby for the other woman's live baby. The next morning the woman who woke with a dead baby recognized what had happened. Solomon offered to cut the live baby into two parts and give each woman her half. This was acceptable to the woman whose baby had died but the true mother begged Solomon to give the other woman the baby. In the rapidly growing early church the duty to serve widows was placed on seven men "...full of the Holy Spirit and wisdom..." (Acts 6:3) Ask God daily to give you wisdom. A Godly man should use spiritual wisdom to make right decisions in all matters of life.

May 8
The Significance of Mothers in a Man's Life

"Honor your father and your mother, that your days may be long upon the land which the Lord your God is giving you." Exodus 20:12
"Now when Jesus had come into Peter's house, He saw his [Peter's] wife's mother lying sick with a fever. So He touched her hand, and the fever left her." Matthew 8:14-15
"Houses and riches are an inheritance from fathers, But a prudent wife is from the Lord." Proverbs 19:14

In today's devotional time the three scripture verses address three different kinds of mothers as they relate to a man. In Exodus, the fifth of the Ten Commandments requires that a man honor his mother. In the Gospel of Matthew Jesus cared for Peter's mother-in-law and healed her. In Proverbs you are reminded of the value of your wife who, when she has your children, becomes a mother to be revered. Mothers have historically and continue to serve as foundations for families. It is your mother, your mother-in-law and the mother of your children who makes a house a home, nurtures the children, supports a man's career and prays for you and your family in good and in hard times. Don't take mothers for granted. Other than a few exceptional circumstances, your mother nurtured you as an infant, sent you off to school with clean clothes, got up nights when you were sick, comforted you in disappointments and prayed for you every day. Tell the mother(s) in your life how much you love and appreciate them. Honor them through work and deed.

May 9
The New Values Menu

"There is a way that seems right to a man, But its end is the way of death". Proverbs 14:12
"...that we should no longer be children, tossed to and fro and carried about with every wind of doctrine, by the trickery of men, in the cunning craftiness of deceitful plotting, but, speaking the truth in all things into Him who is the head – Christ..." Ephesians 4: 14-15

During a professional conference, I went with a group of colleagues for my first visit to a well-known, one-of-a-kind barbeque rib restaurant. When I asked for the menu the waiter and my "friends" burst our in laughter. This restaurant only served ribs and sandwich bread. No menu was needed. That reminds me of a time growing up when we all understood what our values and those of America were. They were based generally on Biblical principles. There was a very clear understanding of the difference between right and wrong, between good and evil and between guilt and innocence. Those lines have blurred. Today, there is a menu of values from which to choose in order to fit an individual's beliefs. Your children are targets in this satanic movement in which Biblically-based values are considered outdated and intolerant of immorality and godlessness. As a Godly man remain vigilant to what your children read, watch, listen and with whom they associate. And pray fervently for them, teaching them Christ-centered values. Instill in them the values based on the solid rock – Jesus Christ. Explain to them no menu is needed.

May 10
One Way Only

"Jesus said to him, 'I am the way, the truth, and the life. No one comes to the Father except through Me'." John 14:6
"And if it seems evil to you to serve the Lord, choose for yourselves this day whom you will serve...But for me and my house, we will serve the Lord." Joshua 24:15

There are some 4,000 "faith groups" in the world. Is it possible that some of these 4,000 religions can be right and we'll all end up in heaven if we believed in "a god"? I know professing Christians who believe people who worship other gods with good intentions will be in Heaven. There is only one way – through Jesus Christ. Though salvation is found through simple faith in His Son Jesus Christ, there is ample evidence to confirm that every Biblical record of Jesus' earthly life is historically factual. In his book, "The Case for Christ", Lee Strobel, an award-winning journalist with the *Chicago Tribune* and atheist, began his investigation in 1979 for evidence that Jesus was who He claimed to be – God. "For two years", he says, "I read books, interviewed experts, asked questions, analyzed history, explored archaeology, studied ancient literature, and for the first time in my life I picked apart the Bible verse by verse." (5) In 1981, after an exhaustive investigation, he admitted that his "objection to Jesus also had been quieted by the evidence of history." Lee Stroble accepted Jesus Christ as his Savior and is now a teacher/pastor. Praise God today for making that way possible.

May 11
<u>Dealing with Difficult Children</u>

"Children, obey your parents in the Lord, for this is right. Ephesians 6:1
"And you fathers, do not provoke your children to wrath, but bring them up in the training and admonition of the Lord." Ephesians 6:4
"The rod and rebuke give wisdom, but a child left to himself brings shame to his mother." Proverbs 29:15
"And he arose and came to his father. But when he was still a great way off, his father saw him and had compassion on him, and ran and kissed him." Luke 15:20

For you who have children you already know that parenting can be one of the most difficult responsibilities and challenges you face in a lifetime. Today's scriptures offer simple deep, rich wisdom in dealing with your children. In Ephesians, Paul commands your children to obey you. He admonishes you not to provoke them to the point of anger but train them in the things of God. In Proverbs, Solomon says that discipline instills wisdom. And in the fifteenth chapter of the Gospel of Luke is the familiar story of the prodigal son which tells you to love your children unconditionally just as God loves you. With each stage of your children's growth, your role will change. But as Stephen Bly writes, "We will always be Mom and Dad. Neither distance nor neglect can break the bonds that tie us to them." (6) By the time we learn to be parents our children are grown. Don't go it alone – seek God for wisdom and patience in raising the children who He entrusts to you. Bathe your children in prayer every day and live so that they see Christ in you.

May 12
A Man's Legacy

"The Lord God of heaven...who spoke to me and swore to me, saying, 'To your descendents I give this land,'... Genesis 24:7
"By faith he was commended as a righteous man, when God spoke well of his offerings. And by faith he still speaks, even though he is dead." Hebrews 11:4 NIV
"Therefore, since all these things will be dissolved, what manner of persons ought you to be in holy conduct and Godliness." II Peter 3:11

A legacy is often associated with money, land, or gifts left to others following the death of a person. A man with billions of dollars, owns a world-renowned corporation, and has accumulated valuable land would leave a legacy of great wealth to his children and family. After the money is spent, the corporation dissolved and his fame forgotten what will remain of his legacy? The kind of legacy you, as a Godly man, should desire to leave your children is not excessive money or property. You should leave a legacy so much more valuable to your children, to your family and to all those who know you. Your legacy should be the enduring influence of your unwavering faith, your integrity, your Godly wisdom and your love for others. This legacy lives on and will be treasured more than any amount money. That indelible inspirational mark you make on the lives of others will be passed on to future generations. A song written and recorded by Nichole Nordeman includes these lyrics: "I want to leave a legacy. How will they remember me? Did I choose to love? Did I point to You enough to make a mark on things?" (7)

May 13
<u>The Danger of Apathy</u>

"Woe to you who are at ease in Zion, and trust in Mount Samaria..." Amos 6:1
"Therefore let him who thinks he stands take heed lest he fall." I Corinthians 10:12
"Therefore let us not sleep, as others do, but let us watch and be sober." I Thessalonians 5:6

Apathy is perhaps the most subtle, unintentional condition a nation, a church or an individual can lapse into. It can slowly lull a man to sleep spiritually. You may face the threat of apathy even as a long-time Christian. You become apathetic and get into a spiritual slumber when you are not actively serving others, encouraging those in despair and boldly witnessing that causes your adversary, the Devil, to attack you. You may have lost that passion of joy that you felt when Christ washed you clean from sin's penalty. In his book, "Six Battles Every Man Must Win", Bill Perkins confesses his struggle to stay focused on spiritual goals and service for Christ. "Like a lot of men, I tend to lose my focus. I forget the radical changes God brought to my life, and I find it easy to get trapped in an eddy of spiritual passivity." (8) You simply don't see it coming. Then, hopefully, a sermon, a prayer or a scripture will shake you awake and you'll realize you've drifted away from close fellowship with Jesus. Pray today that the Holy Spirit will fill you anew and restore your joy and passion. Renew your commitment to your Lord.

May 14
I'll Do It My Way

*"Then the Lord said to Moses, saying...Speak
to the rock and it shall bring water for them out of
the rock..." Numbers 20:7-8
"Then Moses lifted his hand and struck the
rock twice with his rod; Then the Lord spoke to
Moses and Aaron, 'Because you did not believe
Me, to how hallow Me in the eyes of the children of
Israel, therefore you shall not bring this assembly
into the land which I have given them'." Numbers
20:11-12*

This story of Moses and the rock is a sad one. Recently,
I shared this story with my daughter during a teachable
moment about obedience to God. Her reaction was not
unusual: "After all Moses did, it doesn't seem fair that God
would not allow him to enter the promise land." Read the
entirety of this story. Moses was so angry at the disobedience
of the people and that he, too, became disobedient and struck
the rock instead of speaking to it as commanded. God still
allowed water to flow from the rock for the people. Moses
was held to a high standard. He was anointed and called of
God to be a spiritual leader. Do you accept the Holy Spirit's
guidance when He speaks to you? Or do you do it your way?
The lyrics to Frank Sinatra's song, "My Way", are sadly true
for some men: "For what is a man? What has he got? If not
himself – then he has naught. To say the things he truly feels,
and not the words of one who kneels." As a Godly man you
can rely on the Holy Spirit to live a God-purposed life.

May 15
Real Friends

"A man who has friends must himself be friendly, but there is a friend who sticks closer than a brother." Proverbs 18:24
"Greater love has no man than this, then to lay down one's life for his friends." John 15:13

Genuine friends are rare. Observing my son as he grew up provided for me what real friends are about. In the first grade he befriended a kid named Brandon. We had no idea that Brandon and my son would be close knit friends for life. The relationship which began in elementary school would take them through Cub Scouts, little league baseball, high school football, camping trips and more pranks and trouble than Tom Sawyer and Huckleberry Finn. As fraternity brothers in college their relationship became a bond of loyalty and commitment that neither quarrels, girls or times of separation has yet to diminish. Both moved to a larger city where they started their careers and families. If either called the other with a crisis, the response would be immediate. Jonathan and David developed a friendship during a time when Jonathan's father, King Saul, was stalking David to take his life (I Samuel 18). Jonathan proved to be a friend by saving David's life and unselfishly conceding his legal right as heir to Saul's throne to David. Real Godly friends are supportive, encouragers and trustworthy accountability partners. Cherish your close friends and be one.

May 16
That Masculine Spirit

"And what more shall I say? For the time would fail me to tell of Gideon and Barak and Samson and Jephthah, also of David and Samuel and the prophets: who through faith subdued kingdoms, worked righteousness, obtained promises, stopped the mouths of lions, quenched the violence of fire, escaped the edge of the sword, out of weakness were made strong, became valiant in battle, turned to flight the armies of the aliens,..." Hebrews 11:32-34

Television sit-coms several decades ago portrayed men as hard working, masculine and, sometimes, rabble rousers. On "The Honeymooners" Jackie Gleason played the part of a common working man. During the 1970's sit-com "All in the Family", Archie Bunker was a lower middle class, blue collar worker who frequently argued with his more liberal son-in-law. Somewhere around the 1980's, the roles of men in sit-coms were emasculated with effeminate leading characters. God made you with a masculine heart and mind. It is His purpose for you to harness these male hormones into a passion for spiritual battles. Of course, men should have a sensitive side and a gentle but strong personality. Manhood requires that masculine spirit, willing to be decisive and take action. Jesus' displayed anger toward the moneychangers in God's house. John Eldridge says: "He [a man] must have a cause to which he is devoted even unto death, for this is written in the fabric of his being. That is why God created you – to be his ally, to join Him in the Great Battle." Ask God to use your masculine nature as a Godly man to be a role model for younger men as you serve Christ through serving others.

May 17
<u>In It for the Long Haul</u>

"But you must continue in the things which you have learned and been assured of, knowing from whom you have learned them..." II Timothy3:14
"But none of these things move me; nor do I count my life dear to myself, so that I may finish my race with joy and the ministry which I received from the Lord Jesus..." Acts 20:24

The Apostle Paul admonishes men to stay the course and finish the race. All too often, men start their spiritual race energetically only to gradually lose their first love. God told Jeremiah, "Before you were born I sanctified you; I ordained you a prophet to the nations." (Jeremiah 1:5) You were created for a purpose. It is a wonderful experience to be borne again and receive God the Holy Spirit. But it takes a real man to fight spiritual battles, obeying God in every part of his life. Life's stress of marriage, a job, children, finances and temptations seem overwhelming for many men. Stu Weber writes, "The true measure of a man is not in his physical power, in the skill of his hands, in the quickness of his wit, or in his ability to pile up possessions. True, manly courage is best seen in his willing to make and keep promises – though all hell should oppose him." (8) Though you may grow weary, never give up. Stay the course!

May 18
Anxiety and Worry

"Be anxious for nothing, but in everything by prayer and supplication, with thanksgiving, let your request be made known to God." Philippians 4:6
"Therefore I say to you, do not worry about your life…" Luke 12:22
"Do not fret – it only causes harm." Psalm 37:8

Throughout the Bible we are told not to be anxious or worry. Yet, even a man with the toughest outer shell worries. As David emphasized, worry doesn't do any good but only causes harm. Emotional harm, physical harm and spiritual harm can come from anxiety and worry. Everyone gets stressed, becomes anxious and worries at time in their lives. But to allow anxiety and worry to become a pattern suggests a lack of faith in God and His promises. In fact, Jesus commanded that you not worry because it is worthless since God is in control of everything. In the book **Natural Relief for Anxiety** (9), written from a secular viewpoint, the authors offer some good advice on how to reduce your anxiety and worry if prescribed medications are not recommended by your physician. The very first recommendation is to get in touch with "your higher power". The authors recommend prayer, meditation, reading spiritual literature, spiritual fellowship and compassionate service. Sound familiar? That is precisely what the Bible instructs us to do. We can deepen our personal spiritual relationship with the Holy Spirit and learn to trust Jesus with all of our problems.

May 19
Put a Smile on your Face and Be Happy

"Happy is he who has the God of Jacob for his help..." Psalm 146:5
"Rejoice in the Lord always. Again I will say, rejoice!" Philippians 4:4
"This is the day the Lord has made; we will rejoice and be glad in it" Psalm 116:24

In his 1988 platinum album entitled <u>*Simple Pleasures*</u>, the multi-talented Bobby McFerrin's song, "Don't Worry, be Happy", hit the top of the charts with a message that caused listeners to sing along and feel just a little better for the moment. In life it is often difficult to conjure up a smile and to be really happy. There come those times when people hurt your feelings, those times when you are stressed over a problem and times when your heart is saddened by the death someone dear to you heart. You grow stronger spiritually during your spiritual valleys and trials of life. Yet, God does want you to be happy. When you're happy, you illuminate encouragement to the otherwise mundane, sad world around. People tend to want to be around happy people and happiness can be contagious. Those who know of your profession as a Christian should see you happy most of the time. Pray today that the Holy Spirit will remind you of the many blessings for which you should be happy. You should smile because God is control of your problems.

May 20
Tell Her She Looks Good

"O my love, you are as beautiful as Tirzah, lovely as Jerusalem, awesome as an army with banners! My dove, my perfect one, is the only one..." Song of Solomon 6:4, 5, 9

"And Mordecai had brought up ...Esther, his uncle's daughter, for she had neither father or mother. The young woman was lovely and beautiful." Esther 2:7

Want your wife to be more romantic and want to meet your number one desire? First, love her as Christ loved the church and gave himself for it. Second, engage in conversations she wants to have with you and show her you are interested her and her thoughts and dreams. And third, tell her often and sincerely that she is beautiful and her effort to look good pleases you. Just as men need sex and need to be respected for their manhood, women need to be told that they are attractive and loved. Several times, Solomon described his awe of a beautiful woman with pleasing physical features. Okay, men, let's be honest. Not every wife looks as good as she did when you first laid eyes on her. And chances are many of you don't either. But it is important that both husbands and wives keep themselves in good physical condition for each other. You still want to feel that arousal when you watch her change clothes. Tell her in creative ways how she still has your attention and you'll always love her.

May 21
The Influence of Entertainment

"But evil men and imposters will grow worse and worse, deceiving and being deceived. But you must continue in the things which you have learned and been assured of, knowing from who you have learned them," II Timothy 3:13-14
"Set your mind on things above, not on things of the earth." Colossians 3:2
"...bring every thought into the obedience of Christ," II Corinthians 10-5

Men and families are bombarded daily by a wide variety of sordid, seductive and vulgar entertainment. You hear it on radio stations; you can hear and see it on television and in movies. It's on stores' bookshelves and sold in music stores in every mall in every city. Lyrics and video games glorify everything from illegal drugs to rape to murder. Your children are constantly blitzed by this explicitly immoral entertainment. As Godly man you too are confronted by Satan with this Godless entertainment. What's a guy to do to avoid and resist the onslaught of temptation? How are you to keep your children protected from vile music, videos, movies and magazines? First, you take a stand and say with Joshua, "But as for me and my house, we will serve the Lord." (Joshua 24:15) Let your litmus test be, "Does this glorify God?" or "What would Jesus do?" Remove all forms of this ungodly entertainment from your home and vehicles. When you listen to Christian music, your mind and spirit become in tune with the Holy Spirit. Pray today that you will be a warrior for God and remove it and resist it in the name of Jesus.

May 22
<u>Prayer</u>

"Pray without Ceasing" I Thessalonians 5:17
"I desire that men pray everywhere, lifting up holy hands, without wrath or doubting" I Timothy 2:8

Our pastor just began a series of sermons on prayer entitled "Pray". The simple definition of prayer which he gave was: "Prayer is personal communication with God." In his book "What God Does When Men Pray", William Carr Peel explores the significance of and the results of praying men. He writes: "There is no doubt about it. Prayer takes some getting used to for most of us. Plenty of artificial barriers, which have nothing to do with the essence of prayer, make us feel like outsiders. Religious traditions – such as the use of a special language, being in a certain posture, the necessity to recite certain formulas, or being in a specific place – all needlessly keep us from experiencing the joy of prayer." (10) Our perfect example of prayer is Jesus. Jesus communicated often with God the Father. With all the attributes of humanity, Jesus needed to pray often. On the very night of His betrayal, Jesus was praying on the Mount of Olives. Men, if you don't have a special time to spend communicating with God, begin today. If you begin with five minutes, you will experience Gods peace and the presence of the Holy Spirit. Prayer must be an essential part of your day – not an option.

May 23
What about War?

"So the women sang as they danced, and said: 'Saul has slain his thousands and David his then thousand'." I Samuel 18:7
"To everything there is a season, A time of war, and a time for peace." Ecclesiastes 3:1, 8
"Or what king, going to make war against another king, does not sit down first and consider whether he is able with ten thousand to meet him who comes against him with twenty thousand?" Luke 14:31

War originates, not from God's will, but from the sinful nature of mankind. Perhaps surprisingly, the Bible, in general, does not condemn all war. Though Jesus taught peace, He never openly and directly condemned war. In one of his parables in today's third scripture, He uses an analogy of a king's war strategy in determining whether or not to go to war. When enemies threatened His people, God usually sent them into battle.

Following forty years wandering in the wilderness, Moses gave orders to go in and possess the Promised Land, Canaan. The Israelites were commanded to defeat those who opposed them. Moses commanded, "Begin to possess it, and engage him [King Sihon] in battle." (Deuteronomy 3:24). The Israelites defeated King Og and the sixty cities under his rule. America has engaged its enemies in war throughout history. While not all wars are of God, war has always been part of the human condition. Many Godly men and women have made the ultimate sacrifice for America. Pray for peace and pray for those who fight for justice and freedom. Ask God to give us Christian leaders who will follow His orders.

May 24
Men in Battle

"The total number of chief officers of the mighty men of valor was two thousand and six hundred. And under their authority was an army of three hundred and seven thousand five hundred, that made war with mighty power to help the king [Uzziah] against the enemy." II Chronicles 26:10, 13

"Then one of the servants answered and said, 'Look, I have seen the son of Jesse the Bethlehemite, who is... a mighty man of valor, a man of war...'" I Samuel 16:18

As on this writing, United States troops are in battles in Afganistan and Irag. Our country is on the precipice of military action in North Korea, China, Iran, and other hotspots. It's easy to forget about those who suffer death, loss of body parts and suffering – far away from home where families wait and pray. Some of you know first hand the trauma, fear and deprivation of battle. That's why we celebrate Memorial Day. Tom Soddart, a photojournalist embedded with the U.S. Marines in Iraq, captures the essence of men in battle and writes: "The men have been fighting all night on nighttime patrol. They've just been told one of their comrades has been killed. They're sitting by the waterway, exhaustion on their faces. The adrenaline is flooding, but tiredness and grief are overwhelming them. It is a moment that shows...well, it shows just how awful war can be. It shows how awful war really is." (11) Every single day, pray for those in battle to protect you and preserve "one nation under God." Today, invoke the peace and protection of the Holy Spirit on each soldier who serves for you.

May 25
Graduations and Commencements: A Father's Advice

"My son, hear the instruction of your father..."
Proverbs 1:8
"Now the days of David drew near that he should
die, and he charged Solomon his son, saying: 'I go
the way of all the earth; be strong, therefore, and
prove yourself a man. And keep the charge of the
Lord your God: to walk in His ways, to keep His
statutes, His commandments, His judgments, and
His testimonies...that you may prosper in all that
you do and wherever you turn.'" I Kings 2: 2-3

Jurist Oliver Wendell Holmes, Jr. once said, "Young man, the secret of my success is that at an early age I discovered that I was not God." (12) If only men would learn that lesson early in life and trust God in every aspect of their lives. David's final words of wisdom to his son Solomon serve as one good model. The Apostle Paul imparted Godly advice to young Timothy, Paul's son in the Lord. In II Timothy 2:1 he writes, "You therefore, my son, be strong in the grace that is in Christ Jesus." What bit of wise advice would you give your son or daughter on the day which marks the "commencement" of a new stage in his or her life - graduation from high school or college or a professional school? As a Godly man, hopefully you have modeled the truths of God and demonstrated a Godly character that will offer volumes of wisdom to your children. Words of encouragement and challenge to put God first are wise counsel that will last a lifetime.

May 26
What the Bible Says About Homosexuality

"Do not be deceived. Neither fornicators, no idolaters, nor adulterers, nor homosexuals, nor sodomites, now thieves no covetous, no drunkards, nor revilers, nor extortioners will inherit the kingdom of God." I Corinthians 6:9-10
"If a man lies with a male as he lies with a woman, both of them have committed an abomination." Leviticus 20:13
"Likewise also the men, leaving the natural use of the woman, burned in their lust for one another, men with men committing what is shameful, and receiving in themselves the penalty of their error which was due." Romans 1:27

The Bible is clear on the issue of homosexuality. It is an abomination to God. Webster defines abomination as "extreme disgust and hatred". God hates sin and, like adultery, fornication, lying and murder, homosexuality contradicts holiness. The homosexual act violates the very intent of God's purpose for creating man and woman, male and female. Within the marriage relationship God views sex between and man and a woman as a good. Gay Rights activists promote the homosexual lifestyle as acceptable. Their political influence is strong. As of this writing, Massachusetts legally recognizes same-sex marriage and several states have legalized same-sex unions. Homosexual males are a thousand times more likely to contract AIDS/HIV than the general heterosexual population. To disagree with the Gay agenda is to be labeled homophobic or intolerant. God needs men to "stand in the gap" and affirm the truth. Teach your children the truth. And pray that God will have mercy on

America. History teaches us that many countries which were defeated militarily were already crumbling from within as a result of moral and spiritual decay.

May 27
About Tomorrow

"...whereas you do not know what will happen tomorrow. For what is you life? It is a vapor that appears for a little time and then vanishes away." James 4:14

"Do not boast about tomorrow, for you do not know what a day may bring forth." Proverbs 26:1

"Therefore do not worry about tomorrow, for tomorrow will worry about its own things. Sufficient for the day is its own trouble." Matthew 6:34

Contemplate for a moment how much of your time is spent of thinking about tomorrow. My guess is that you think more about tomorrow's plans, issues, problems and opportunities than those of today. You think of your job, your children, your health, your finances and your spiritual relationship with God in terms of tomorrow. It is not necessarily wrong to plan for the future and prepare for the unexpected. But is important that in doing so you recognize that today, not tomorrow, is where God wants you to focus and serve Him. So how should we deal with tomorrow? First, you should not become so preoccupied with tomorrow that you miss serving God and others today. Secondly, stay prepared for tomorrow in all areas of your life. Thirdly, do not fear, worry or be anxious about what you really don't know about tomorrow. And finally, remember that God holds tomorrow and will be there and in control. Ask God to give you wisdom for today and peace about tomorrow.

May 28
Your Eyes are the Window to Your Mind

"For all that is in the world – the lust of the flesh, the lust of the eyes, and the pride of life – is not of the Father but is of the world," I John 2:16

"The lamp of the body is the eye. If therefore your eye is good, your whole body will be full of light. But if your eye be bad [evil], your who body will be full of darkness." Matthew 6:22-23

"And from the roof he [David] saw a woman bathing, and the woman was very beautiful to behold." II Samuel 11:2

Of all the issues which men face, I am confident that control of the eyes is at the top of the list. If you don't have a problem with your eyes wandering to some attractive woman, then stop reading now. As a man, once this tempting image penetrates your eyesight, it goes directly to the brain where your mind makes the decision to yield or resist. If you are not sanctified daily with a fresh filling of the Holy Spirit, that image and those thoughts will lead you to sinful behavior. Your battle with lust and sin begins with your commitment to control what your eyes dwell on. Obviously, you can't walk around with your eyes closed. You will see and be in the company of attractive women. The secret is to stay aware of the danger in looking with lust. If you're daily walking in fellowship with the Holy Spirit, He will immediately convict you when a glance becomes a gaze. He will strengthen you to keep your eyes and mind from straying. Remember, controlling what your eyes look upon requires daily surrender to Jesus.

May 29
Men's Bible Studies: Building Fellowship and Growing in God's Word

"All scripture is given by inspiration of God, and is profitable for doctrine, for reprove for correction, for instruction in righteousness, that the man of God may be complete, thoroughly equipped for every good work." II Timothy 3:16-17

"...not forsaking the assembling of ourselves together, as is the manner of some, but exhorting one another, and so much more as you see that Day approaching." Hebrews 10:25

The old cliché that "no man is an island" has particular application for Christians who make no effort or commitment to fellowship with other believers. Praying in private is a wonderful experience. Carving out quiet time for studying God's Word strengthens you. Attending church is a time to praise and glorify our Lord. However, too often, men avoid the commitment to join a men's-only Bible study/fellowship group. Regular fellowship opportunities enable you to get to know other men's struggles. It provides men a place to better learn what the Bible says about the real issues they face. Rick Warren emphasizes small group fellowship: "If you want to cultivate real fellowship, it will mean meeting together even when you don't feel like it, because you believe it is important. The first Christians met together every day! Fellowship requires an investment of time." (14) As a Godly warrior, have courage to find a men's Bible study and commit to regular participation. Consider beginning one if one is not available. It will be well worth your investment of time and effort. You'll become a stronger man for it.

May 30
Visit The Sick, Elderly and Prisoners

"...'for I was hungry and you gave Me food; I was thirsty and you gave Me drink; I was a stranger and you took Me in; I was naked and you clothed Me; I was sick and you visited Me; I was in prison and you came to Me'." "...Assuredly, I say to you, in as much as you did it to one of the least of these my brethren, you did it to Me." Matthew 25:35, 36, 40

Perhaps you feel that dealing with your own struggles is enough for you to handle. So you avoid thinking of the less fortunate people near you with needs greater than yours. As a Christian, God has plans for you to fit in His purpose to serve. Though the call to foreign missions is a high calling to serve and share Jesus Christ, you don't have to go to South America to find people desperate for someone to care for and encourage. Within driving distance of your home there are thousands of lonely, hurting, hopeless people. Step outside of your box and visit a nursing home one day and just walk down the halls. Make a call to a local jail or correctional facility and ask if any inmate(s) would welcome a visitor or Bible study. Afraid or reluctant? Henry and Tom Blackaby put it this way: "God will reveal through our relationship with Him His plans and purposes for us. God didn't call us to be successful. God called us to be obedient."(15) You cannot sit on the sidelines and let others go for you. Listen to the Holy Spirit when He nudges you to go and serve.

May 31
Resisting Temptation

"But each one is tempted when he is drawn away by his own desires and enticed." James 1:14
"Be sober; be vigilant; because your adversary the devil walks about like a roaring lion, seeking whom he may devour. Resist him, steadfast in the faith..." I Peter 5:8-9
"...bringing every thought into captivity to the obedience of Christ." II Corinthians 10:5

While all men are tempted to sin, the struggles with certain temptations are more difficult for some men than others and the variation in the kinds of sins exceeds the imagination. Some men are almost uncontrollably drawn to gambling. Integrity issues such as fraud, extortion and illegal schemes are particularly tempting for some men. Pornography addition, drug addition, cheating, lying, homosexuality and issues make up a short list of the many enticements which cause men to be tempted. Due to the masculine nature that men have, the most universal temptation is lust. Male hormones, the natural attraction to some women and a particular environment creates opportunities. As a Godly man, married or single, you are likely to struggle with sexual thoughts many times a day. There is no "cure". It is a daily battle you must fight and win. Prayer, Bible study, worship and a close Christian friend are vital weapons. But your mind is the real battleground and you must, with the Holy Spirit's presence, work on controlling your thoughts and avoiding that first "innocent" comment or second look. Whatever your temptation, don't entertain the thoughts. Ask Jesus to sustain you and then trust him.

REFERENCES FOR MAY

1. Max Lacado, "Traveling Light" (W. Publishing Group) 2001 p.16
2. Webster's Ninth New Collegiate Dictionary (A Merriam-Webster Inc., Springfield Massachusetts) 1991, p. 278
3. Eugene Peterson, "Leap Over A Wall"(HarperCollinsP ublishers, New York, New York) 1997 p.200
4. "The Complete Christian Dictionary for Home and School" (ALL NATIONS, Ventura, California) 1992 p.792
5. Lee Strobel, "The Case for Christ", (Zondervan, Grand Rapids Michigan) 1998, p. 14,265
6. Stephen A. Bly, "Once a Parent, Always a Parent" (Tyndale House Publishers, Wheaton, Illinois) 1993, p.10-11
7. Nichole Nordeman, "Legacy" (Ariose Music administered by EMI Christian Music Group) 2002
8. Stu Weber, "The Heart of a Tender Warrior" (Multnomah Publishers, Sisters, Oregon) 2002 p.33
9. Edmund J. Bourne, Arlene Brownstein and Lorna Garano, "Natural Relief for Anxiety" (New Harbinger Publications, Inc. Oakland California) 2004 p.188-189
10. William Carr Peel, "What God Does When Men Pray" (Navpress, Colorado Springs, Colorado) 1993 p. 16
11. Tom Stoddart, "Tom Sodddart's War" ("Life". Time Incorporated, New York, NY) 2005 p. 73
12. Kathryn and Ross Petra, "Age doesn't matter unless you're cheese" (Workman Publishing, New York) 2002 p. 223
13. The HIV/AIDS Surveillance Report, U.S. Department of Health and Human Services, Centers for Disease Control, National Center for Infectious Diseases, Division of HIV/AIDS through December 2002

14. Rick Warren, "The Purpose Driven Life" (Zondervan, Grand Rapids, Michigan)2002 p. 150-151
15. Henry and Tom Blackaby, "The Man God Uses" (Broadman and Holman Publishers, Nashville Tennessee) 1999, p. 107

June 1
Through the Roof...Faith in Action

"And when they could not come near Him because of the crowd, they uncovered the roof where He was. So when they had broken through, they let down the bed on which the paralytic was lying." Mark 2:4

We grew up playing little league baseball, fishing, hunting and racing our motorbikes. Most everyone thought Wayne and I were brothers, instead of cousins. In time we went our separate ways. But I prayed daily for his salvation. Forty years later we moved back near our home. I had just embarked on a new career at a nearby university and Wayne was jobless, drunk and in the advanced stages of cirrhosis of the liver. For forty years my prayer for him had not changed his heart. While he was in and out of the hospital I often prayed for his body and soul. One fall evening as we sat by his nursing home bed re-living our childhood, the Holy Spirit helped me ask him if he would like to ask Jesus into his heart. In a sane, sober mind, he said "Yes". We prayed together. He confessed his sin and accepted Jesus. During his remaining weeks of his life, his family reported amazing changes in his spirit. God miraculously answers our prayers. He may ask you to connect actions with your faith. Pray, believe and act in obedience. Then expect God to answer in His time and within His purpose.

June 2
A Man with a Vision

"Then he said unto them, 'You see the distress that we are in, how Jerusalem lies in waste, and its gates are burned with fire. Come and let us build the wall of Jerusalem, that we may no longer be a reproach'." Nehemiah 2:17

"Where there is no vision, the people perish;" Proverbs 29:18, KJV

Nehemiah served as King Artaxerxes' cupbearer and had opportunities to be in the King's presence. Several men from Judah told Nehemiah of the destruction of Jerusalem with the walls broken down and the gates burned. Nehemiah's first reaction was to sit down and weep. Then he began to pray and fast. He waited and prayed four months for the right time to approach the King for permission to go to Jerusalem and rebuild the walls. King Artaxerxes granted his request and provided everything Nehemiah needed. As a great leader, Nehemiah first assessed the situation by viewing the devastation. When he returned he charged the people to "Come and let us build..." He had a vision from God and passionately shared his vision. The people followed Nehemiah and worked from daylight until dawn. Through adversity and threats, they continued to build. When they were fearful Nehemiah encouraged them: "Do not be afraid of them. Remember the Lord, great and awesome..." (Nehemiah 4:14). Every man needs a vision from God. There are spiritual battles to fight, spiritual walls to be built, the hungry to be fed and souls to be won. Ask the Holy Spirit to give you a vision, passion and courage to fulfill God's purpose.

June 3
A Father's Love for His Son

"'As for Mephibosheth', said the King, 'he shall eat at my table like one of the king's sons'." II Samuel 9:11
"And the son said to him, 'Father, I have sinned against heaven and in your sight, and am no longer worthy to be called your son'." "But the father said to his servants, 'Bring out the best robe and put it on him, and put a ring on his hand and sandals on his feet'." Luke 15:21-22

There is special importance of the father-son relationship. This relationship is the foundation of your salvation. Jesus is the Son of God the Father. Jesus described this relationship and demonstrated it constantly. Want to be a Godly father? A Godly father loves his son unconditionally. A Godly father understands issues and problems his son faces. A Godly father wants to be with and talk often with his son. A Godly father wants what is best for his son. In today's scriptures we see a natural father and a father figure who, despite circumstances of their sons' lives, they loved their sons unconditionally when others showed little or no concern. David took in and took care of his best friend's son, Mephibosheth, as his own. The prodigal son's father welcomed his undeserving son back home with tears and open arms. Pray that the Holy Spirit will give you a heart to love your son unconditionally as God loves you. Pray for him and strive to be his model that he respects.

June 4
<u>**Take Time to Talk with Your Children**</u>

*"You shall teach them diligently to your chil-
dren, and shall talk of them when you sit in your
house, when you walk by the way, when you lie
down, and when you rise up." Deuteronomy 6:8*
*"Then they brought little children to Him, that
he might touch them; and He said to them [his
disciples], 'Let the little children come to me, and
do not forbid them; for of such is the kingdom of
God." Mark 10:13-14*

I must admit that I regret not spending enough time with
my children. I regret, too, that the time I did spend with
them I was not always focused on them. But what pains me
most is that I missed many opportunities to affirm them as
the beautiful and extraordinary individuals they were/are.
Bill Perkins expresses this so well: "As a father you play a
crucial role in the battle for the heart of your children. Your
affirmation and love will do more to fortify them against the
enemy than you can imagine." (1) Make time to share the
many blessing which God has abundantly given to you, to
your wife and to them. As you sit around the breakfast or
dinner table (a family tradition too often abandoned) listen to
them, offering guidance when asked. Weave into the conversation spiritual applications to their issues and challenges.
Remember: Let nothing - not your job, not your community
activities, not your favorite sport, or not your friends - take
away time you should be spending to be with your children.
This is the purpose for which God made you a father. You
will never regret it.

June 5
<u>Natural Disasters: Why?</u>

"And behold, I Myself am bringing flood waters
on the earth, to destroy from under heaven all flesh
in which is the breath of life; everything that is on
the earth shall die Genesis 6:17
"You will be punished by the Lord of hosts
with thunder and earthquake and great noise, with
storm and tempest and the flame of devouring fire."
Isaiah 29:6
"The Lord has His way in the whirlwind and in
the storm." Nahum 1:3

Hurricane Katrina recently hit the coasts of Alabama, Mississippi and Louisiana leaving unprecedented destruction and loss of lives. Since New Orleans was about 10 feet below sea level, protected from the ocean only by levies which broke, the City flooded like a fishbowl. The death toll was in the thousands. The Bible contains many instances of natural disasters, sometimes God sent. Jesus, Peter, Paul and John (in Revelations) foretold of our present earth's destruction. Theological positions as to God's role in natural disasters leave uncertainty. Natural disasters have occurred since the fall of man. When catastrophic disasters occur you may ask "Why, Lord?" Anne Graham Lotz' book entitled "Why?" offers questions many have. Why did thousands die on September 11, 2001? Why do young men die in wars? "Why does God allow bad things happen?" (7) You may never know the "why?" Job didn't understand "why?" Yet he said, "Though He slay me, yet will I trust Him." (Job 13:15) Now, meditate on this: "I lay my 'whys?' before Your cross in worship kneeling, my mind beyond all hope,

175

my heart beyond all feeling; and worshipping, realize that I in knowing You, don't need a "why?" – Ruth Bell Graham

June 6
Restored and Renewed

"He makes me to lie down in green pastures; He leads me beside the still waters. He restores my soul;" Psalm 23:2-3

"...and be renewed in the spirit of your mind, and that you put on the new man which was created according to God, in true righteousness and holiness." Ephesians 4:23-24

"Therefore we do not lose heart. Even though our outward man is perishing, yet the inward man is being renewed day by day." II Corinthians 4:16

You, like every other Christian man who will get spiritually and emotionally weary. The daily problems of dealing with adversity and resisting allurements of the devil can create spiritual battle fatigue. God knows this and provides "still waters" from which you can drink and gain sustenance. God the Holy Spirit wants to renew, restore and refill you afresh with His strength everyday. "The Shepherd knows your every need. He knows you will grow weary... He can strengthen you: through His word, through others or through your circumstances." (2) Many sincere Godly men struggle with their battles and their strongholds on their own only to become increasingly discouraged. Charles Stanley says it so well: "Every day, ask the Holy Spirit to fill your life anew with His life-giving, joy-producing, comforting, guiding, renewing presence." (3) You cannot allow the demands of life, though they may be necessary and worthy, to sap your energy and make you spiritually anemic. As a Godly warrior ask the Lord to renew you in mind and spirit. He will restore you as you draw closer to Him in pray. God loves you.

June 7
<u>Adultery and It's Lasting Consequences</u>

"For this is the will of God, your sanctification: that you should abstain from sexual immorality; that each of you know how to possess his own vessel in sanctification and honor,... that no on should take advantage and defraud his brother in this matter, because the Lord is the avenger of all such, as we have forewarned you and testified." I Thessalonians 4: 3- 5

There is an alarming rate of increase in adultery in our society. As a Christian man, you know that you are not immune from this temptation. The media, a vacuum of values and your testosterone make you vulnerable everyday. Your natural man is subject to thoughts, fantasies and arousal in almost in any situation from a trip to the grocery store to a routine day at work. Gordon Dalbey writes: "Christian men understand that they cannot in their own human power overcome themselves and the natural desires of the flesh." (4) The Bible is very clear on adultery's disastrous consequences. Stuart Briscoe asks: "What about the harm done to spouses by cheating partners? Who can measure the sense of betrayal, who can calculate the weight of rejection, and who can plumb the depth of pain? Who knows the impact on bewildered children, and who can calculate the cost of broken homes?" (5) Following David's adultery with Bathsheba his success as God's anointed began to unravel. This is, perhaps your toughest battle as a Godly warrior - one you cannot afford to lose! "Freedom to choose...is not about conquering desires, but rather about surrendering to God." (6) Ask God to strengthen your resolve to resist this sin.

June 8
Are You in the Right Church?

*"Now you Philippians know also that in the begin-
ning of the gospel, when I departed from Macedonia,
no church shared with me concerning giving and
receiving but you only." Philippians 4:15*

The church is not only a building but a gathering of fellow
Christians. The Bible instructs us "And let us consider one
another in order to stir up love and good works, not forsaking
the assembling of ourselves together..." (Hebrews 10:24-
25) Choosing to become part of a church family is a major
decision to be bathed in prayer. You should be certain that
the church is founded on Word of God as measured by the
Holy Scriptures. A fundamental principle of every church
should be a strong emphasis on service to those outside
of the local church in the community, in other states and
in foreign missions. Jesus modeled service and sacrifice as
did the early Christian churches. The incident of Pashher,
the priest, striking Jeremiah serves as a reminder that even
pastors, ministers and church staff members can miss God's
purpose, having personal agendas. Are you being suffi-
ciently feed spiritually from sermons and Bible studies? Is
there a men's fellowship/accountability group? Seek God
for a discerning spirit in choosing to be part of a Spirit-lead
church. You need spiritual growth and opportunities to serve
others.

June 9
Dealing With Difficult People at Work

"For a great and effective door was opened to me, and there are many adversaries." I Corinthians 16:9

"But so it happened, when Sanballet heard that we were rebuilding the wall, that he was furious and very indignant and mocked the Jews." Nehemiah 4:1

You probably spend many hours each week at work. Your work is important to you and to your family. Your work is where you want to be happy and successful. No matter where you work, if you work with people you will inevitably encounter difficult employees. The Bible contains many instances of God's people who, in their efforts to serve Him, faced adversity and criticism from difficult people. Nehemiah was led to rebuild the wall of Jerusalem. God gave His blessings, the King supported him and his fellow Israelites joined in the work. But Nehemiah faced criticism and threats from other Israelites. You too experience opposition and uncooperative people at work. John C. Maxwell writes: "Take heart; there are certain general rules you can put into practice that will enable you to work more effectively with problem people. (1) Love them unconditionally; (2) Ask God for wisdom in working with them; (3) Stay emotionally healthy yourself; (4) Do not elevate people to positions of leadership in order to rescue them; and (5) Be honest with God, yourself and them." (8) Today ask the Holy Spirit to equip you with wisdom, patience and love.

June 10
Facing Persecution for Your Faith

"Blessed are those who are persecuted for righteousness sake, for theirs is the kingdom of heaven."
Matthew 5:10
"Yes, all who desire to live godly in Christ Jesus will suffer persecution" I Timothy 3:12

Since Jesus' ascension and the beginning of the Christian church, Christians have been persecuted. In a *New York Times* editorial, A.M. Rosenthal lists some of these countries where Christians are experiencing severe persecution, to include death for their faith. "They evidence a worldwide trend of anti-Christian persecution based on two political ideologies – Communism and militant Islam." (9) Reports of the death of Christian missionaries are seldom included in today's media reports. The persecution of Christians in America has increased dramatically during the past three decades. Hard line secular groups such as the American Civil Liberties Union are making a concerted effort to take your Christian freedoms from schools, public places and speech. Of great concern is the attack and persecution on individual Christian freedoms such as the prohibition of wearing a small cross necklace at work and the elimination of any reference to God from a valedictorian's speech. Our founding fathers opposed recognizing and establishing a national religion. However, they clearly intended to insure and protect the freedom of religion from government interference and constraint. As a Godly man, you will experience persecution. Whenever you do rejoice that your life reflects Christ so that others know that you are a Christian.

June 11
Faith in Action

"By faith Noah, being divinely warned of things not yet seen, moved with Godly fear, prepared the ark for the saving of his household..." Hebrews 11:7

"Do you see that faith was working together with his {Abraham} works, and by works faith was made perfect?" James 2:22

Do you have faith in God? Are you willing to step out in faith and obey God? Godly men, when led by the Holy Spirit, need to obey God in spite the circumstances. Former Coach Bill McCartney felt led of God to begin a ministry to reach men for Jesus. In 1990 Coach McCartney shared his vision with a friend. Within a year, through the prayers and work of other Godly men, the first Promise Keepers conference was held drawing 4,200 men. In 2000 Promise Keepers celebrated its 10th anniversary having reached 5 million men. In 1959 John Osteen obeyed a call from God to begin a church. He started a church in an old feed store in Houston, Texas. God did the rest. From there to Lakewood Church, his son followed the footsteps of his late father as senior pastor. In 2005 they moved into a new worship center, a converted sports arena. Over 57, 000 people attended the Grand Opening. (10) Acting in faith is not for wimps, but Godly warriors. It requires courage. Your call may not involve a major undertaking. If it is but to share your testimony with others believe for courage to do so and the Holy Spirit will give you the right words.

June 12
Death and Dying

"Whereas you do not know what will happen tomorrow. For what is your life? It is even a vapor that appears for a little time and then vanishes away." James 4:14

"...and it is appointed for men to die once but after this the judgment." Hebrews 9:27

"The sting of death is sin, and the strength of sin is the law. But thanks are to God, who gives us the victory through our Lord Jesus Christ." I Corinthians 15:56-57

You may seldom think of death, especially your own. If you're a young man you may feel invincible. No one wants to discuss death over a cup of coffee. Few, to include Christians, talk much about heaven. Fewer people will broach the subject of hell. If you are middle-aged or older, you may have begun to face the reality of death. At fifty-six, I am beginning to grasp the reality that life is a vapor which lingers but for a moment. Death is inevitable. You are not immune. God knows the number of your days. Only God know the "why" and the "when" of your death. The Reverend Billy Graham writes, "Christians are not immune to the fear of death. Death is not always a beautiful release, but an enemy which separates. There is a certain mystery to it. It does not respect the young or the old, the good or the evil, the Christian or the heathen." (11) Keep a strong grip on your assurance of eternal salvation. Jesus' sacrifice at Calvary defeated death's permanence and guarantees you life beyond this world. You will simply leave your human body with all of its imperfections and be ushered by God into a new glorious body.

June 13
The Human Condition for the Just and the Unjust

"For He makes His sun rise on the evil and on the good, and sends rain on the just and the unjust."
Matthew 5:45
"What then? Are we better than they?" "For all have sinned and fall short of the glory of God."
Romans 3:9, 23

Years ago, I believed that a genuine Christian would not sin, would not be sick, and would be protected from bad things that happen to the unsaved and to faithless Christians. As I matured spiritually and observed the reality of the human condition, I realized that Christian men committed adultery like unbelievers and that Godly men died with cancer just like unsaved men. I had the same question that James Dobson posed: "How can an infinitely loving and just God permit some people to experience lifelong tragedy while others seem to enjoy every good and perfect gift?" (12) No human mind can adequately answer that question. But God does bless His children in many special ways and sometimes He chooses to heal, to provide and to make a way when there seems to be no way. Paul declares, "Now unto Him who is able to do exceedingly abundantly above all that we ask or think…" (Ephesians 3:20) You are, as was Jesus, subject to nature, the actions of evil men and death. When bad things happen to you, instead of asking "why?" ask "why not?" Trust God in all things and don't be anxious over that which you have no control.

June 14
Keeping Your Cool

"Be angry, and do not sin:" do not let the sun go down on your wrath, nor give place to the devil."
Ephesians 4:26-27
"So Moses' anger became hot, and he cast the tablets out of his hands and broke them at the foot of the mountain." Exodus 32:19

You are going to get angry. Sometimes becoming angry and acting on it is good. But it can also be a sinful to be angry. Jesus was angry when He overturned the tables and ran out those who were selling animals in the temple courts. (John 2:15) That is considered righteous indignation. Peter, however, displayed anger that is not Godly when he cut off the right ear of one of the chief priest's servants. (John 18:10) Men are prone to express their anger in different ways such a profaning, bottling it inside or through aggressive behavior. Men associate anger and action as being masculine, tough, or courageous. It is part of the male dominance God gave you. But as a Godly man, you're should not let your anger become sin. Anger must be under the control of the Holy Spirit. Traffic grid lock, getting cut off in traffic, insults at work, and arguments with your wife, losing you job and other things can set ablaze of anger within you. Though you will get angry, do not sin! Cool off and let it go. If you're prone to get angry often, ask God to for more patience. Prayerfully consider anger management counseling and seek the Lord's help.

June 15
The Role of the Holy Spirit in Your Life

"But the Helper, the Holy Spirit, whom the Father will send in My name, He will teach you all things, and bring to your remembrance of the things that I have said to you." John 14:26
"...that He would grant you, according to the riches of His glory, to be strengthened with might through His Spirit in the inner man." Ephesians 3:16

One of the most confusing subjects among many Christians is the Holy Spirit. You should not be uncertain as to whom the Holy Spirit is and what His role is today. He is part of the Trinity of God. The Trinity is God the Father, God the Son and God the Holy Spirit. The Holy Spirit is referenced numerous times as being active in the Old Testament. God the Holy Spirit was present with men and enabled men to do a work or preach a word from God the Father. Jesus promised His disciples that He would send another Helper [the Holy Spirit]. He said "...for *He dwells with you* and shall *be in you.*" (John 14:17) Today we receive the indwelling of the Holy Spirit when we accept Jesus. The Holy Spirit lives *in us.* Charles Stanley lists seven works of the Holy Spirit in our lives: 1. The Holy Spirit convicts us of sin; 2. He regenerates us; 3. He teaches and guides us; 4. He comforts us; 5. He gives us spiritual gifts; 6. He imparts His nature to us; and 7. He refines and transforms us so that we become more like Jesus. (13) Pray today and every day asking the Holy Spirit to fill you anew for the day ahead.

June 16
Your Personal Budget: What's God got to do with it?

"So let each one give as he purposes in his heart, not grudgingly or of necessity; for God loves a cheerful giver. And God is able to make all grace abound toward you, that you, always having sufficiency in all things, may have an abundance for every good work." II Corinthians 9:7-8

In both the Old and New Testaments, since Abraham, God has required His followers to tithe and give an offering. In Deuteronomy 12:11 Moses relayed God's command to tithe and give offerings. In Luke 11:42 Jesus chastises the Pharisees for all of their rules and rituals, yet He affirms their practice of tithing. I can attest to life-long experiences on this issue. When I tithe and give offerings for a righteous purpose, my financial needs are always met with blessings. During the two or three times that I felt that I couldn't afford to tithe and didn't, my income simply wouldn't meet my budget requirements. Our family debt increased and our financial circumstances deteriorated. Each time the Holy Spirit would lead me to tithe despite my insistence that giving a tenth of my income would result in disastrous financial woes. Not true! Without exception, when I began tithing again my family and I began to prosper financially and my money didn't run out before the month did. God's economy doesn't make sense to a secular world. But obedience in this area of worship will cause you to prosper.

June 17
Your Responsibility for Abandoned Boys

"As for Mephibosheth, 'said the king [David]',
he shall eat at my table like one of the king's sons."
II Samuel 9:11
"Pure and undefiled religion before God ad the
Father is this: to visit orphans and widows in their
trouble, and to keep oneself unspotted from the
world." James 1:27
"To Timothy, a beloved son..." II Timothy 1:2

In today's first verse, David had found that the disabled son of Jonathan was alive and called for him. David made Mephibosheth as one of his own sons in honor of Jonathan, David's loyal and close friend. In the second verse, James exhorts Godly men to visit orphans. IT is probable that you live in a community in which there are boys and teen-agers whose fathers have abandoned them. According to the National Fatherhood Initiative, almost 40% of America's chil-dren living in single-parent families will experience poverty before they reach age eleven. Children without fathers are at greater risk for behavioral problems. As a Godly man, you can make a difference in a boy's life by encouraging him, providing specific needs as approved by his mother or guardian. You or, perhaps, your son can invite him to church and/or a church activity. Be open to opportunities when the Holy Spirit leads you to be a Christ-like father figure that can change to life of a boy or young man.

June 18
Life's Storms and God's Provision

"Now when neither sun nor stars appeared for many days, and no small tempest beat on us, all hope that we would be saved was finally given up. "...then Paul stood in the midst of them and said, 'Men...I urge you to take heart, for there will be no loss of life among you..." Acts 27:20-22

Nature can be harsh and brutal. Devastation and death by hurricanes, tornados, flooding, lightening and earthquakes take a horrific toll on people's lives. When Hurricane Katrina flooded New Orleans in 2005 many people had no place to go. The storms of life can also be cruel and destructive. You will face storms in which you feel that you cannot survive. Your storm may be the of betrayal of your spouse, dark clouds of depression, a career washed away, a terminal illness or death which shakes your faith or the fury of unrelenting winds of temptation against your mind. You have a place of safety from the storms of life. David writes "And in the shadow of Your wings I will make my refuge, until these calamities have passed by." (Psalm 57:1) Your trust and faith in Christ must be strong enough to sustain you through your storms. The words of an old song ring true: "Hold me fast, let me stand in the hollow of Thy hand, Keep me safe 'till the storm passes by." (14) Jesus never promised that we would have no troubles in our lives. He did, however, promise to be with us until the end of time. Thank Him now for His constant presence.

June 19
Men Just Want to Have Fun

"So the boys grew. And Esau was a skillful hunter, a man of the field." Genesis 25:27
"You are fair, my love, And there is not a spot in you. Come with me from Lebanon, my spouse, With me from Lebanon. You have ravished my heart...Your lips, O my spouse, Drip as the honeycomb;" Song of Solomon, 4:7, 8, 9, 11 - Entitled 'The Beloved'

Part of your God-created masculine soul is that need for adventure, competition and having fun. He wants you to have courage, passion, joy and desire – for good and righteous things. Men find fulfillment in adventures like auto and bike racing, rugged football, mountain climbing and white water rafting. Many men find it fun to get up at 4:00 am, at 25 degrees and head for the woods to hunt. For others, it's fishing all day in the blistering sun. You should also have enthusiasm in your spiritual walk. Psalms of David uplifted and made people happy: "This is the day that the Lord has made; We will rejoice and be glad in it. (Psalm 118:24) Your body was created with testosterone and within God sanctioned marriage you should enjoy the pleasure of sex. But remember; God never gives you an excuse to sin by putting fun above obedience to His Word. John Eldredge writes, "A man just won't be happy until he's got adventure in his work, in his love and in his spiritual life." (15) Be thankful to God for creating you to have fun and to enjoy manhood as you faithfully serve Him on your journey from here to eternity.

June 20
Seasons of a Man's Life: Summer

"Now learn this parable from the fig tree: When its branch has already become tender, and puts forth leaves, you know that summer is near." Mark: 13:28
"David was thirty years old when he began to reign..." II Samuel 5:4

As the temperature rises, fruit is beginning to grow and kids are on summer vacation, spring turns to summer gradually and without notice. Nature has changed with different characteristics and with the anticipation of growth. So is life as a young man in his mid-to-late twenties gradually moves into another season in which he will change, grow and come into full bloom. For the next fifteen to twenty years he will mature, make critical life decisions and find opportunities. During these years a man usually marries, begins a family, and finds success in his career. It is a season for building a strong spiritual foundation, strengthening his Godly values and discovering God's purpose. A young David, known as "a man after God's own heart" stepped into his first real job - King of Israel at the age of thirty. During the next twenty years he became a mighty warrior and a great leader. He also succumbed to the temptation of murder and adultery. A man should establish his commitment to Christ early in his adult life. He should also commit to nurturing his wife and children. It can be a wonderful, fulfilling season for the Godly man who has a made-up mind to follow Jesus.

June 21
Passion for Spiritual Victories

"But His word was in my heart like a burning fire shut up in my bones; I was weary of holding it back, and I could not. But the Lord is with me as a mighty awesome one. Jeremiah 20:9, 11
"Then David danced before with all his might..."
II Samuel 6:14

Today you have the victory in Christ and you should look forward to life with great anticipation! You face daily battles in which the Holy Spirit strengthens you and guides you away from sin and harm. Or you may face major crises in your life in which you cling to faith and trust in God. Remember Paul's words in I Corinthians 15:57: "But thanks be to God, who gives us the victory through our Lord Jesus Christ." Winston Churchill, in a radio broadcast rallied the French against German occupation. He said: "Never stop, never weary, and never give in." (16) You win a spiritual battle everyday that you live a Godly life, every time you pray or read His word. God has and does answer your prayers. Too often Christians tend to take blessings for granted. Take a cue from Jeremiah and David and discover the excitement and joy in their gratitude and of love God. Become passionate for God's goodness and blessings and spread your joy with others.

June 22
Your Role as Head of the Family

"Hear, my children, the instruction of a father, and give attention to know understanding..." **Proverbs 4:1**

"For the husband is head of the wife, as also Christ is head of the church. Husbands, love you wives, just as Christ loved the church and gave Himself for her." Ephesians 5:23, 25

Despite the feminist movement and those who have attempted to emasculate you as head of your home and family, God's word remains God's standard for a man's role in his family. In our society, the roles of both men and women are constantly changing. In many families, both parents work outside the home to gain the income they want for their standard of living for their children. It is preferable for a mother to spend as much time as possible raising and nurturing her little ones. Yet, some women find it necessary to work outside the home, insuring their children receive proper care. Women sometimes earn more than their husbands. While this can create an esteem issue for your masculine spirit, it does not change God's word that you are the head of the wife and the home. As a Godly husband, you are to insure the discipline of your children, lead in major decisions and be the spiritual leader of your family, while valuing the importance of your wife in these areas. You are to love, respect, and adore your wife. And always be the model Godly man for your children. This will require you to remain in fellowship with your Lord.

June 23
Gentleness: A Fruit of the Spirit

"But the fruit of the Spirit is love, joy, peace, longsuffering, kindness, goodness, faithfulness, gentleness..." Galatians 5:22-23
"You have also given me the shield of Your salvation; Your gentleness has made me great." II Samuel 22:36

Gentleness is a masculine trait. Often the word is associated with the characteristic of a mother with her child. But gentleness is a spiritual quality the Godly man. Though David was a might warrior, he relied on the gentleness of God in his life. The Apostle Paul suffered inhumane persecution for preaching Christ. He describes some of his persecution for Christ: "From the Jews five times I received forty stripes minus one. Three times I was beaten with rods; once I was stoned; three times I was shipwrecked;...in weariness and toil, in sleeplessness often, in hunger and thirst, in fastings often, in cold and nakedness –"(II Corinthians 11:24, 25, 27) Yet he writes to the church at Thessalonica: "But we were gentle among you, just as a nursing mother cherishes her own children." (I Thessalonians 2:7) These were real men - men who were fearless and who dared to risk life for Christ. They understood and modeled gentleness. Ask the Holy Spirit to fill you with gentleness and preserving your masculine qualities that God intends you to possess.

June 24
Character Counts

"...but we also glory in tribulations, knowing that tribulation produces perseverance; and perseverance, character; and character, hope." **Romans 5:3-4**
"For you know his proven character, that as a son with his father he served me in the gospel." **Philippians 2:22**

The Complete Dictionary for Home and School defines character as: 1. "The part of a person that makes one different from anyone else; 2. Honesty; integrity, morals, etc." (17) Surveys of high school and university students reveal that a large majority admit to committing plagiarism at least once. We know that reports of white collar crimes such as fraud have increased dramatically. Large corporations have been defrauded and brought down by top CEO's, thus robbing their stockholders of their investments and pensions. In professional sports players have been exposed for illegal drug use and schemes to benefit themselves. It seems a man of character is hard to find. Yet, God makes it clear in His word that character counts. As a Godly man, your character should be unblemished from any unethical and illegal practices and behavior. In 1896 the inventor, Booker T. Washington, said, "Character, not circumstances, makes the man." (18) Knute Rockne, Notre Dame's legendary football coach said, "The one thing no one can ever take away from you is your integrity." (19) You have the opportunity through the Holy Spirit's presence and by living a life modeled after Jesus to be a man of character.

June 25
<u>No one Ever Said It Would Be Easy</u>

"Yes, and all who desire to live godly in Christ Jesus will suffer persecution." II Timothy 3:12
"But may the God of all grace, who called us to His eternal glory by Christ Jesus, after you have suffered a while, perfect, establish, strengthen, and settle you. I Peter 5:10
"Before I was afflicted I went astray, But now I keep Your word." Psalm 119:67

Life can be full of hard knocks, disappointments and grief. I can say without equivocation that the overwhelming number of difficulties in my life resulted from bad choices which I made. Then there are Satan's constant attempts to prevent me from being all that God wants me to be. Every day you rise you can expect adversity. It stems from man's sinful nature. As a Christian, you are not immune from the struggle between the old natural man and the new spiritual man. Paul, one of the most passionate men for Christ, expressed his struggle in Romans 7:19, 21: "For the good that I will to do, I do not do; but evil I will not do, that I practice. I find then a law, that evil is present with me, the one who wills to do good." You seldom hear from pulpits that living a Godly life is spiritual warfare and it's not easy. You would be without hope had it not been for the price for sin which Jesus paid for you on the cross and the presence of the Holy Spirit. That is why despite the struggle against sin, you will experience times of joy and peace that passes understanding.

June 26
Slip Sliding Away

"For Demas has forsaken me, having loved this present world and has departed to Thessalonica..."
II Timothy 4:10
"For they all [Jesus' disciples] Him and fled."
Mark 14:50
"They have forsaken the right way and gone astray, following the way of Balaam the son of Beor, who loved the wages of unrighteousness." II Peter 2:15

Paul Simon one of the well-known duos of the 1960's and 1970's, *Simon and Garfunkel,* wrote the song entitled "Slip Sliding Away" The last stanza includes these words: "God only knows, God makes His plan... Believe we're gliding down the highway, when in fact we're slip sliding away." Whether the term is "forsaking", "flee", "gone astray" or "departed", they can be descriptive of once Godly men who have fallen away from their first love and their daily walk with the Holy Spirit. They're slip sliding away from their personal relationship with the Holy Spirit and from God's purpose for their lives. It seldom happens abruptly or intentionally. A Godly man doesn't wake up one morning and say to himself, "I'm throwing in the towel" or "God, I quit!" It is a gradual and subtle sliding away from prayer, from Bible study and from church attendance - lulled into apathy. Once you have experienced His love and peace, you can never be truly happy living away from Him. Today ask God as David did in Psalm 51:12: "Restore to me the joy of your salvation." He will respond with His love, mercy and sufficient grace.

June 27
What Do You Treasure?

"For where your treasure is, there your heart will be also." Luke 12:34
"For we brought nothing into this world, and it is certain we can carry nothing out" I Timothy 6:7

What do you really cherish the most? Is it money? Is it your land? Is it your position at work? Is it some recreation? My father was a blue collar worker who worked in harsh conditions for forty seven years. After twenty nine years working in the ore mines he was laid off when the mines closed. He eventually found another job and from that point in his life he seemed to be consumed with working for retirement. Working overtime, he paid for our modest home. He patiently waited, hoping to have many healthy years to enjoy retirement. He did retire, achieving that which he treasured most only to discover that he had terminal cancer. He lived less than one year from retirement. Some men scheme to find that opportunity which will produce instant wealth. Stuart Brisco says: "Money or wealth can be that which we possess or that which possesses us. If it's the former, it can be a blessing. If it's the latter, our love for it becomes a root of all kinds of evil." (20) Ask the Holy Spirit to search your heart and show you the good and right things to treasure.

June 28

Give God Praise for His Goodness, Love and Grace

*"Praise the Lord! Praise the Lord, O my soul!
While I live I will praise the Lord; I will sing praises
to my God while I have any being." Psalm 146:1-2
"Oh that men would give thanks to God for His
goodness..." Psalm 107:8*

God is great, God is good. But do you fully comprehend
the depth of His goodness, love, and grace? Are you truly
grateful for His blessings heaped upon you every day? And
do you thank Him and praise Him for who He is and what
He does for you? Some men only go to God in prayer when a
crisis or need arises. Others spend their time in prayer asking
for things and seeking God's intervention. Jesus' model for
prayer begins with "Our Father in heaven, Hallowed be Your
name. Your kingdom come. Your will be done on earth as
it is in heaven." (Luke 12:2) God desires your praise. You
should begin every prayer with praise and thanksgiving to
God. Praise Him for who He is. As creator of all things, He
is mighty and omnipotent. Praise Him for His goodness and
grace. He sent His Son to sacrifice His life to pay the penalty
for your sin. Then praise Him for His immeasurable blessings to you, to include eternal life, your material things, your
health, your family, your church and the presence of the Holy
Spirit. Praise lifts your spirit and enhances your communion
with your Heavenly Father.

June 29
Watch, Stand Fast, Be Brave, Be Strong

"Watch, stand fast in the faith, be brave, be strong." I Corinthians 16:13
"Continuing earnestly in prayer, being vigilant init wit thanksgiving…" Colossians 4:20
"You therefore, my son, be strong in the grace that is in Christ Jesus. You therefore endure hardship as a good soldier of Jesus Christ. No one engaged in warfare entangles with the affairs of this life, that he may please him who enlisted him as soldier." II Timothy 2:1, 3, 4

During the time when Nehemiah and the Israelites were re-building the walls of Jerusalem, they were threatened and intimidated by those who sought to stop Nehemiah's God-sanctioned task. They stayed on watch. While half of them worked the other half stood watch with spears, shields, bows and breastplates. As Paul admonished the Ephesians, "Put on the whole armor of God that you may be able to stand against the wiles [scheming] of the devil."(Ephesians 6:11) Never allow your adversary, the devil, slip the world's culture into your home. In both of today's scripture verses Paul says, "Be strong". Your spiritual strength is directly proportional to the time you spend in prayer, Bible study, worship and fellowship with Godly men. Stand your ground and engage your adversary when he tempts you and inundates your family with things which represent a valueless culture. Never allow evil and those who represent Godless beliefs to intimidate you. You are not defenseless. Invoke the name of Jesus and "having done all, stand".

June 30
Our Advocate to God

"My little children, these things I write to you, so that you may not sin. And if anyone sins, we have an Advocate with the Father, Jesus Christ the righteous. And He Himself is the propitiation for or sins, and not for ours only but also for the whole world" I John 2:1-2

Webster defines *advocate* as "one that pleads the cause of another". As a Christian, you are not exempt from committing sin because you have to battle with the flesh with its weaknesses, its desires of the flesh and its Adamic nature. Thus, you may hear some refer to Christians as "saved sinners". However, this verse does not give you a license to practice sin. The first part of this verse sets the tone John's intention in his writing. John, one of Jesus' twelve apostles, is clear in his message that you should not sin. In verse four of this chapter, John leaves no doubt as to his position. "He who says 'I know Him' and does not keep His commandments, is a liar, and the truth is not in him." Yet John knows that believers have not yet reached perfection and may stumble and fall into temptation. Therefore, Jesus Christ, who sits at the right hand of the Father and "pleads our cause" to the Father, is your advocate when you sin. When you confess your sin, your sin is forgiven. Then seek restoration in prayer through the Holy Spirit to renew your first love.

REFERENCES FOR JUNE

1. Bill Perkins, "Six Battles Every Man Must Win" (Tyndale House Publishers, Inc, Wheaton, Illinois) 2004 p.71
2. Henry T. Blackaby and Richard Blackaby, "Experiencing God Day-By-Day." (Broadman and Holman Publishers, Nashville, Tennessee) 1997 p. 59
3. Charles F. Stanley, "Living in the Power of the Holy Spirit" (Nelson Books, Nashville Tennessee) 2005 p. 96-97
4. Gordon Dalbey, "Healing the Masculine Soul" (W. Publishing Group, Nashville, Tennessee), 2003 p. 81
5. Stuart Briscoe, "Vital Truths to Shape Your Life" (Tydale House Publishers, Inc., Wheaton, Illinois) 2002 p. 112
6. Dalbey, p. 83
7. Anne Graham Lotz, "Why?" (W. Publishing Group, Nashville, Tennessee) 2004 p. 19
8. John C. Maxwell, "Be a People Person" (Chariot Victor Publishing, a division of Cook Publishing, Colorado Springs, Colorado) 1989 p.112-113
9. A.M. Rosenthal, "Persecuting the Christians", *The New York Times,* Editorial Page, February 14, 1997
10. Promise Keepers Website, (Promise Keeper Headquarters, Denver, Colorado) Copyright 2005
11. Billy Graham, "Death and Life After" (W. Publishing Group, a Division of Thomas Nelson, Nashville, Tennessee) 1987 p. 9
12. James Dobson, "When God Doesn't Make Sense" (Tyndale House Publishers, Inc. Wheaton, Illinois) 1993 p. 112
13. Stanley, p. 74 – 77
14. Mosie Lister, "'Till the Storm Passes By" (Mosie Lister Publications, Tampa, Florida) 1958
15. John Eldredge, "Wild at Heart" (Thomas Nelson Publishers, Nashville, Tennessee) 2001 p. 200

16. James C. Humes, "The Wit & Wisdon of Winston Churchill" (Harper Perennial, A Division of Harper-Collins Publishers) 1995 p. 23
17. *The Complete Christian Dictionary for Home and School* (ALL NATIONS and distributed by Gospel Light, Ventura, California) 1992 p. 97
18. Alex Barnett, "The Quotable American" The Lyons Pres, Guilford, Connecticut) 2002 p.145
19. John Heisler, "Quotable Rockne" (Towle House Publishing, Nashville, Tennessee) 2001 p.105
20. Briscoe, p. 151

July 1
Dealing with Prejudice

"But a certain Samaritan, as he journeyed, came where he was. And when he saw him, he had compassion on him. So he went to him and bandaged his wounds, pouring oil and wine; and he sat him on his own animal, brought him to an inn, and took care of him." Luke 10:33, 34

"There is neither Jew nor Greek, there is neither slave, nor free, there is neither male nor female; for you are all one in Christ Jesus." Galatians 3:28

Few men can say unequivocally that they have not harbored some "preconceived judgment or opinion" (Webster) toward someone of a different faith, a different race, a different culture, or a different social-economic status. As a Godly man you should not prejudge or treat anyone differently because of their distinctive characteristics. Don't paint everyone in a category with the same broad brush. In the preceding verses in Luke 10 in which the Samaritan cared for a man who had been robbed and beaten, a Jewish priest and a Levite had passed by without offering assistance. The Jews despised Samaritans who were Gentiles. Yet, it was a Gentile man who demonstrated love and mercy toward the distressed stranger. It is bad behavior of others which we should find intolerable, not the color of their skin or the size of their home. You may struggle with prejudice. Ask the Holy Spirit to enable you not to prejudge others based on the behavior of a few and to remind you that Christ died for *all* men – to include you who were once a sinner lost without Christ.

July 2
Caring for Aging Parents

"Honor your father and your mother, that your days maybe long upon the land which the Lord your God is giving you." Exodus20:12
"...and he [David] said to the king of Moab, 'Please let my father and mother come here with you, till I know what God will do for me'. So he brought them before the king of Moab, and they dwelt there with him all the time David was in the stronghold." I Samuel 22:3-4

Aging is a fact of life. Everyone wants to live a long time, but no one wants to be "old". As the aging process takes its toll on your parents' lives to the extent that they need assistance with routine activities and in the ability to properly care for themselves it is your responsibility to provide your support and assistance. This is clearly God's will. Caring for your father and mother is a part of the marriage and family relationship which God ordained. In other cultures and about a half century ago in our society, aging parents who could no longer function independently were taken into the home of an adult child to live and receive care until death. Today's culture in which both spouses work full-time, parental care-taking has changed similarly as has child rearing. While this is a time of stress, difficult decision-making and guilt for you, remember the emotional pain your parents are experiencing. "Our culture places such value on self-reliance that aging parents, especially those who survived the Depression, resist acknowledging weakness." (1) Respect their dignity. As David did, you must make provisions to care for your parents and do so with gentle love, respect and gratitude they deserve.

July 3
<u>God's Love is Abundant</u>

"Now hope does not disappoint, because the love of God has been poured out in our hearts by the Holy Spirit who was given to us." Romans 5:5

"And we have known and believed the love that God has for us. God is love, and he who abides in love abides in God, and God in him." I John 4:16

"...to know the love of Christ which passes understanding; that you may be filled with all the fullness of God." Ephesians 3:19

There is no human being that can fully comprehend the love of God. Try as you may, it is unfathomable to the mind. Yet you can experience a fullness of His love as you walk in the Spirit and allow Him to love you. The basic tenet of your salvation is the love God has for you. It is important that you understand that God really loves you and He wants to bless you. If you do not deeply believe that, it will be difficult for you to trust God and have faith in God. Perhaps no words better describe God's love than those penned by Fredrick M Lehman in the early 1900's in the song, *"The Love of God"*. The lyrics of the third stanza and the refrain so eloquently describe His love: "Could we with ink the ocean fill and were the skies of parchment made, were ev'ry stalk on earth a quill and every man a scribe by trade, to write the love of God above would drain the ocean dry, nor could the scroll contain the whole though stretched for sky to sky. O love of God, how rich and pure! How measureless and strong!" This love He pours out on you.

July 4
Dare to Be Free

"Afterward Moses and Aaron went in and told Pharaoh, 'Thus says the Lord God of Israel': Let My people go, that they may hold a feast to Me in the wilderness" Exodus 5:1

"But God be thanked that though you were slaves of sin..." "And having been set free from sin..." Romans 6:17-18

Today America celebrates Independence Day. We recognize when our founding fathers signed the Declaration of Independence which declared the colonies to be a sovereign government from the rule of the British Government. Since then, America has stood as a symbol of freedom. But it didn't come without opposition. The Revolutionary War was waged between this new government and the British, in part, to gain religious freedom. "In declaring their independence from earthly power and authority, our Founding Fathers declared their dependence upon Almighty God: 'With firm reliance on the protection of divine Providence'."(2) There are some similarities in this American event and that of God setting His people free from slavery under the Egyptian King Pharaoh nearly 3,500 years ago. God sent Moses to persuade King Pharaoh to set the Israelites free from hard labor bondage. It began with God's declaration of independence - "Let my people go". Though opposed by Pharaoh they were freed. God set all mankind free when He sent His Son Jesus to serve as a sacrifice for our sin so that we are free from the sting of eternal death. Be grateful on this special day for what happened in 1776 as well as that ultimate victory the cross.

July 5
America: Built on a Foundation of Prayer

"If My people who are called by My name will humble themselves, and pray and seek My face, and turn from their wicked ways, then will I hear from heaven, and I will forgive their sin and heal their land." II Chronicles 7:14
"Blessed is the nation whose God is the Lord, The people He has chosen as His own inheritance." Psalm 33:12

The freedoms we hold dear in American are under attack by a satanic secular movement which is at work in organizations, among some government officials, in the media and in individuals who use their wealth and status to denigrate God and our Judeo/Christian heritage. As a Godly man, it is important that you teach your family and share with others that America was built on a foundation of prayer and faith in Almighty God. Freedom of religion and from religious intolerance is the primary reason the Pilgrims sailed to America. From the first meeting in Congress until this writing, every session of Congress is opened with prayer. Most presidents have recognized God. Samuel Adams stated: "We have this day restored the Sovereign, to Whom alone men ought to be obedient. He reigns in heaven and ...from the rising to the setting of the sun, may His Kingdom come." (3) In his Gettysburg Address, Lincoln included: "—that this nation, under God, shall have a new birth of freedom—" (4) Never acquiesce your heritage of a nation built through prayer under God. Proclaim that we can continue to be blessed as a nation only when we acknowledge God as Supreme.

July 6
Patriotism and God

"And I looked, and arose and said to the nobles, to the leaders, and to the rest of the people, 'Do not be afraid of them. Remember the Lord, great and awesome, and fight for your brethren, your sons, yours daughters, your wives and your houses.'."
"For who is this uncircumcised Philistine, that he should defy the armies of the living God?" I Samuel 17:26

In his Farewell Address, George Washington said: "Of all the dispositions and habits which lead to political prosperity, religion and morality are indispensable supports. In vain would that man claim the tribute of patriotism who should labor to subvert these great pillars of human happiness..." (5) Patriotism is the love for one's country. During World Wars I and II, patriotism was strong in our country. The nation was united against the axis of evil and the tyrants who threatened the world. Almost every American was willing to sacrifice in some way to support our troops who were scattered throughout Europe, the Pacific and other parts of the world. As a lad David proved himself to be a courageous patriot for Israel when he refused to allow the army of Israel to be defied by a Philistine giant. While God wants you to demonstrate your patriotism to your country, he also desires your patriotism to Him and to the coming new heaven and earth which He has promised. Love America, but remember you are just a stranger passing through on a journey to your eternal land of promise.

July 7
<u>What the Bible Says about Alcohol</u>

"He causes the grass to grow for the cattle, and vegetation for the service of man, that
He may bring forth food from the earth, and wine that makes glad the heart of man,"
Psalm 104:14-15
"At last it [wine] bites like a serpent, and stings like a viper." Proverbs 23:32
"And when they ran out of wine, the mother of Jesus said to Him, 'They have no wine'." Jesus said to them, 'Fill the water pots with water'. And they filled them to the brim. When the master of the feast had tasted the water that was made wine,"
John 2:3, 7, 9

You have heard opposing views on alcohol consumption. Some pastors declare that the wine used in the Bible was grape juice and not intoxicating. Others teach that it was intoxicating, citing numerous scriptures to that effect. I find no definitive mandate in the scriptures against the moderate use of alcohol. Neither the Old Testament nor the New Testament prohibits the consumption of alcohol in moderation. Yet, the scriptures send a strong message of warning about the pitfalls of intoxicating drink. No doubt you know the devastating effects of alcohol on some relative or friend. The consequences extend far beyond the one who drinks to excess. Marriages are destroyed, families suffer hurt and shame and children become innocent victims. Also, as a believer you should avoid behavior and habits which offend fellow believers. And, you may have a genetic or hereditary predisposition to alcohol addiction. Your best choice is to refrain from alcohol. If you do drink, you are stepping into potentially perilous waters and your witness as a Godly man is at risk for being diminished. Read the scriptures on this issue and pray fervently that God will give you wisdom to make the right choice.

July 8
Preference or Purity?

"Let not him who eats despise him who does not eat, and let not him who does not eat judge him who eats; for God has received him." Roman 14:3
"And those who are Christ's have crucified the flesh with its passions and desires. If we live in the Spirit, let us also walk in the Spirit." Galatians 5:25-26

Often we find contention among church members over doctrinal issues. Church denominations can often be distinguished by minor interpretations of scriptures which have no eternal consequence. As a believer and committed Christian, you will be faced with controversial issues. Some of these issues in your local church may include what is appropriate attire for church, the choice between traditional and contemporary music and the method of administering the Lord's Supper. These represent but a few of the petty issues with which some Christians become obsessed. Most of them should not become stumbling blocks to your faith and fellowship. Among denominations you will find hard and fast beliefs on such issues as musical instruments or no musical instruments in worship, the wearing or not wearing of cosmetics and jewelry, and the role of women in the church. All of these are matters of preference which Paul addressed in today's scriptures. They do not determine a person's salvation. Issues such as baptism, immorality, being borne again in the Spirit and the virgin birth are issues of purity. These are essential to your faith in Christ and are not to be compromised. Seek the Holy Spirit to show you if the issue is one of preference or purity.

July 9
Vacation: Leave the Cell Phone at Home

"That you give him rest from the days of adversity," Psalm 94:13
"And they rested on the Sabbath according to the commandment." Luke 223:56
"He departed to the mountain by Himself alone." John 6:15

"There's a world where man and nature live in perfect harmony and time sways to the rhythm of a lover's heart. And life couldn't be more perfect. So your time is as free from worries as it is full of pleasures." (6) Sounds wonderful, doesn't it? This vacation ad sends a message of tranquility and relaxation. You need that. Your wife needs that with you. In a fast-paced society in which many of you live and work you need time to rest your heart and mind and allow the Holy Spirit to restore your inner man. As in today's scriptures, Jesus grew tired and withdrew Himself to rest and commune with His Heavenly Father. My wife and I occasionally have opportunities to get away for rest and restoration. I notice with increasing frequency that people who have driven or flown hundreds of miles to get away from the "rat race" are constantly talking on their cell phones with business partners and customers - not really leaving their stressors behind. Leave your cell phone at home and experience solitude, communion with the Holy Spirit and much-needed time alone with your wife.

July 10
Marriage May End, Fatherhood Doesn't

"For this reason a man shall leave his father and mother and be joined to his wife, 'and the two shall become on flesh'; so then they are no longer two, but one flesh." Mark 10:7- 8

"But if anyone does not provide for his own, and especially for those of his household, he has denied the faith and is worse than an unbeliever." I Timothy 5:8

No marriage, including yours, is immune to divorce. Nearly every study done on divorce in America finds that there is little difference in the rate of divorce among church-goers and non-church-goers. A study conducted at Rutgers University notes that "the American divorce rate today [2003] is more than twice that of 1960." (7) If you are married treasure that relationship and protect it. With a few exceptions, divorce is not an option. The abandoned spouse and the children experience feelings of rejection and betrayal. Children are perhaps the real victims even when a divorce is somewhat amicable. When men become divorced, it is critical that, while their marriage may have ended, their responsibilities as a father have not. A man should spend time with his children, support them, instill in them Christian values and assure them of his love for them. In Proverbs God gives fathers instructions to share with their children: "My son, do not forget my law, but let your heart keep my commands;… Let not mercy and truth forsake you; bind them around your neck, write them on the tablet of your heart, and so find favor and high esteem in the sight of God and man." (Proverbs 3:1, 3, 4)

July 11
"It's not about *Me*"

But none of these things move me; nor do I count my life dear to myself, so that I may finish my race with joy, and the ministry which I have received from the Lord Jesus, to testify to the gospel of the grace of God." Acts 20:24
"Let no one seek his own, but each one the other's well-being. "I Corinthians 10:24

Our society emphasizes self gratification and being the center of one's world. No doubt you have been engaged in a conversation with a friend or relative who talked incessantly about themselves. Or perhaps you know someone who obsesses about their problems and illnesses. It's always about *"me"*. A *"me"* attitude contradicts everything the Bible teaches. It flies in the face of the Cross. Every great and God-anointed man in the Bible counted their lives as loss to God's calling and purpose. Moses left the grandeur of the palaces in Egypt and committed his life to God's call to "suffer with the righteous". For David, success was never about *"me"* but always about God. So many selfless men like Jeremiah, Abraham, the committed eleven disciples of Jesus, and the Apostle Paul gave up much to suffer and serve God and others. Today, ask the Holy Spirit to search your heart and see if there is too much *"me"* in your life and not enough of others. The lyrics of a song I recall from long ago say it so well: "Others, Lord, yes others. Let this, my motto be. Help me to live for others that I might live like thee."

July 12
Your Days Are Numbered

"The days fashioned for me, when as yet there were none of them." (Psalm 139:16)
"Return and tell Hezekiah the leader of My people, 'Thus says the Lord, the God of your father: I have heard your prayer, I have seen your tears; surely I will heal you. And I will add to your days fifteen years'." II Kings 20: 5-6
"It is appointed to man once to die..." Hebrews 9:27

The occasion of your death is not a popular topic. It is as if that death comes only to someone else, especially older people. There is an avoidance to face the realization that your days are numbered according to God's timing. Billy Graham says, "The truth is that all of us have our time to die. The conspiracy of silence which so often surrounds death today cannot change that fact." (8) As a borne again man, you have no need to fear death. It is our last enemy and has already been defeated by Jesus' death and resurrection. Yet, you should gain a profound perspective about life by acknowledging that tomorrow has no guarantee. Therefore, it is important that you live every day and make every decision as if it were your last. "If we don't give our full attention to death, but spend our lives avoiding the subject and obscuring it with euphemisms, we diminish our lives. (9) As you commune with the God the Holy Spirit, ask Him to keep you focused on what really matters. Know God's purpose for your life and engage it as if today is your last.

July 13
<u>Pride</u>

"Pride goes before destruction and a haughty spirit before a fall." (Proverbs 16:18)
"For from within, out of the heart of men, proceed evil thoughts, adulteries, fornications, murders...pride, foolishness." Mark 7:21-22
"But He gives more grace. Therefore He says: 'God resists the proud, but gives grace to the humble'." James 4:6

The word "pride" has two different meanings. One is a "reasonable justifiable self-respect" which you should have. The other, "inordinate self-esteem: conceit" is denounced by God. This kind of selfish pride causes men to elevate themselves above others. They have a feeling of self-sufficiency and an attitude of arrogance. This contradicts Jesus' teachings on humility, servant-hood and self sacrifice. Pride is listed among such sins as adulteries and murders in today's first scripture verse. Max Lucado writes: "God hates arrogance. He hates arrogance because we have nothing to be arrogant about. Don't take success too seriously. Counteract this pride with reminders of the brevity of life and the frailty of wealth." (10) Some Christians are unaware that they have become prideful. Pride often accompanies success, wealth and/or position. It doesn't take very much success or a very significant position to engender pride in some men's hearts. When this occurs, it becomes evident to others. Ask the Holy Spirit to search your heart and attitude and reveal to you any unrighteous pride. Pride will render you ineffective for God and disrupt fellowship with others. Always accept success as a blessing from God. Without God, you are an empty, meaningless soul.

July 14
Sin, Confession, Repentance, and Restoration

"What shall we say then? Shall we continue in is that grace may abound? Certainly not! How shall we who are dead to sin live any longer in it?"
Romans 6:1-2

"If we confess our sins, He is faithful and just to forgive us our sins and to cleanse us from all unrighteousness." I John 1:9

"Brethren, if a man is overtaken in any trespass, you who are spiritual restore such a one in a spirit of gentleness..." Galatians 6:1

As a Godly man, you will sometimes stumble in areas of your spiritual life and sin. It is important that you know how to take care of that sin immediately, lest it overcomes you and you fall into its pit. It is absolutely critical that you acknowledge your sin and face it and its consequences. You cannot hide sin! You acknowledge your sin by confessing it and, Jesus, your advocate with the Father will forgive your sin, though there will be consequences. While some say that confession is sufficient, the Bible is clear that you are to repent, or "to turn from sin..." (Webster). Jesus told the woman caught in adultery and the leper at the pool of Bethesda to "go and sin no more". To insure that you have the strength to resist the devil and a particular temptation, spiritual restoration is needed. This is a time in which you surround yourself with accountability partners, intensely seek God to make you whole and put on the whole armor of God. God will always forgive. But there are no shortcuts.

July 15
<u>Light Up Your World</u>

"Let your light so shine before men, that they may see your good works and glorify you Father in heaven." Matthew 5:16

"For you once were darkness, but now you are the light of the Lord. Walk as children of light." Ephesians 5:8

"You are the sons of light and sons of the day. We are not of the night nor of darkness." I Thessalonians 5:5

Light dispels darkness. It the darkest room or cave, a small match when lit will illuminate the darkness as if the darkness is pushed out. Most criminal activity, both property crimes and crimes against persons, is committed during the cover of night. Jesus told his disciples, "that light is come into the world, and some men loved darkness rather than light because there deeds were evil." (John 3:19) You are a reflection of THE light, Jesus Christ. Wherever you are, your presence should be like the match in the pitch black darkness - illuminating and reflecting Christ-like character-istics. Henry and Richard Blackaby write: God's desire is to fill you with His light. He wants you to shine as a brilliant testimony of his presence and power in your life." (11) God needs you to seek Him with all of your heart and to let the light of Jesus within you light up your world for God. Your light will shine in direct proportion to your proximity to the source of light – Jesus Christ. Time spent in prayer, Bible study and walking in the Spirit will keep your light bright in a dark world.

July 16
The Obsession with Pleasure

"Now the ones that fell among thorns are those who, when they have heard, go out and are choked with cares, riches, and pleasures of life, and bring forth no fruit to maturity." Luke 8:14

"But know this, that in the last days perilous times will come: For men will be loves of themselves, lovers of money, boasters, proud, unthankful, unholy...traitors, headstrong, haughty, lovers of pleasure more than lovers of God," II Timothy 3:2-4

Look on any bookstore magazine rack and you'll see a plethora of magazines with titles related to pleasure of one kind or another. The *Vision, Global Business and Pleasure* magazine is designed to combine business with pleasure. Sports, travel, home decorating, sexual exploitation and pornography fill the shelves for the pleasure or those seeking happiness and fulfillment. We live in a pleasure-obsessed society ranging from healthy themes of exercise, golf, fitness, sexual perversion, violence for fun and illegal drug use. Today's scriptures describe man in his abandonment of righteousness and the obsessive-compulsive desire of pleasure. God wants his children to have pleasure in the right things and for the right reasons. In Psalm 15:11 David speaks to God saying, "You will show me the path of life; In Your presence is fullness of joy; At Your right hand are pleasures forevermore." As a Godly man you must not become caught up in this world's epidemic of pleasure seeking. Obsession with any pleasure is about self and does not glorify God. Enjoy wholesome pleasure in moderation, especially in living a life with the assurance of God's blessings and His promise of eternal life.

July 17
<u>When the Unrighteous Prosper</u>

"But as for me, my feet had almost stumbled; my steps had nearly slipped. For I was envious of the boastful when I saw the prosperity of the wicked. Their eyes bulge with abundance; they have more than heart could wish. Behold, these are the ungodly, who are always at ease; they increase in riches. When I thought how to understand this, it was too painful for me – until I went into the sanctuary of God; then I understood their end... God is the strength of my heart and my portion forever."
Psalm 73:2- 3, 7, 12, 26

I encourage you to read Psalm 73 in its entirety. Asaph, one of David's chief musicians, expresses his frustration of the righteous as they view the prosperity of those who do not serve God. After Asaph bemoans the prosperity of the unrighteous, he goes into the sanctuary of God. There God reveals to him the brevity of their wealth and pride. God gives Asaph a new eternal perspective of what true prosperity is and what it is not. Today, we read reports of corporate CEO's who have wickedly defrauded stockholders. They suddenly lose their position, wealth and power. In II Samuel 1:19 David laments the fall of Saul, King of Israel: "How the mighty have fallen." The unrighteous may prosper here on earth, but their hands are empty in their coffins. Paul wrote to Timothy (I Timothy 6:7): For we brought nothing into this world, and it is certain we can carry nothing out." Be careful not to set your heart on the riches and on accumulating wealth. Rather place your trust in God who will meet your needs here on earth. He has eternal riches awaiting you beyond this world.

July 18
An Attitude of Gratitude

"O give thanks to the Lord, for He is good! For His mercy endures forever." Psalm 136:1

"...giving thanks always for all things to God the Father in the name of our Lord Jesus Christ, submitting to one another in the fear of God." Ephesians 5:20-21

Do you comprehend how great God is and how He abundantly blesses you? We tend to take God's daily blessings for granted. A few years back, I had the opportunity to serve as the interim director of Pastoral Care and Membership at a large church. A major portion of my time was dedicated to visiting hospitals, nursing homes and the home bound. Walking the halls of the children's hospital where death was eminent for some was heart rendering. Particularly painful for me were my visits to nursing homes where in room after room the elderly, once full of vitality, lay helpless and lonely. I encountered parents of newborns who had just received word that their long-awaited baby had died. I had the opportunity to serve meals at a Christian shelter for the homeless. Leather-like skin and premature wrinkles marked many faces. Despite the plight of these people, I found an attitude of gratitude among them just for my visit. Though you too have struggles, you should be overflowing with praise to God. Have you recently considered how blessed you are? Make time when you pray to show God your attitude of gratitude for His love and blessings.

July 19
<u>**Being Angry with God**</u>

Then God saw their works, that they turned from
their evil way; and God relented from the disaster
that He had said he would bring upon them, and He
did not do it." Jonah 3:10
"But it displeased Jonah exceedingly, and he
became angry." Jonah 4:1
"But David became angry because of the Lord's
outbreak against Uzzah; and he called the name of
the place Perez Uzzah [outburst against Uzzah] to
this day." II Samuel 6:8

Sometimes when life seems unfair and your circumstances unjust, you may become angry with God. Men can allow anger to overwhelm them and their faith. If you have been angry with God because He didn't come through for you when you needed Him, you're in the company of men like David, Jonah and Moses. David said, "Be angry, and do not sin" (Psalm 4: 4) Despite your humanity you are spiritual being with special relationship with God. It is not necessarily wrong to be angry with God. Eugene H. Peterson writes: "Our anger can be a measure of our faith. Believers argue with God; skeptics argue with each other." (12) Bad things do happen to good people and Christians are not immune. God *is* there. His grace and love never waiver. Our finite minds cannot understand the all-knowing mind of God. James Dobson writes: "He will not parade His plans and purposes for our approval. He wants us to believe and trust Him despite things we don't understand." (13) Release your anger. For your heart's sake seek God for release from anger and be restored to full fellowship with Him.

July 20
God has Plans for You

"For I know the plans I have for you," 'says the Lord'. "They are plans for good and not for disaster, to give you a future and a hope." Jeremiah 29:11 NIV
"Now the Lord spoke to Paul in the night by a vision, 'Do not be afraid, but speak, do not keep silent; for I am with you, and no one will attack you to hurt you; for I have many people in this city." Acts 18:9-10

Yes, God has plans for you! He had plans for you before you were born. David's writes: "The days fashioned for me, when yet there was none of them." (Psalm 139:18) That may be difficult for you to comprehend. Maybe you work hard but never seem to get recognition or achieve success. Many men measure their success for God in terms of their talents, skills and abilities or lack thereof. Consequently, they hinder what God wants to do through them. It's not about you, but about God. It is *your* need, not God's, to find what He has planned for you. But to know God's plan, you need to draw near to Him and allow the Holy Spirit to fill you so that you can hear when He speaks. "Your love relationship with God prepares you to be involved in God's work by developing God-centered living. Focusing your attention on God's plans, purposes and ways rather then your own is essential." (14) To grow as a Godly man and a spiritual warrior you must yield to God's purpose whether it seems an insignificant chore or a bold step in a ministry. Open your heart, become willing and be passionate for God.

July 21
<u>An Optimistic Perspective</u>

"If that be the case, our God whom we serve is able to deliver us from the burning fiery furnace, and He will deliver us from your hand, O king. But if not...," Daniel 3:17-18

"Now unto Him who is able to do exceedingly abundantly above all that we ask or think..." Ephesians 3:20

"For in the time of trouble He shall hide me in His pavilion...He shall set me high upon a rock." Psalm 27: 3, 5

You have bad days and good days and days on which optimism is hard conjure up. You have daily spiritual battles. You know that from personal experience. Some come in the form of major onslaughts by Satan in which you feel failure, fear and faithlessness. But most often it is those little irritants to which you respond with worry. It would be naive to think you will always have an exuberate attitude. On the other hand, neither should you always look at the glass half empty. Many of you, even on your good days, simply refuse to be optimistic about anything. This kind of thinking, in reality, is a sure sign of your lack of trust in God and in his enduring faithfulness. In his book, "Don't Sweat the Small Stuff", Richard Carlson writes; "Somehow, it's the little stuff, not the big stuff that we struggle with the most. My suggestion is that we all strife to become a little more accepting of life and take it as it comes, put things in perspective." (15) Remember that God *is* in control. Therefore, be optimistic.

July 22
Earth, Wind and Fire...Then a Small Voice

"Then He said, 'Go out, and stand on the mountain before the Lord.' And behold, the Lord passed by, and a great and strong wind tore into the mountains and broke the rocks in pieces before the Lord, but the Lord was not in the wind; and after the wind an earthquake; and after the earthquake a fire, but the Lord was not in fire; and after the fire a still small voice." I Kings 19: 11-12

Listening to God is, perhaps, one of the most neglected attributes of Christians. Prayer is often no more than a one-way conversation of asking for things from God as if He were Santa Claus. Do you find a quiet place to be alone in prayer and keep your mind and heart in tune with the Holy Spirit listening for what He has to say? When your relationship with the Holy Spirit becomes one in which you commune with Him and become in tune with Him, you will sense His presence and hear what God is saying. In their book, "Hearing God's Voice", Richard and Henry Blackaby write: "When God speaks, he does not give new revelations about Himself that contradicts what He has already reveled in Scripture. Rather, God speaks to give you application of His Word to the specific circumstance in your life." (16) In whatever circumstance you find yourself, if you will be still and listen, God the Father will speak to you through the Holy Spirit and guide you through His Word giving you peace and assurance that He cares. Don't wait for an earthquake or thunder to find what He has to say. He is there now in a "still small voice".

July 23
Returning to the Father

"Have mercy upon me, O God, according to Your lovingkindness; according to the multitude of Your tender mercies, blot out my transgressions. Wash me and I shall be whiter than snow. Created in me a clean heart, O God, and renew a steadfast spirit within me. Restore to me the joy of Your salvation, and uphold me by your generous Spirit."
Psalm 51: 1, 7, 10, 12
"And the son said to him, 'Father, I have sinned against heaven and in your sight, and am no longer worthy to be called your son'." Luke 15: 21

We have all been guilty of straying during our walk with God. While the scriptures encourage believers to constantly pray and walk in the Spirit, God knows that we are but dust and earthen vessels. "Straying" may range from simply not being fervent in spirit and become lethargic in our efforts to serve Christ. Or, it may be the falling out of fellowship with our Lord where we cease to pray and become disobedient in areas of your life. In whatever circumstances you've found your self, you must return to your Father. Returning requires more than just getting back in your former routine and turn over a new leaf. It requires acknowledging your "absent without leave". It requires you to repent, or pull away from your sinful inclinations. It requires you to ask Jesus to cleanse your heart and mind so that you are renewed in spirit. You will also need to seek full restoration in your fellowship with the Holy Spirit and with fellow Christians who may have witnessed your spiritual falling away. Know this: God's love never fails. He is waiting for you to return so that He can welcome you back into fellowship.

July 24
<u>Facing Disaster: Take Heart</u>

"We are hard-pressed on every side, yet not crushed; we are perplexed, but not in despair; persecuted, but not forsaken; struck down, but not destroyed..." II Corinthians 4: 8-9
"When my heart is overwhelmed; lead me to the rock that is higher than I." Psalm 61:2

On September 11, 2001 the World Trade Center was brought down killing near 3,000 innocent people including children. On December 26, 2004 the most powerful earthquake in forty years erupted in the Indian Ocean near Sumatra killing hundreds of thousands of people. On August 20, 2005 Hurricane Katrina took more than 1,200 lives in five southeastern coastal states and destroyed most of the City of New Orleans. In these disasters people lost their homes, businesses, cars, personal possessions and, worst of all, members of their families. Why? You may ask that question when death takes your wife or your child. You may ask 'why?' when your house burns to the ground. The Bible is clear that no matter what happens, God's love and grace are sufficient. Anne Graham Lotz writes: "His joy has balanced my pain. His power has lifted my burdens. His peace has calmed my worries. His grace has been more than adequate to cover me. His strength has been sufficient to carry me through. His love has bathed my wounds like a healing balm." (17) No matter what happens and you don't understand "why?' never waiver in your faith. God is in control and knows best. Trust and rest in Him.

July 25
Sing!

"But at midnight Paul and Silas were praying and singing hymns to God, and the prisoners were listening to them." Acts 16: 25
"My heart is steadfast, O God, my heart is steadfast; I will sing and give praise." Psalm 57:7
"Let the word of Christ dwell in you richly in all wisdom, teaching and admonishing one another in psalms and hymns and spiritual songs, singing with grace in your hearts to the Lord." Colossians 3: 16

Perhaps it is our culture or a man thing which cause some men to refuse to sing – especially in church. Though many of us cannot carry a tune, God wants us to worship Him in song. One of the first musicians and foremost musicians was David. He used song and dance to express his love for God and to proclaim to the Israelites that God was great and awesome. Christians in the early church used songs for praise and encouragement. The lyrics, along with the music help us memorize songs to bless us time after time. We can then pass on songs to our children and their children. The early composers such as Bach and Beethoven composed music and lyrics exclusively for the church. It is not important to God how well you can sing. It is important to Him that you sing His praises and worship Him in song. Christian music, both traditional hymns and contemporary music, have inspiring messages which can embolden us and encourage us. Sing. Sing in church. Sing in your car or truck. Sing in the shower. Just sing the praises for God and magnify His name. Lifting your voice in song can lift your spirits.

July 26
<u>Seven Times Seventy: Don't Give Up</u>

"In Him we have redemption through His blood, the forgiveness of sins, according to the riches of His grace." Ephesians 1: 7
"My little children, these things I write to you, so that you may not sin. And if anyone sins, we have an advocate with the Father, Jesus Christ the righteous. And He Himself is the propitiation for our sins..." I John 2: 1-2

During my childhood and early teenage years I took to heart the evangelist's warnings that Christians must never sin, and to do so would result in certain damnation unless through much agony, strenuous repentance took place immediately. I believed that I had to be perfect and if I made a mistake, to include a fleeting bad thought, I would go straight to hell unless I repented immediately. Consequently, I did not really feel God's love, grace and mercy that I know now. I didn't understand the significance of the cross and the penalty from sin that Jesus paid for me. Have you felt that because you can't seem to "get it right" that eventually God will stop forgiving you? When you accepted Jesus as your Savior and Lord, you became one of God's children. You don't have a license to sin and sin has consequences. As Paul said, "Shall we continue in sin that grace may abound? Certainly not! How shall we who have died to sin live any longer in it?" (Romans 6: 1-2) But as a Godly man, you will stumble and sin but you are not to practice sin. Be assured that God will always, through His love and grace, forgive you.

July 27
<u>Time Alone In Prayer</u>

"Now when Daniel knew that the writing was signed, he went home. And in his upper room, with the windows open toward Jerusalem, he knelt down on his knees three times that day, and prayed..." Daniel 6: 10

"But you, when you pray, go into your room, and when you have shut the door, pray to your Father who is in the secret place; and your Father who sees in secret will reward you openly." Matthew 6: 6

Today, some men typically work far more than 40 hours per week. Many men commute in bumper-to-bumper traffic to and from work often taking more than an hour each way. With the cell phone and the high-tech mini- laptop computer there are few times and places a man cannot be contacted. Once home the television is the centerpiece of attention with several hundred stations from which to choose. Perhaps after a hectic day, a man deserves to sit back in his favorite recliner and watch some T.V. or continue his work via his computer. As a Christian man, you find it difficult to carve out a time to be alone with God. But oh how so important it is! Bob Barnes writes: "People do what they want to do. I find morning – before the telephone starts to ring or I get involved in the day's activities – to be the best time for me to be alone with God." (18) Today, commit a private place and a quiet time to pray before getting into the fray of work and your hectic schedule of activities. And while you're driving to work learn to commune with the Father and receive spiritual sustenance for the day ahead.

July 28
Unheralded Acts of Kindness

"But a certain Samaritan, as he journeyed, came where he was, and when he saw him, he had compassion on him, So he went to him and bandaged his wounds, pouring on oil and wine; and he set him on his own animal, brought him to an inn, and took care of him. Luke 10: 33-34

Few and far between will you find the individual who will give of self to help another. The story Jesus shares about the Good Samaritan stands a model of unheralded kindness. The Samaritan's compassion, hands-on care and monetary sacrifice are starkly contrasted to the other passer-bys who avoided this poor destitute man. They refused to stoop to the level to help a Samaritan. Inconvenience, touching the bleeding man and spending money on him outweighed their Godly love. You may give to the United Way or to a Christmas charity. You may give to foreign missions through your local church. But have you passed by someone who was hurting, lonely or hungry? You don't have to look far to find these people. Your community is full of lonely people. A simple "I'm praying for you", a touch or some form of assistance expresses God's love. Such acts of kindness do not bring recognition to you, no tax deduction or no "good citizen award". Ask God to show you hurting, emotionally wounded and lonely people who are overlooked and passed by. Then demonstrate your love as did the Samaritan, roll up your sleeves and share Jesus' love in a real meaningful way.

July 29
Study the Word

"Be diligent to present yourself approved to God, a worker who does not need to be ashamed, rightly dividing the word of truth." II Timothy 2:15
"...and that from childhood you have known the Holy Scriptures, which are able to make you wise for salvation through faith which is in Christ Jesus" II Timothy 3: 15
"How sweet are Your words to my taste, sweeter than honey to my mouth!" Psalm 119: 103

God's Word is a cornerstone of your faith in Jesus Christ. Unfortunately, there are so many Christians who have been saved for many years who seldom read the Bible and, consequently, are not familiar with what God has to say to them. As a Godly man, it is essential that you make Bible study an integral part of everyday. Further, as a Godly father, it is your responsibility to read Bible stories to your children, model Bible study at home and include scripture reading in family traditions and holidays. Your children should witness the strength, wisdom and holiness in your life as a result of your studying and living by God's Word. Ask God to give you a love and hunger for His Word. As you read, allow the Holy Spirit to reveal what God has to say to you. The *Voice of Martyrs* organization's book entitled "Heroic Faith" so eloquently express the value of God's written Word: "When we are thirsting for God's touch in our lives, the Bible is an oasis that floods us with a sense of his power. It is like the refreshment and awe we experience when we stand beneath a cascading waterfall." Love and cherish God's Word.

July 30
Missions: You Don't Have to Go to Africa

"...for I was hungry and you gave me food; I was thirsty and you gave me drink; I was a stranger and you took me in; I was naked and you clothed Me; I was sick and you visited Me; I was in prison and you came to Me" Matthew 25: 35-36

"...there arose a complaint against the Hebrews by the Hellenists because their widows were neglected in the daily distribution. 'Therefore, brethren, seek out from among you seven men of good reputation, full of the Holy Spirit and wisdom, whom we may appoint over this business'." Acts 6: 1, 3

Growing up in the church I heard the accounts of missionaries in far away countries that suffered and died for their faith in God. I was so afraid that God would call me to the mission field. As I grew older I didn't feel the call to foreign missions on my life and felt relieved. However, we do not "escape" Jesus' great commission to His witnesses both in our community but in other parts of the world. At home, all around us the mission fields are ripe for harvest. There are people who have never been approached with the gospel within a short distance from your home. The sick, the elderly, the lonely, the hurting and the hungry all around you become your mission field. Such charitable services such as "Meals on Wheels" provide warm lunches for many of the homebound and elderly. John Hudson Tiner prays: "Sometime I find it easier to give from a distance than to become personally involved in situations. Help me, Lord, to fulfill the mission to serve others." (28) Men, don't turn away when you are called to reach others with the gospel.

July 31
<u>Men, It's Okay to Cry</u>

"For He will deliver the needy when he cries."
Psalm 72: 12
"So David and his men came to the city, and there it was, burned with fire; and their wives, their sons, and their daughters had been taken captive. Then David and the people who were with him lifted up their voices and wept, until they had no more power to weep." I Samuel 29: 3-4
"Jesus wept." John 11: 35

God created men to be masculine. Men's masculine nature exhibits characteristics of the warrior, the champion and the protector. Men fight, box, play football, labor in risky jobs and hunt wild game. Years ago there was a T.V. commercial in which a rugged, tough-looking man rode up on his horse enjoying his Marlboro...referred to as "Marlboro Country". That captured, for many, what a real man was. "Men are taught from boyhood that "real men" don't cry, aren't sensitive, don't allow any emotion that could be construed as weakness." (21) Men often hold in or conceal emotions of anger, hurt, loneliness, grief, guilt, sympathy, and even overflowing joy. It's okay for you to cry. Crying releases your deep-seated emotions and brings relief when you can no longer carry your burden or withhold your joy. The Bible has many examples of real men who cried. When you let go and weep, you become pliable as clay in the potter's hands. God can take these moments of to touch your heart, express His care and offer answers to battles you've been fighting for years. Never be ashamed to cry. And fathers, never tell you son that real men don't cry.

REFERENCES FOR JULY

1. Hugh Delehanty and Elinor Ginzler, "Caring for Your Parents", (Sterling Publishing Co. Inc, New York, New York, an AARP endorsed book) 2005, p. 5
2. Toby Mac and Michael Tait, "Under God" (Bethany House Publishers, Bloomington, Minnesota) 2004, p. 18
3. Ibid.p. 19
4. Michael Waldman, "My Fellow AMERICANS" (Sourcebooks Inc. Napersville, Illinois) 2003 p. 56
5. Ibid.p. 12
6. Travel Impressions, *Where to Retire*, Volume 12, Number 6, November/December 2003 (magazine), (*Where to Retire*, Houston Texas, Alan Fox, Editor and Publisher) p. 86-87
7. The National Marriage Project, "Unions 2003", (Rutgers University, Piscataway, New Jersey) 2003 p. 23
8. Billy Graham, "Death and the Life After" (W Publishing Company, A Division of Thomas Nelson, Nashville, Tennessee) 1987 p. 2
9. Eugene H. Peterson, "Leap Over a Wall" (HarperCollins Publisher, San Francisco) 1997 p. 218
10. Max Lucado, "Traveling Light" (W Publishing Company, A Division of Thomas Nelson, Nashville, Tennessee) 2001 p.72, 75
11. Henry T. and Richard Blackaby, "Experiencing God" (Broadman and Holmes Publishers, Nashville, Tennessee) 1997 p. 52
12. Eugene H. Peterson, "Run With The Horses" (Inter Varsity Press, Downers Grove, Illinois) 1983 p. 103
13. James Dobson, "When God Doesn't Make Sense" (Tydale House Publishers) 1993 p.236-237

14. Henry T. Blackaby and Claude V. King, "Experiencing God" (Broadman and Holman Publishers, Nashville, Tennessee) 1994 p. 73
15. Richard Carlson, "Don't Sweat the Small Stuff" (Hyperon, New York, New York) 1998 p 153-154
16. Henry T. and Richard Blackaby, "Hearing God's Voice" (Broadman and Holman Publishers, Nashville, Tennessee) 2002 p. 18
17. Anne Graham Lotz, "Why" (W Publishing Company, a Division of Thomas Nelson Publishing, Nashville, Tennessee) 2004 p.25
18. Bob Barnes, "15 Minutes Alone with God" (Harvest House Publishers, Eugene Oregon) 1995 p. 8
19. *Voice of Martyrs* (organization), "Heroic Faith" (W. Publishing Group, a division of Thomas Nelson, Inc., Nashville, Tennessee) 2002 p. 50
20. John Hudson Tiner, "Prayers and Promises for Men", (Barbour Publishing, Ulrichsville, Ohio) 2003 p. 128
21. Patrick A. Means, "Men's Secret Wars", (Fleming H. Revell, Grand Rapids, Michigan) 2004 p. 84

August 1
<u>A Conqueror and a Hero</u>

"So David inquired of the Lord, saying, 'Shall I go up against the Philistines? Will you deliver them into my hand?' And the Lord said to David, 'Go up, for I will doubtless deliver the Philistines into your hand'. So David went to Baal Perazim and David defeated them there; and he said, 'The Lord has broken through my enemies before me, like a breakthrough of water'." II Samuel 5: 19-20

Sir, you have already called to be a conqueror and a hero by God. Among the last words Jesus spoke to his faithful disciples as he ascended into the clouds were, "But you shall receive power when the Holy Spirit has come upon you;" (Acts 1:8) As a Godly man, you're in a daily spiritual battle with Satan, with evil people and with the old sinful nature within you. Armed with the "whole armor of God" you and filled with the Holy Spirit's power you will be a conqueror and a hero. You're in the battle to win and you will win as long as you know the source of your power. You must understand that you are a hero in an ongoing spiritual war for your soul, for your family and for a world without God. John Eldridge says, "Every man has a battle to fight, a great mission to his life...You have a specific place... a mission God made you for." (1) Praise God today for your role as a conquering, heroic warrior!

August 2
Golf: Common Ground

"For by on Spirit we were all baptized into one body – whether Jews or Greeks, whether slaves or free – and have all been made to drink into on Spirit." I Corinthians 12: 13
"Then Peter opened his mouth and said: In truth I perceive that God show no partiality. But in every nation whoever fears Him and works righteousness is accepted by Him." Acts 10: 34-35

Golf is a game that is enjoyed by the young and the old, by men and by women and it is a common denominator worldwide. For the millions of amateur golfers who play regularly it is a stress reliever, a social event and competition. It is an opportunity where Godly men can share their testimonies during 18 holes of play. It provides Christian brothers the chance to share what's on their hearts, encourage each other and discuss common issues. In golf tournaments men from different backgrounds are often mixed into teams, offering you the opportunity to demonstrate your Godly character and let your values be a Godly example. If you haven't played golf, consider doing so for its benefits to you. If you do play, ask the Holy Spirit to make you more aware of circumstances that you can make a difference in someone's life by sharing Jesus' love. As you walk or ride from hole to hole, enjoy God's beautiful creation. Take every opportunity to share your testimony with a fellow golfer.

August 3
"My Utmost for His Highest"

"Yet indeed I also count all things loss for the excellence of the knowledge of Christ Jesus my Lord that I may know Him and the power of His resurrection, and the fellowship of His sufferings, being conformed to His death." Philippians 3: 8, 10

"My utmost for His highest" – an unmatched phrase that overflows with deep spiritual implication – stirs the hearts of Godly men and women. Oswald Chamber's Christian Classic devotional is a compilation of his lectures given during the early 1900's. In it, Chambers directly tells you what kind of commitment you must have to God the Father, God the Son and God the Holy Spirit. It will stir your spirit, renew your faith and change your daily walk with God. Oswald Chambers goes straight to the heart of his message: "We shall all feel very much ashamed if we do not yield to Jesus on the point He has asked us to yield to Him. To get there is a question of will…but a surrender of will, an absolute and irrevocable surrender on that point. Shut out every other consideration and keep yourself before God for this one thing only – My Utmost for His Highest. I am determined to be absolutely and entirely for Him and for Him alone." (2) That's heavy. It separates the "real men" from the timid. It demands that you step out of the boat. Ask God for the courage to accept this challenge.

August 4
The Love of Money

"For the love of money is a root of all kinds of evil, for which some have strayed from the faith in their greediness, and pierced themselves through with many sorrows." I Timothy 6: 10

"But Peter said to him, 'Your money perish with you, because you thought that the gift of God could be purchased with money'!" Acts 8:20

Money is necessary to exchange for goods and services. It is okay to have money, to save money and to plan your retirement with enough money to live comfortably. But when money becomes your obsession it can drive you to greed and selfishness. God wishes to bless Christians. He expects you to be a good steward of the money which He entrusts to you. When Peter was approached by a man who wanted to purchase the Holy Spirit-filled power, Peter rebuked him. Our world is full of men who believe that their money can buy them happiness and peace…if only they could have more money. The love of money will consume both men and women causing them to indulge in lavish life styles which they believe will satisfy the emptiness which can only be filled by Jesus Christ. Christians often become envious of those who have wealth, big homes and expensive cars. As Solomon said, "All is vanity". In cautioning Timothy about the danger of seeking riches, the Apostle Paul makes a very interesting statement: "For we brought nothing into this world and it is certain we can carry nothing out." Think about that and ask God help you wisely use the money He provides.

August 5
<u>Servant-Leaders Rely On God</u>

"Therefore, brethren, seek out from among you seven men of good reputation, full of the Holy Spirit and wisdom, who we may appoint over this business..." Acts 6:3

"Then He came to Simon Peter. And Peter said to Him, 'Lord, are You washing my feet?'" John 13:6

Whatever your career role or position in any organization to include your church you will have opportunities to lead others and collaborate with others to complete a task or reach a goal. Jesus was the supreme example of a servant-leader. He called the "twelve" to follow Him and He led them into new realms of serving others unselfishly. He modeled this in His many encounters. Peter protested when his Lord and Master stooped to wash his feet. This act of humility by Jesus, the Son of God, negates any excuses you may have to not get elbow to elbow with those who may be your subordinates or volunteers and serve along side them. In his book, "The 21 Indispensable Qualities of a Leader", John C. Maxwell offers a few fundamental characteristics of a servant-leader:

- Puts Others Ahead of His Own Agenda
- Possesses the Confidence to Serve
- Initiates Service to Others
- Is Not Position-Conscious
- Serve Out of Love

When given the opportunity to lead others in any kind of endeavor, be a servant-leader. This is not common among many of today's CEO and managers. It will set you apart and reflect your walk in Christ.

August 6
Knowing Christ

"...that I may know Him and the power of His resurrection, and the fellowship of His suffering, being conformed to His death," Philippians 3:10
"To know the love of Christ which passes knowledge; that you may be filled with all the fullness of God." Ephesians 3:19

Today's scriptures are both written by Paul – one in a letter the Philippians and one to the Ephesians. Paul had this deep, genuine desire to know Jesus intimately. His thirst to know more about Christ was never satisfied during his life on earth. Paul expresses his desire to know God when he wrote: "To know the love of Christ which passes knowledge" and "that I may know Him". Paul was willing to suffer as his Lord had suffered. He gladly proclaimed Jesus to those who would throw him in jail. Through his obedience, his joy of suffering, his daily prayer life and seeking Christ, Paul probably came to know Christ as few others have. Oswald Chambers wrote: "Fruit bearing is always mentioned as the manifestation of an intimate union with Jesus Christ. When once we get intimate with Jesus we are never lonely, we never need sympathy, we can pour out of all the time without being pathetic." (3) Begin today to seek to know Jesus more intimately by continuous communing with Him and by yielding to His voice. Your impact will be tremendous when you are in pursuit of knowing Him better.

August 7
Ready to Give, Willing to Share

"To Timothy, a beloved son...as without ceasing I remember you in my prayers night and day." II Timothy 1:2-3
"Let them do good that they be rich in good works, ready to give, willing to share..." I Timothy 6:18

As you read this and have your prayer time, think of someone who may be struggling with loneliness, or someone who may have a long-term illness, or someone who is hurting inside. Perhaps a visit with them will lift their spirits. For others, a brief phone call will be encouraging. Tell them you are praying for them. A thoughtful card or a note enables you to better express your genuine care and your intercession for them. Through the leading of the Holy Spirit you can take a small step in helping someone to find hope in their seemingly hopeless circumstances. This is what the Apostle Paul did to encourage and build up young Timothy, Titus, Philemon and the new churches which he had helped establish. I recall a day when I was especially "down" at work and received a letter from a former young employee with a simple message of gratitude, sharing how I made a difference in his life. Immediately, my discouragement disappeared and I couldn't hide my smile. It gave me courage and a renewed purpose to continue encouraging others as they matured and began their career beyond college. Take a few minutes and make that call or send that note...prayerfully.

August 8
Controlling Your Thoughts

"For as he thinks in his heart, so is he." Proverbs 23:7

"Casting down arguments and every high thing that exalts itself against the knowledge of God, bringing every thought into captivity to the obedience of Christ." II Corinthians 10:5

Everyday there is a battle raging in your mind between the Spirit and the flesh. This battle is especially difficult because you don't always recognize Satan's devious strategies to invade your thoughts with things which are contrary to your walk in Christ. You may experience these mental assaults during times and in some circumstance in which you are least spiritually on guard. At other times you'll be blindsided by when you feel the closest to God thinking you're invincible to certain evil thinking and inclinations. Neil T. Anderson explains it this way: "Don't think that Satan is no longer interested in manipulating your mind in order to accomplish his purposes. Satan's perpetual aim is to infiltrate your thoughts with his thoughts and to promote his lie in the face of God's truth. He knows that if he can control your thoughts, he can control your life." (4) I have struggled with bringing my thoughts "to the obedience of Christ". Let's stay alert and daily recognize that we can do nothing without His strength and intervention in our lives. I encourage you to assess your daily thoughts and seek God to give you peace and a sound mind...one that "is stayed on Him" (Isaiah 26:3).

August 9
Making the Right Decision

"And if it seems evil to you to serve the LORD, choose for yourselves this day whom you will serve, whether the gods which your fathers served that were on the other side of the River, or the gods of the Amorites, in whose land you dwell. But as for me and my house, we will serve the LORD." Joshua 24:15 "Cleanse your hands, you sinners; and purify your hearts, your double-minded." James 4:8

Throughout the time when my two children were growing up in our home, I made every effort to teach them and guide them into making right decisions. I shared with them that they should make the decisions and a commitments in their hearts and minds in the "now" as to their spiritual values and what behaviors were unacceptable. I explained that it is critical that they not wait until the time of temptation to make choices. Many men are double-minded about spiritual issues and their decisions. Some men operate on the principle of "situational ethics". In other words, they wait on making fundamental spiritual decisions until being faced with a temptation and crisis of belief. It is then when they are most vulnerable to making the wrong decision. Consequently, a double-minded philosophy makes it difficult to make the right decision at the moment of temptation. You have no doubt been guilty of being double-minded about some issues. Ask God to search your heart and ask His Holy Spirit to strengthen your faith. Determine that your decisions in future compromising circumstances have already become a foregone conclusion. Victory in the face of temptation is faith-building and will bring you tremendous joy.

August 10
When the Holy Spirit Speaks

"While Peter thought about the vision, the Spirit said to him, "Behold, three men are seeking you. Arise therefore, go down and go with them, doubting nothing; for I have sent them." Acts 10:19-20

"For we do not know what we should pray for as we ought, but the Spirit Himself makes intersession for us..." Romans 8:26

Do you ever wonder what some Christians mean when they say that God directed them to do or say a certain thing? There are few reported events where God speaks audibly to people as He did in the Old Testament. Just before Jesus was crucified and ascended to the Father, He told His disciples that the Father would send the Holy Spirit to comfort and guide them (John 14:26). Perhaps you have experienced the Holy Spirit whispering in your ear or giving you inclinations and impressions as to what to do or say in a given situation. Maybe you have experienced this but were unsure if they were from the Holy Spirit or if they were your own thoughts. So how do you develop and experience such a relationship in which you know the Holy Spirit is guiding you? Search the scriptures which refer to the working of the Holy Spirit and begin to seek God to gift you with discernment so you will recognize the voice of the Spirit. Focus on Jesus everyday and walk in the Spirit. Your daily walk with God, facing temptations and dealing with adversity will become easier as you listen when He speaks.

August 11
<u>Count Your Blessings Today</u>

"Blessed be the Lord, who daily loads us with benefits, the God of our salvation! Selah. Psalm 68:19
"Blessed be the God and Father of our Lord Jesus Christ, who has blessed us with every spiritual blessing in the heavenly places in Chris..." Ephesians 1:3

Do you really comprehend and appreciate the abundant blessings which you and your family receive each day from God? As our first scripture says, He "daily loads us with benefits". But when you have accumulated excess debts, when your money runs out before the month does or when you are out of work, you may question why God doesn't meet these needs. God did not promise you wealth, He promised to be with you and bless you no matter what you face. This may come in forms of peace of mind, wisdom to handle our finances or the blessing of a family. It is important to count every blessing which comes from God, despite your circumstances. Pray that you will become aware and grateful for each blessing God grants you – both small and great. There is an old saying: "I complained because I had no shoes, until I met a man who had not feet." In the little book *"Prayers & Promises for Men"* a portion of a prayer says: "I acknowledge the rich blessings that you have showered upon me. Let me focus on what You have done for me and rejoice in all the blessings You give me." (5) Trust God. He will supply your needs.

August 12
Complaining is Contagious

"These are grumblers, complainers, walking according to their own lusts; and they mouth great swelling words, flattering people to gain advantage." Jude 1:16

"Now when the people complained, it displeased the LORD; for the LORD heard it, and His anger was aroused. So the fire of the LORD burned among them, and consumed some in the outskirts of the camp." Numbers 11:1

Have you ever worked with a fellow employee who constantly complains? Or have you ever been guilty of being a chronic complainer at work, at home or at your church? Complainers cause strife and discouragement among others. It is clear that God is not pleased with complainers – especially Christians. As a Godly man you should not complain, but be an encourager in whatever circumstances you find yourself. The man who complains demonstrates his lack of the joy, trust, thankfulness and confidence in the grace of God. If you are convicted of this negative habit begin by praying, asking the Holy Spirit to make you aware of each time you feel like complaining. Focus on God's blessings. Let your heart by joyful, praising God for who He is. You will find that by doing so you will experience God's peace and contentment. The Apostle Paul who perhaps suffered more than any other early church evangelist was able to say, "Not that I speak in regard to need, for I have learned in whatever state I am, to be content." (Philippians 4:11) Regardless of your circumstances, don't complain. Let the joy of the Lord be your strength.

August 13
Changes in Our Lives...It's That Time of Year

"If you walk in My statutes and keep My commandments, and perform them, then I will give you rain in its season..." Leviticus 26:3-4
"All of its spring leaves will wither, and no great power or many people will be needed to pluck it up by its roots." Ezekiel 17:9

As autumn nears seasonal changes become gradually evident. Green leaves of summer slowly give way to shades of yellow, gold and orange. As the autumn wind blows, leaves begin to fall. You too are or will experience change as you grow older into your middle-aged years. Maybe you're still strong, hard-working and living life to its fullest. But as summer turns to fall, the signs of change creep up on you. The gray begins to show, the hair thins and a few wrinkles crease your face. Billy Graham writes: "Each of us is on a journey, inevitably moving from one stage to another until its conclusion...young adulthood slips into middle age; middle age advances toward the mature years; the mature years give way to old age." (6) As you ease ever so gradually into the autumn of life, you will experience the "empty nest" when your children leave home. You may be faced with the care of your aging parents. Older, middle-aged men often face age discrimination in the workplace. And you will discover that temptation is not just a young man's issue. Remain faithful and stay focused on God's purpose for your life. Above all, enjoy this time in your life, resting in God's proven grace and strength.

August 14
<u>Never Ignore a Child</u>

"But when Jesus saw it, He was greatly displeased and said to them, "Let the little children come to me, and do not forbid them; for of such is the kingdom of God." Mark 10:14
"And Samuel said to Jesse, 'Are all the young men here?' Then he said, 'There remains yet the youngest, and there he is, keeping the sheep.'" And Samuel said to Jesse, "Send and bring him. For we will not sit down till he comes here." So he sent and brought him in. Now he was ruddy, with bright eyes, and good-looking. And the LORD said, 'Arise, anoint him; for this is the one!'" 1 Samuel 16:11-12

God loves all children. His love for children and His special purposes for children are described through important events in the Bible. Today's scriptures are examples of God's love and destiny for children. I've noticed that many men ignore the presence of a child. The brutal reality is that some men consider children as insignificant and, in some instances, a bother. Recall your childhood. Do you remember those adults who were gave their attention to you? Do you painfully remember the adults who ignored you? There is an epidemic of fathers who walk out and abandon their own children. Years ago, we had a seasoned pastor who never forgot the name of a child. When he visited a home he focused on each child, being sure he got their names correctly. Then, weeks later when a family with seven children went up front to become church members our pastor would, without any prompt or notes, introduce the parents' and each child's names with accuracy. Your attention and acknowledgement of a child will make a lasting impression and raise their self esteem. If Jesus took time to focus on children, you should do no less.

August 15
<u>Strength Training: Spiritual Growth</u>

"Therefore we also, since we are surrounded by so great a cloud of witnesses, let us lay aside every weight, and the sin which so easily ensnares us, and let us run with endurance the race that is set before us," Hebrews 12:1

"Therefore I run thus: not with uncertainty. Thus I fight: not as one who beats the air. But I discipline my body and bring it into subjection, lest, when I have preached to others, I myself should become disqualified." 1 Corinthians 9:26-27

If you are a fan of such sporting events as football, basketball, baseball, soccer, boxing, running, or other endurance athletic competitions, you know that they all have a few fundamentals for success. Each individual athlete must train and discipline their bodies for maximum performance. They must also focus their minds on each practice, each workout and each competition. Teams with such individual efforts are usually known as "winners". They finish the game, race or course because they have prepared themselves to endure until the finish. As a Godly man, you too should discipline your body and mind to stay focused on God's purpose for your life and to be battle-ready for Satan's assaults of temptations and problems. By practicing daily prayer, Bible study, regular worship and connections with other Christian men you will build the stamina to stay in the race. The reason so many men succumb to temptation and live defeated lives is because they fail to stay spiritually fit and daily grow stronger in Christ. Ask God today to help you make it a part of your life to practice spiritual strength training every day.

August 16
Fasting and Prayer

"However, this kind does not go out except by prayer and fasting." Matthew 17:21
"So when they had appointed elders in every church, and prayed with fasting, they commended them to the Lord in whom they had believed." Acts 14:23

Fasting and prayer have potent power for the Godly man. Fasting is often misunderstood. But fasting is a form of worship and denial of self before God. We often hear or read the slogan, "Prayer changes things". When coupled with prayer, fasting has tremendous effects on whatever you face. Throughout the New Testament fasting was used when facing Satan's oppression or when seeking spiritual strength and God's intervention. Jesus, our perfect example, fasted for forty days and forty nights. From that point He was empowered to resist fleshly lusts and to defeat Satan. "Jesus takes for granted that His disciples will observe the pious custom of fasting. Strict exercise of self-control is an essential feature of the Christian's life. [Fasting] is to make the disciples more ready and cheerful to accomplish those things which God would have done." (7) Fasting and praying for others will bring results. Some fast for a week while others fast a day or a meal. Never do harm to your health. Do not neglect drinking water during your fast. Fast as the Holy Spirit directs. When facing life's crises, you may feel the need to separate yourself for a time to fast and pray. God will honor your passion and devotion.

August 17
Men Must Stand for Right

"Watch, stand fast in the faith, be brave, be strong." 1 Corinthians 16:13
"Therefore, brethren, stand fast and hold the traditions which you were taught, whether by word or our epistle." 2 Thessalonians 2:15

You have probably heard the often used phrase, "If you don't stand for something you'll fall for anything". That rings no more true than when applied to God's man. Being a Godly man who stands for truth in every situation is not for sissies. It requires a man who walks in the Spirit and stands by his convictions based on God's Word. The 1962 movie, "To Kill a Mockingbird" is a story of a man called Atticus Finch, played by Gregory Peck, who took an unpopular stand in the face of threats and against the prevailing culture. Atticus Finch defended a black man who was not guilty as charged. Despite attempts and threats by the town's people, Atticus stood firm. Though the black man was found guilty and justice failed, Atticus left the courtroom with a clear conscience knowing that he had stood for the right. It is noteworthy that his young son observed his father throughout his ordeal. You too will have opportunities to defend truth and stand against Satan's attempt to discredit Christ and those who believe in Him. And your children will be watching. Paul told the Ephesians, "Put on the whole armor of God that you may be able to stand…" (Ephesians 6:11)

August 18
Take Responsibility for Your Sin and Mistakes

"Then Samuel went to Saul, and Saul said to him, 'Blessed are you of the LORD! I have performed the commandment of the LORD. But Samuel said, 'What then is this bleating of the sheep in my ears, and the lowing of the oxen which I hear?'" 1 Samuel 15:13-14

"For I acknowledge my transgressions, and my sin is always before me. Against You, You only, have I sinned, and done this evil in Your sigh..." Psalm 51:3-4

In today's scripture King Saul fails to accept the responsibility of his disobedience to God. God told him not to take flocks of the defeated enemy. Yet, Saul allowed his soldiers to plunder and seize property and animals. When the prophet Samuel confronted him, Saul denied doing this. But the "bleating of the sheep and the lowing of the oxen" exposed his sin. We find David acknowledging his sins of adultery and murder. He asks God to cleanse him and "renew a right spirit within" him. When you have sinned, your first response should be to go to your Father and confess your sin, repent of it and ask Him to restore you to fellowship with Him. God knows that you are human and humans fail. His provision for your sin is in the death and resurrection of His Son, Jesus Christ. He has already paid the penalty for your sin. But He desires that you come to Him with a broken heart and humble spirit and confess your sin. He wants you to repent and not return to that sin. During your time of restoration, pray earnestly that God will create in you a clean heart and a deeper love for Him.

August 19
<u>Suicide: A Permanent End to a Temporary Problem</u>

"Then he threw down the pieces of silver in the temple and departed, and went and hanged himself." Matthew 27:5
"Then Saul said to his armorbearer, "Draw your sword, and thrust me through with it, lest these uncircumcised men come and thrust me through and abuse me." But his armorbearer would not, for he was greatly afraid. Therefore Saul took a sword and fell on it." 1 Samuel 31:4

Have you ever become so despondent and hopeless that you considered suicide as your way to escape? Men who suffer from depression or find themselves deep in debt or become entangled in an adulterous affair see no logical way out. Hopelessness is a trick of the devil. "Men are five times more likely than women to commit suicide. Men are told from birth that they are not supposed to feel. Fear, sadness, helplessness – these are anathema to the male character." (8) Despite this mindset, suicide is never the answer. As a child of God, you have a helper, the Holy Spirit, who will offer "the peace of God which passes all understanding". This is a battle of the mind that you must win now, before Satan attacks at your weakest moment. Man of God, you are bought with the price of the cross because God loves you and has loved you long before you were born. You already have the victory. Make up your mind today that you will be on guard and not be caught by this lie of the devil. But "lay hold of the hope set before us" (Hebrews 6:18) Jesus came to give you life more abundantly.

August 20
Prayer Requests

"Brethren, pray for us." 1 Thessalonians 5:25
"Is anyone among you suffering? Let him pray. Is anyone cheerful? Let him sing psalms. Is anyone among you sick? Let him call for the elders of the church, and let them pray over him," James 5:13-14

How often do you remember to prayer for a fellow believer who is having a crisis of belief, or who is struggling with a life-threatening illness? When prayer requests are made during church worship or in your Bible study class, do you really listen, jot it down and pray for those requests? Often we simply don't follow through in prayer for fellow believers. The Bible clearly instructs us to pray of one another. Jesus set the example for us to pray for each other when he told His disciples "I pray for you..." (John 17:9) And He wants you to pray for each other and do it daily. Billy Graham so aptly put it this way: "A solitary Christian is a contradiction in terms. We are on a journey together, and God wants us to live the Christian life together." (9) As you pray this day, recall those who have requested prayer for a need. Fervently pray for them that God will encourage them, give them hope and meet their every need.

August 21
<u>Unceasing Prayer</u>

"Therefore we also pray always for you that our God would count you worthy of this calling, and fulfill all the good pleasure of His goodness and the work of faith with power," 2 Thessalonians 1:11

"For this reason we also, since the day we heard it, do not cease to pray for you, and to ask that you may be filled with the knowledge of His will in all wisdom and spiritual understanding;" Colossians 1:9

Intercessory prayer for the church and for fellow believers is God's purpose for every Christian. You do not need a prayer request to intercede on behalf of your family, friends, church members and for your Godly brothers in Christ. Though we should hold each other accountable, the most reliable way is through intercessory prayer. Pray unceasingly that God will strengthen and encourage other believers in Christ. In his book "Prayer", Richard J. Foster says: "Of all our ongoing work in the kingdom of God, nothing is more important then intercessory prayer". (10) Become a prayer warrior. Get up every morning with your prayer list and intercede on behalf of those who minister through full-time vocation, for foreign missionaries, for your family members and for other Godly men who face struggles as you. Paul told the Christians in Colossus, "we...do not cease to pray for you". It is vitally important to encourage those for whom you pray by telling them that you pray for them every day. You cannot imagine how strengthening that is! Begin today and make intercessory prayer a permanent part of your devotional time.

August 22
<u>A Man of Prayer in Family Crises</u>

"But at midnight Paul and Silas were praying and singing hymns to God, and the prisoners were listening to them." Acts 16:25
"And it happened that the father of Publius lay sick of a fever and dysentery. Paul went in to him and prayed, and he laid his hands on him and healed him." Acts 28:8

Have you faced a crisis in your family which seemed overwhelming? Most of us have had those unexpected pitfalls and land mines. Though God has mercifully blessed me in many ways, there have been times when I've felt like Job. As a man it is important to you to be viewed as strong and unflappable in the face of whatever comes. The truth is many men may appear to be as solid as a rock when inside they are trembling with fear and anxiety. That's why it is so important to stay focus on the Rock of Ages and never believe for one minute that we have any strength without Him. David said: "When my heart is overwhelmed, lead me to that Rock that is higher than I." Though a hero and a courageous man, David recognized that circumstances sometimes were so overwhelming that even he was not man enough to stand on his own. Whether you face a trial with illness, divorce, a wayward child, financial disaster, loss of a close family member or chaos in your life, God your Rock is more than sufficient to raise you above the flood waters and help you stand strong through it all.

August 23
The Country Home, the
Pickett Fence and the Rose Garden Illusion

"Whereas you do not know what will happen tomorrow. For what is your life? It is even a vapor that appears for a little time and then vanishes away." James 4:14 "Set your mind on things above, not on things on the earth." Colossians 3:2

When my son was young he and his friends enjoyed riding their motorcycles on nearby country roads. They sometimes passed a beautifully painted white house with a long front porch, big oak trees, and a white picket fence enclosing a yard full of rose bushes. He said that when he grew up he wanted to make that house his home. He is now an attorney in a firm in the city. He and his wife live in a home in the suburbs. Perhaps his dream will someday come true. But many times our fantasies and expectations for earthly wants and ambitions never become reality. Today's scriptures remind us to keep our minds focused on what is eternal, not on our treasures in this life. We are part of the human condition and the devil battles for our hearts and minds. An old sacred hymn says it so well: "And the things of earth will grow strangely dim in the light of His glory and grace." (9) Trust in the Lord and don't set your minds on earthly things. Bask in His love and let your desire be God. All else will be left behind and of no consequence in eternity.

August 24
Everybody Wants to Go
to Heaven, Just Not on the Next Load

"For our citizenship is in heaven, from which we also eagerly wait for the Savior, the Lord Jesus Christ..." Philippians 3:20
"Do not love the world or the things in the world. If anyone loves the world, the love of the Father is not in him... And the world is passing away, and the lust of it; but he who does the will of God abides forever." 1 John 2:15, 17

Do you long for Heaven? Are you really anticipating eternity with great anticipation? Or do you struggle with leaving life here on earth? It is sometimes confusing to differentiate between the thousand years of Christ's reign on earth, Heaven and the Holy City New Jerusalem. I believe such confusion diminishes many Christians focus and desire for Heaven with all of the wonder that await us. For sure we know there will be no night there, no death, no tears, no sorrow and no crying. That should be enough for each of us to get excited about our eternal destination. Perhaps your faith is being tried regarding the reality of Heaven. Today's culture is so self-centered that we find the belief of life after death hard to grasp. Search the Bible for scriptures related God's plan for us after this brief, temporary life. Discover that for a thousand years you will rule in a new earth. You will see the New Jerusalem coming down from Heaven. Paul wrote: "If in this life only we have hope, we are of all men most pitiable". Prayerfully seek God to create in you a longing to be with Him.

August 25
<u>Your Priorities – Today</u>

"This is the day the LORD has made; We will rejoice and be glad in it." Psalm 118:24
"Come now, you who say, 'Today or tomorrow we will go to such and such a city, spend a year there, buy and sell, and make a profit; whereas you do not know what will happen tomorrow.'" James 4:13-14

Many men, young and old, find themselves overloaded with commitments. They become so busy that each day seems like a blur and at the end of the day it seems that nothing of any significance has been achieved. Work is usually near the top of priority lists. Social and civic activities, family time and recreational/entertainment are typically on the list. Many Christian men simply have not set their priorities in the proper order. Often, time spent in prayer and reading His Word is either low on the list or not on it at all. The Psalmist David spoke of rising early in the morning to praise the Lord for His goodness, His blessings and His marvelous creation. Sad but true, we read and hear of men of all ages zealous about their work and plans for the future that unexpectedly face death before the sun arises the next day. It behooves us to slow down, assess our priorities and ask God to help us firmly dedicate a daily time of prayer and worship with Him a top priority. Scheduling your devotional time with God first thing each day puts Him first and better prepares you to meet the day's challenges with His peace.

August 26
<u>A Man's Frustration with Responsibilities</u>

"And Jesus, walking by the Sea of Galilee, saw two brothers Simon called Peter, and Andrew his brother, casting a net into the sea; for they were fishermen. Then He said to them, "Follow Me, and I will make you fishers of men." Matthew 4:18-19
"For everyone to whom much is given, from him much will be required; and for whom much has been committed, of him they will ask the more." Luke 12:48

Being a man, a husband, a father, an employee, a manager, a church leader, a community "mover and shaker" and/or a loyal friend translates to a heavy load of responsibilities. Men seem driven with some extra amount of adrenaline to achieve in their careers. They often take on a home mortgage, an auto loan and all that comes with success. Unfortunately, with each additional responsibility come higher bills, more stress, more time committed to tasks and less time spent with family and attending to spiritual matters. Consequently, sometimes after years of overload, they face increasing health problems, anxiety, anger, frustration and depression. Jesus expects men to accept responsibilities as they successfully reach goals and fulfill their commitments. But He never intends us to overload ourselves and neglect the most important part of living. That is our trust and obedience to Him and to fulfilling His purpose. If you find yourself tied in knot and so stressed that road rage becomes an issue, it is time to seek God and Godly counsel for you, for your family and for others around you. If you are frustrated with responsibilities and complicated issues in your life take them to the one who said to the raging ocean, "Peace, be still".

August 27
Become a Man of Wisdom

"Happy is the man who finds wisdom, and the man who gains understanding;" Proverbs 3:13
"If any of you lacks wisdom, let him ask of God, who gives to all liberally and without reproach, and it will be given to him." James 1:5

Godly men should seek wisdom from God. It is not a genetic trait, nor an achievement. It is borne through a close walk with God, knowledge of His word and having a keen hear to what the Holy Spirit says. Wisdom is so often thought to be reserved for the elderly. That notion would assume that someone who has been a Christian for 25 years must have a deep, close walk with God. The truth is, some Christians simply do not grow in their walk with Christ, and thus they may have one year of growth in Christ twenty-five times! Wisdom comes from more than just having lived long. Author Eugene Peterson describes wisdom this way: "Wisdom is the art of living skillfully in whatever actual conditions we find ourselves. It...has to do with honoring our parents and raising our children, handling our money and conducting our sexual lives, going to work and exercising leadership, using works well and treating friends kindly, eating and drinking healthily, cultivating emotions within ourselves and attitudes toward others that make for peace." (12) Ask God for wisdom and it will be given to you. Ask God for wisdom and consider Eugene Peterson's descriptors of wisdom.

August 28
God's Man and Harmful Habits

"Or do you not know that your body is the temple of the Holy Spirit who is in you, whom you have from God, and you are not your own?" 1 Corinthians 6:19

"But now you yourselves are to put off all these: anger, wrath, malice, blasphemy, filthy language out of your mouth." Colossians 3:8

Healthy living is a popular topic these days. Books, magazines and marketed programs are devoted to the best strategies to become healthier physically. God made our bodies and when we are born again into His family, He expects us to take care of our "temple of the Holy Spirit". It is sad to see pastors and preachers stand in front of a congregation one hundred pounds overweight and out of shape. That tells the members of the congregation that this man of God has little self-control and is not totally surrendered to God's purpose for his life. Paul said that he must keep his body in shape so that he could continue to preach the Gospel. There are habits which, in excess, are not pleasing to God. Our temper, excessive eating or drinking and anything harmful to our bodies should be stopped in obedience to Christ. As a Godly man, you are to be an example to others. Ridding yourself of bad habits will be good for you and those who observe your life. Become a healthy man in body and spirit, walking daily in the love of God.

August 29
You've Packed the Suitcase

"Only take heed to yourself, and diligently keep yourself, lest you forget the things your eyes have seen, and lest they depart from your heart all the days of your life. And teach them to your children and your grandchildren..." Deuteronomy 4:9
"Train up a child in the way he should go, and when he is old he will not depart from it." Proverbs 22:6

It is that time of year when many parents prepare to see their children leave home and move off to college. This signifies a major change for parents and their children. You may try to guide them, give advice and control them to some degree but your words of wisdom now may have little influence. John Crowle, former University of Alabama star football player, is Director of Big Oak Ranch in Alabama. He devotes his life to rescuing and nurturing children in need of a good home, love and spiritual guidance. He says to parents that once that "suitcase" is packed around age fifteen, there is little a parent can do to impact that child. Therefore, it is very important that you devote yourself to instilling God's word, strong values and faith in God in your children from their earliest years until that "suitcase" is full and shut. If this fall or in falls to come you get that lump in your throat and those tears in your eyes as you unload your child's belongings in some college dormitory or apartment and drive back home, be sure you'll have a peace that you packed the right things of God for their life's journey.

August 30
"This is Just the Way I Am"

"And do not be conformed to this world, but be transformed by the renewing of your mind, that you may prove what is that good and acceptable and perfect will of God." Romans 12:2

"That you put off, concerning your former conduct, the old man which grows corrupt according to the deceitful lusts," Ephesians 4:22

Often Christians are confronted with a sin or a short-coming. Some may be harmful and/or hurtful to others. As a man, husband and father, you want to be respected, make right decisions and to be right in what you say and do. However, when you are overcome with a sin or fault do you make excuses or rationalize the circumstances? There is a rationale that is often used. It goes something like this: "Hey, it's not my fault. That's just the way I am and I can't help it." It is the natural man or the "old man" that prefers to blame something or someone else for your wrongdoing. It is reminiscent of the phase Flip Wilson, the comedian, frequently used – "The devil made me do it". Ask God today if there is any fault or wrongdoing in your life with which you need to deal and seek His strength to overcome. Confess, repent and be fully restored to fellowship with Christ. When you do so you will gain the respect of fellow believers and your family. You can restore your character and integrity only when you are man enough to accept responsibility for your actions.

August 31
Beyond the Spiritual Maintenance Mode

"And He said to me, 'My grace is sufficient for you, for my strength is made perfect in weakness.' Therefore most gladly I will rather boast in my infirmities, that the power of Christ may rest upon me." 2 Corinthians 12:9

"And Stephen, full of faith and power, did great wonders and signs among the people." Acts 6:8

In today's secular culture Godly men full of the Holy Spirit are needed to stand in the gap. Though there are a lot of Christian men who provide for their family and serve in their church, many are spiritually anemic. Our secular culture has attempted to emasculate men in our God-given roles as leaders and warriors in our homes, workplaces and society. Few and far between are Godly men who are filled with the Spirit and full of a working faith. How many of us are as passionate about winning people to Christ as we are about our favorite football team? You may be a Christian man who serves in your church, has daily devotions and teach a Sunday school class. That is certainly commendable. But if you live in a maintenance mode and have become satisfied with the spiritual status quo, you're living beneath your privilege. People all around you are in need of someone to share Jesus with them. Seek God and ask Him to fill you with the Holy Spirit, give you a passion to reach the lost and anoint you with Holy boldness to do so. Become a light for those in darkness.

REFERENCES FOR AUGUST

1. John Eldridge, "Wild at Heart" (Thomas Nelson, Publishers, Nashville, Tennessee) 2001 p. 141
2. Oswald Chambers, "My Utmost for His Highest" (Discovery House Publishers, Grand Rapids, Michigan) 1963 p. 1
3. Ibid, page 7
4. Neil T. Anderson, "The Bondage Breaker" (Harvest House Publishers), Eugene Oregon) 2000 p. 61
5. Barbour Publishing Company, "Prayers & Promises for Men", (Barbour Publishing, Inc., Uhrichsville, Ohio, 2003) p. 56
6. Billy Graham, "The Journey" (W Publishing Group, Nashville, Tennessee) 2006, p. 289
7. Dietrich Bonhoeffer, "The Cost of Discipleship", (Simon and Schuster, New York) 1995, p. 169
8. Richard O'Connor, "Undoing Depression" (The Berkley Books Publishing Group, New York, New York) 1997 p. 181
9. Graham, 127
10. Richard J. Foster, "Prayer: Finding the Heart's True Home", (HarperSanFrancisco, New York, New York) p. 1992
11. Lemmel, Helen H., "Turn your eyes upon Jesus", (Singspirations, Inc., Nashville, Tennessee), 1922
12. Garborg's Inc., "Wisdom for the Workplace" (Garborg's Inc.P.O. Box 20132, Bloomington, MN 55420) p. 46

September 1
<u>Are You Ready for Some Football?</u>

*"Brethren, I do not count myself to have appre-
hended; but one thing I do, forgetting those things
which are behind and reaching forward to those
things which are ahead, 14 I press toward the goal
for the prize of the upward call of God in Christ
Jesus." Philippians 3:13-14*

It's that time of year when football fans at all levels get
their adrenalin revved up and get ready to adorn themselves
in their favorite team shirt, hat and other paraphernalia. There
is a slight hint of fall and football in the air. High school,
college and professional football teams begin with high hopes
of finishing their seasons as number one and winning the
first place trophy. If you are a football fan (fanatic) you are
probably already anticipating your team's winning season.
As a Christian man, football brings out that masculinity deep
down within you. Perhaps you played football at one or more
levels. You have experienced that toughness, courage and
passion to defeat the players lined up across from you. If you
have not played, you vicariously experience those emotions
on Friday nights and on Saturday and Sunday afternoons. Do
you experience this level of passion for winning the very real
spiritual game of life - the battle for your life? Ask Christ to
place within you that determination and passion which Paul
spoke of in today's scripture. Become passionate for living
for Christ and reaching the goal set before you.

September 2
A Team Effort

"Then I said to the nobles, the rulers, and the rest of the people, 'The work is great and extensive, and we are separated far from one another on the wall. Wherever you hear the sound of the trumpet, rally to us there. Our God will fight for us.' So we labored in the work, and half of the men held the spears from daybreak until the stars appeared." Nehemiah 4:19-21

In the game of football winning requires teamwork. Of the football standouts who were recipients of the coveted Heisman Trophy, not one of them would say they were awarded the prize without the support of ten other players. As you watch football games this fall and winter pay close attention to the coordination of plays which can be achieved only by teamwork of all eleven men on the field. As a Seattle Seahawk, Shaun Alexander scored 28 touchdowns in one season and went on to be that year's NFL MVP and led his team to the NFL Superbowl. His teammates know his heart and respect him and he depends on them to get him into the end zone. His Christian testimony and passion for Christ have been and continue to be his top priority in life. (1) Teamwork is about supporting each other and working together to win. The great professional football coach Vince Lombardi once said "Winning isn't everything, it's the only thing" (2) Godly men should come together as a team in their community, at their workplace and in their church to build up one another so that all win in the spiritual game of life.

September 3
Practice and Discipline Makes a Team

"If you know that He is righteous, you know that everyone who practices righteousness is born of Him." I John 2:29
"But I discipline my body and bring it into subjection, lest, when I have preached to others, I myself should become disqualified." I Corinthians 9:27

Knute Rockne, the legendary Notre Dame Football coach is known for the many quips and quotable statements he made. A couple of those pertinent to today's topic include: "And don't forget the only way to gain perfection is to practice it until it becomes a habit... (3) And "Pick the right men, teach them how to do things perfectly, then make them practice, practice, practice. (4) God seeks men who are willing to discipline themselves to the point where serving others through His Spirit becomes a habit. There are simply no excuses we can make to God for not being spiritually conditioned and Spirit-filled to accomplish His purpose. Through fellowship with other Godly men holding up one another we can take our communities and our workplaces and our families from Satan's bondage. It is difficult to stay prayed up and walking in the Spirit. Yet, following Paul's self-disciplined life as an example to reach others with the gospel, Godly men can practice praying, practice studying God's Word and practice keeping ourselves spiritually conditioned. Start today with a prayer and a commitment to practice daily.

September 4
Spiritual Power for You

"Now to Him who is able to do exceedingly abundantly above all that we ask or think, according to the power that works in us..." Ephesians 3:20

"But you shall receive power when the Holy Spirit has come upon you; and you shall be witnesses..." Acts 1:8

Power. This word has a special meaning to men. It conjures up masculine thoughts and emotions as strength, being a hero, a man capable of rescuing others and extraordinary ability to overcome threats and enemies. In today's scriptures the Apostle Paul spoke of power with which every believer is endowed. The power of God was demonstrated through men called of God to accomplish great things. Sampson, David, Moses, Jesus' disciples, Steven and the Apostle Paul are but a few men who God anointed with His power. God still endows you and me with His power. His power is often stifled by our lack of belief and our reluctance to surrender ourselves totally to Him. You have access to power this day to fight back evil, to overcome temptation and to bring someone to the saving knowledge of Jesus Christ. It has nothing to do your ability or your talent. Spiritual power comes from being full of the Holy Spirit. It produces boldness, passion and changes the hearts of men. In prayer seek God for a renewal and a filling of the Holy Spirit's power.

September 5
Labor Day: A Tribute to the American Worker

"Whatever your hand finds to do, do it with your might; for there is no work or device or knowledge or wisdom in the grave where you are going."
Ecclesiastes 9:10
"For even when we were with you, we commanded you this: If anyone will not work, neither shall he eat." 2 Thessalonians 3:10

My Dad often reminded me the "Work is honorable. Never look down on any man who is working, whether he is digging a ditch or hauling other people's trash." Notable men of the Bible who we, at first glance, do not associate with labor performed menial labor. David, who became King of Israel, once tended sheep and ran errands for his brothers. Moses, after enjoying the royalty of the King's son, later tended sheep. Paul, an educated Roman with authority, gladly gave it all up for the sake of the Gospel and supported his ministry by making tents. For the Godly man, work can include his career or vocation. But God has recruited you to work in His Kingdom. James said "Thus also faith by itself, if it does not have works, is dead." (James 2:17) Working for God can take on various forms from sharing His word, working on a mission trip, helping you neighbor, serving in a volunteer capacity at your church, ministering to the less fortunate, etc. Today as we celebrate those who labored to make this country great, remember that God has a work for you.

September 6
Blue Collar or White Collar: All Are Equal in Christ

"Then I said to the nobles, the rulers, and the rest of the people, "The work is great and extensive, and we are separated far from one another on the wall. Wherever you hear the sound of the trumpet, rally to us there. Our God will fight for us." So we labored in the work, and half of the men held the spears from daybreak until the stars appeared." Nehemiah 4:19-21
"There is neither Jew nor Greek, there is neither slave nor free, there is neither male nor female; for you all are one in Christ Jesus." Galatians 3:28

Often, even in the church and among Christians, there is a chasm among men and women stemming from differences in race, in socio-economic status, the type of career, the social status within a political/social community and/or physical appearance. God sees all of us as his children and gives not preferential treatment to any of His children. James says: "My brethren, do not hold the faith of our Lord Jesus Christ, the Lord of Glory, with partiality." (James 2:1) Godly men are not immune from falling into the mindset of discriminatory preference. Unfortunately, an elitist attitude happens inside the church. This is not to say that we should not enjoy the company and association with those like us. However, we should approach and treat every Christian brother as equals, no matter their race or social standing. We should worship with those different than us, converse with them and give them the "right hand of fellowship". Join me in prayer today that we not be guilty of showing partiality to those who, by this world's standards, are better than any others. At the foot of the cross the ground is level.

September 7
Falling Down

"For we all stumble in many things. If anyone does not stumble in word, he is a perfect man, able also to bridle the whole body." James 3:2
"But as for me, my feet had almost stumbled; my steps had nearly slipped. For I was envious of the boastful, when I saw the prosperity of the wicked." Psalm 73:2-3

We have all stumbled in many ways and we have all sinned. Lest you feel that you are especially weak and fall into sin, our "heroes" and great men of the Bible had their times of falling down. Though there are too many to name, a few include Moses, David, Sampson and Peter. Moses, called of God to deliver the Israelites out of bondage, later disobeyed God and, in anger, struck the rock instead of speaking to it. David, who God called a man after His own heart, committed adultery with Bathsheba and had her husband killed. Sampson, borne to be a Nazirite (dedicated to God for his lifetime), was a womanizer. And Peter, who after being called by Jesus to become one of His twelve disciples, denied that he knew Jesus. Not one of these men escaped consequences of their sin. Yet, in every case, God used them for His purpose despite their failures. Eugene Peterson says this about David's sin: "David's sin, as enormous as it was, was wildly outdone by God's grace." (5) Never feel that because you have sinned God discards you or no longer loves you. Genuinely seek restoration. God's greatest purpose for your life may be just ahead.

September 8
The Secularist Attack on Your Religious Freedom

"Yes, and all who desire to live godly in Christ Jesus will suffer persecution." II Timothy 3:12

"Now Saul was consenting to his death. At that time a great persecution arose against the church which was at Jerusalem; and they were all scattered throughout the regions of Judea and Samaria, except the apostles. And devout men carried Stephen to his burial, and made great lamentation over him. As for Saul, he made havoc of the church, entering every house, and dragging off men and women, committing them to prison." Acts 8:1-3

Christianity has come under increasing attacks from secularists, atheists and others who seek to push Christianity or anything associated with Christianity out of public view. Many of these individuals, groups and the federal courts are using their money, influence and power to abolish the rights of Christians which are guaranteed by the U.S. Constitution. Writing about modern day persecution against the Church, David Limbaugh states: "Anti-Christian discrimination occurs in a variety of contexts throughout our culture, from the public sector to the private sector, in the mainstream media and in Hollywood, in the public education system and in our universities." (6) In her book, *The Godless: The Church of Liberalism,* Ann Coulter writes: "While secularists are always comparing conservative Christians to Nazis, somehow it is always the godless who is always doing the genocides." (7) As a Godly man you will be called to defend the faith. Be alert to the new "tolerance" and "relativism" which are being used to brainwash your children.

Stand up and be courageous against attempts to remove your Constitutional religious freedom.

September 9
When It Becomes Your Idol?"

"Set your mind on things above, not on things on the earth." Colossians 3:2
"But know this, that in the last days perilous times will come:" Timothy 3:1

Webster defines "idol" as "a symbol of an object of worship: a false god or a form or appearance visible but without substance." The Israelites became impatient and rebellious while wandering in the wilderness. Their dissatisfaction with God's timing caused their faith to wane. They turned to craven images to worship. When Moses returned with the Ten Commandments he found the people indulging in sinful behavior turning from the God to a "form without substance." Have you similarly allowed other gods or idols to have more of your thoughts and time than God? At times when all seems to be going well, you may be lulled into self-sufficiency, not feeling the need for God as at other times. Consequently, you may unknowingly find other "objects of worship". Instead of worshipping God on Sunday mornings you rationalize that "I can worship God on the golf course just as well as at church". Or, with work, family, and civic responsibilities, say "I just cannot squeeze in that men's Bible study." Is God still God in your life? Ask Him to search your heart and mind for any "idols" in your life. Be reminded that you are never, even for a moment, sufficient or equipped for life without God.

September 10
<u>Reduce Your Anxiety</u>

"Be anxious for nothing, but in everything by prayer and supplication, with thanksgiving, let your requests be made known to God;" Philippians 4:6
"And let the peace of God rule in your hearts, to which also you were called in one body; and be thankful." Colossians 3:15

Men are plagued by worry and, anxiety to a greater degree than traditionally believed. "Real men don't cry. Real men are emotionally tough. Real men just deal with it." These are myths. I think Psalm 37:8 precisely expresses the outcome of worrying: "Do not worry. It only causes harm." Worry and anxiety indicates a lack of trust in God and that He is not big enough to handle your perplexities. Men want to believe that they really control. For years, I tried to control the behavior of my college-aged children. It simply did not happen! So, I worried and allowed anxiety to rule my thoughts. In the end all of my worrying and anxiety produced nothing but harm. Most of our anxiety over circumstances in our lives and over the behavior of others is harmful to our emotions, our health and our relationships with those around us. While medication may be needed, first consider talking with another Godly man, to your pastor and/or to a Christian counselor. Seek the scriptures and pray for that "peace that passes all understanding". Begin to worship your Lord with more praise and thanksgiving. That will dispel so much worry. And most importantly, let go and let God.

September 11
The Enemy's Attack on America: A Wake-up Call

"For we do not wrestle against flesh and blood, but against principalities, against powers, against the rulers of the darkness of this age, against spiritual hosts of wickedness in the heavenly places. Therefore take up the whole armor of God, that you may be able to withstand in the evil day, and having done all, to stand." Ephesians 6:12-13

America is under attack both internally and externally. The focus: Christianity. As Christians in our own county which was founded by God-fearing men and on the precept of religious freedom, we now face persecution, ridicule and judicial assault as never before in the history of this country. David Limbaugh states: "Discrimination against Christians and the suppression of Christian religious expression pervade our society, and its perpetrators are legion. (8) From outside our borders a similar enemy has attacked our nation with the tragedy of 9/11 in attacks on the Pentagon and the World Trade Center. This enemy is fighting a religious war against Christianity and the American way. Jihad has been declared against America and has wide-spread support throughout the Arab world. America is facing an increasing hostile world, none of which are Christian nations. Some of these nations no longer respect America and would like to eradicate Christianity. It behooves you and me to seek God while He may be found. Commit to be Spirit-filled and be strong in the Lord. You should not fear nor panic. Our trust is in the creator of all things. Let His peace rule your heart and mind. And He has already given us the victory.

September 12
Remember When God Came Through

"For indeed he was sick almost unto death; but God had mercy on him, and not only on him but on me also, lest I should have sorrow upon sorrow." Philippians 2:27

"Jesus said, 'Take away the stone.' Martha, the sister of him who was dead, said to Him, 'Lord, by this time there is a stench, for he has been dead four days'." John 11:39

"Now when He had said these things, He cried with a loud voice, 'Lazarus, come forth!' And he who had died came out bound hand and foot with grave clothes, and his face was wrapped with a cloth. Jesus said to them, 'Loose him, and let him go.'" John 11:43-44

Do you ever take time to recall some of the times when your back was against the wall or you felt like you were in the bottom of the well? Sure, there are times when God doesn't solve our every problem or meet our every need. To my knowledge, no one – great evangelists, renowned theologians or the wisest, most devoted Bible scholars – knows why He sometimes seems to rush to rescue us and then times when He seems not to hear our cry. But I can testify with a surety that God has miraculously saved the day and answered my prayer when there could be no other explanation. Are you really aware of just what a great and marvelous God you serve? Are you really grateful to God for His blessings? Sadly, we all forget and take God for granted far too much. Today take time to recall those instances and dire circumstances when you called on God and He, without a doubt, met your need. And praise Him for His love and grace and all the daily benefits with which He loads on you. God is good. God is love.

September 13
What Made Them Great Men?

"And when Asa heard these words and the prophecy of Oded the prophet, he took courage, and removed the abominable idols from all the land of Judah and Benjamin and from the cities which he had taken in the mountains of Ephraim; and he restored the altar of the LORD that was before the vestibule of the LORD." Chronicles 15:8

"Now what more shall I say? For the time would fail me to tell of Gideon and Barak and Samson and Jephthah, also of David and Samuel and the prophets: who through faith subdued kingdoms, worked righteousness, obtained promises, stopped the mouths of lions..." Hebrews 11:32-33

Today's scriptures tell us what it took and what it will take today for men of God to become great in service for Him. There are skeptics who say that which compelled the Biblical heroes is not available for us today. Hogwash! The truth is few Godly men today will become fully obedient to Christ. Abandonment and obedience are two characteristics which our Biblical examples possessed. The writer of Hebrews offers a long list of great men who accomplished great things for God. He uses a key word which we will find in all great men of God – Faith. In his book, *Heroic Faith*, Greg Asimakoupoulos and others share qualities of great men. (9) These are: Eternal perspective; Dependence on God; Love of God's word; Endurance: and Self-control. Are these not what God requires of you? Granted, you may not be called into full-time ministry. Yet, you should aspire to possess these spiritual qualities so that you can change our world around you. Don't allow fear and disbelief to thwart your commitment to accomplish great things for God. Rely on Jesus to work in you. For He said, "…without me you can do nothing." (John 15:5) Trust Him today.

September 14
When You Can't Feel God's Presence

"Answer me speedily, O LORD; My spirit fails! Do not hide Your face from me, Lest I be like those who go down into the pit. Cause me to hear Your lovingkindness in the morning, For in You do I trust; Cause me to know the way in which I should walk, For I lift up my soul to You." Psalm 143:7-8
"For we walk by faith, not by sight." 2 Corinthians 5:7

I dare say that few of you have not experienced that time and place when you could feel nothing that resembled God's presence. It is perplexing, especially when you may have a pressing need and want Him to give you His undivided attention. While many report a feeling of joy unspeakable and new peace when they came to know Christ, the assurance of our salvation depends only on our faith in Him – not feeling. Billy Graham says: "Our emotions aren't a dependable gauge of our true standing with God. Emotions come and go, and a faith that is built solely on our feelings will never be secure." (10) Feeling His presence should not be considered a result of our good deeds. When you walk in the Spirit continually, you may well experience the closeness of the indwelling Holy Spirit, but there will be those times when you go to your private place of prayer and God may seem as if He's asleep. Pray anyway. He's listening! He never sleeps and He never slumbers. He is always watching over you. He knows your thoughts and the number of hairs on your head. What an awesome God you serve.

September 15
Opportunities to be a Good Samaritan

"But whoever has this world's goods, and sees his brother in need, and shuts up his heart from him, how does the love of God abide in him?" 1 John 3:17

"And I will very gladly spend and be spent for your souls; though the more abundantly I love you, the less I am loved." 2 Corinthians 12:15

"Spend and be spent' pretty much goes straight to the point. As a Godly man who has received the greatest gift of all from the Omnipotent God of this Universe, you should be aware of needs all around you. They are in City and County jails, in State and Federal penitentiaries, homeless shelters, nursing homes, hospitals, orphanages and a litany of other institutions where hurting, lonely people live. Maybe a church ministry goes there occasionally. But there is always room for you. I served on an interim basis for a relatively large church's Pastoral Care Ministry. Somewhat reluctantly I was faced with many opportunities to visit the sick, the elderly and these bereaved. To my surprise, I received the greater blessing each time I entered a hospital or nursing home room and offered words of encouragement, grasped a wrinkled hand and prayed a prayer sharing God's love and grace. If these opportunities seem too far away or inconvenient, look around you at work, in the grocery store checkout line and sitting beside you at church. Jesus not only commanded us to serve, He set the example. Now take a few moments and sincerely ask God to make you aware of others who need you – a Good Samaritan.

September 16
<u>The Love of God</u>

"Now hope does not disappoint, because the love of God has been poured out in our hearts by the Holy Spirit who was given to us." Romans 5:5
"...to know the love of Christ which passes knowledge; that you may be filled with all the fullness of God." Ephesians 3:19

As a child, I recall listening to the Billy Graham radio telecast and hearing George Beverly Shea sing his rendition of "The Love of God". The words of that beautiful old hymn would send chills up my spine. *"The love of God – how rich and pure, how measureless and strong..."* The older I become the more real and fathomless is God's love. The human mind cannot truly understand God's love. Perhaps the one analogy which resonates, especially with parents, is the relationship of God to His children (you and me) and the relationship between a parent and a child. Good fathers and mothers will sacrifice their lives for their children. Their love runs deep, forgiving the deepest wounds created by a disrespectful and wayward child. "Yes, the first thing that happened when you committed your life to Christ is that God gave you a new relationship. He is now your loving Heavenly Father, and you are His child..." (11) Allow God's love to become new and refreshing today. No matter who you are or what you have done, as a child of God the love of God, "deep and pure", and will keep from now and throughout eternity.

September 17
Christ's Second Coming

"For the Lord Himself will descend from heaven with a shout, with the voice of an archangel, and with the trumpet of God. And the dead in Christ will rise first. Then we who are alive and remain shall be caught up together with them in the clouds to meet the Lord in the air. And thus we shall always be with the Lord." I Thessalonians 4:16-17

"You have heard Me say to you, 'I am going away and coming back to you.' If you loved Me, you would rejoice because I said 'I am going to the Father,' for My Father is greater than I." John 14:28

Jesus promises us in His word that He is returning to gather the redeemed and to destroy this old earth as we know it and replace it with a new earth. God keeps His promises. Yet, there are those of all nations and religions who doubt the second coming of Christ. Have you ever wondered if He is really going to return in the clouds as He said? Peter wrote of those who doubted Jesus' promise to return to earth. He said: "...scoffers will come in the last days, walking according to their own lusts, and saying, 'Where is the promise of His coming? For since the fathers fell asleep, all things continue as there were from the beginning of creation." (II Peter 3:3-4) I believe that the signs of our times all point to the soon second coming of Christ who will come "as a thief in the night". Study the scriptures which foretell and describe the "last days" and the events following Jesus second coming. Or simply read the daily news and the fulfillment of the signs which precede His coming are there. As a Godly man, stay Spirit-filled and share the gospel with urgency.

September 18
<u>Occupy Until He Comes</u>

"But you shall receive power when the Holy Spirit has come upon you; and you shall be witnesses to Me in Jerusalem, and in all Judea and Samaria, and to the end of the earth." Acts 1:8

"Therefore, my beloved brethren, be steadfast, immovable, always abounding in the work of the Lord, knowing that your labor is not in vain in the Lord." 1 Corinthians 15:58

There is a song entitled ***Until Then*** (12) with a theme which reminds the believer of this world's struggles and problems, but points to Christ's second coming. The chorus points to Jesus' return to earth and the continuing hope and praise that the writer will maintain "until then". The words offer great encouragement for those who await Christ's return and need to be renewed in occupying with joy until He does return: "But until then my heart will go on singing, until then with joy I'll carry on..." What a great encouragement to believers which should lift up our hearts as we live here on earth among troubles, wars, disease and death. Until then you are to live every moment of every day as if it were your last. You should take time and praise God for redemption through Jesus Christ which removes any fear of the future. Until then you should touch as many lives as possible through the name of Jesus. On those days which you find most difficult to get through remember that He has saved your from the penalty of sin and will keep you "until then'.

September 19
Honor Your Father

"Honor your father and your mother, that your days may be long upon the land which the LORD your God is giving you." Exodus 20:12

"And Solomon said: 'You have shown great mercy to Your servant David my father, because he walked before You in truth, in righteousness, and in uprightness of heart with You; You have continued this great kindness for him, and You have given him a son to sit on his throne, as it is this day.'" 1 Kings 3:6

Some of you may have no recollection of your father. Others' memories are so awful that you wish you could forget. The lack of strong, positive fathers in the lives of boys has contributed to dysfunctional lives of men. God taught all men (and women) to honor their parents and to show them respect. This is the natural, order of in God's plan. You may be a young man, a middle-aged man or a maturing man, but if you still have your father it is never too late to devote yourself to demonstrating God's love. Time alone listening to your father is invaluable. The time you spend learning things about him which you never knew may help you understand him better. Though your father may have not been the ideal father (whatever that is), you owe him honor and respect. Do things with and for your father whether hunting, fishing, a trip together, a building/repair project or having lunch together. While you both need each other, you will be the beneficiary of gaining an understanding your heritage. After all, you won't always have him around. Honor your father.

September 20
A Father's Wisdom

"I go the way of all the earth; be strong, there-fore, and prove yourself a man. And keep the charge of the LORD your God: to walk in His ways, to keep His statutes, His commandments, His judgments, and His testimonies, as it is written in the Law of Moses, that you may prosper in all that you do and wherever you turn; 1 Kings 2:2-3:8

"My son, pay attention to my wisdom; Lend your ear to my understanding, That you may preserve discretion, And your lips may keep knowledge." Proverbs 5:1-2

Fathers can make a significant difference in a young boy's life and future. At twenty-four both my wife and I were teachers. Life had started in the right direction when, suddenly, my father was diagnosed with cancer and died four weeks later. Though he accepted Jesus only weeks before his death, he had been a strong, positive role model for me. Having a limited education, he had held hard, back-breaking jobs in the ore mines and in a hot, dusty cement plant. From my earliest memories he would share his wisdom with me, at the breakfast table, riding along in our old family car or sitting in the quiet of the woods hunting squirrels or rabbits. He instilled in me values of integrity, a strong work ethic and to owe no man anything for long. He taught me how to work hard along side him. His life was simple. I always knew he loved me – he told me. He was proud of me and everyone in our small town knew it. It's been over thirty years now that I've been a father and I still pass on my father's wisdom. Our Heavenly Father wants to share with us if we will spend time with Him.

September 21
Seasons of a Man's Life: Autumn

"I press toward the goal for the prize of the upward call of God in Christ Jesus. Therefore let us, as many as are mature, have this mind; and if in anything you think otherwise, God will reveal even this to you." Philippians 3:14-15

"Come now, therefore, and I will send you to Pharaoh that you may bring My people, the children of Israel, out of Egypt. But Moses said to God, 'Who am I that I should go to Pharaoh, and that I should bring the children of Israel out of Egypt?'" Exodus 3:10-11

As a man approaches his fifties the autumn of life shows itself in his a few wrinkles, maybe a bit of arthritis and adult children. He can have a new perspective on life. In today's culture a man has a desire to stay competitive longer and continue to work hard and to achieve goals. Some men actually find among the golden leaves of autumn that they can make contributions to family, career, their communities and God with a renewed passion. Their seasoned experiences of life have prepared them for new challenges. Moses took on a new challenge near the autumn of his life. After living in the house of Pharoh until young adulthood, after doing a mundane job for forty years, he became God's man of the hour. He was charged to lead the Israelites out of bondage in Egypt to the Promised Land of Canaan. Reluctantly, Moses accepted his new leadership role. For forty more years up until life's end, he struggled with a rebellious people in the wilderness but took them within sight of Canaan. This could be the best time of your life. Live it as unto the Lord fulfilling His purpose for your life.

September 22
<u>Higher Heights and Deeper Depths</u>

"From the end of the earth I will cry to You, When my heart is overwhelmed; Lead me to the rock that is higher than I." Psalm 61:2
"But those who wait on the LORD Shall renew their strength; They shall mount up with wings like eagles... Isaiah 40:31

Throughout my childhood I recall lying in my bed at night with heavy eyes from a long day at school or play. I could hear my mother praying beside her bed as she did every night. I remember those portions of her prayer which she prayed every night. One phrase lingers in my memory. She prayed: "Oh Lord, lead me into higher heights and deeper depths with you." When I ponder on what she was asking from God I'm led to several scriptures including today's verses. David knew God was his higher rock safe from the overwhelming waves of threats and disillusionment. He watched with awe the eagles spread their magnificent wings climbing high above the storm. Luke tells about Jesus commanding His disciples to launch out into the deep "for a catch" though they had labored all night but came to shore with empty nets. (Luke 5:3, 6) If you are to become a man whom God can use and walk daily in the Spirit, you cannot be satisfied with the mundane walk as a lukewarm Christian. Pray today that God will give you a passion to reach higher heights and deeper depths in Him.

September 23
<u>A Treasure Found on a Graveyard Wall</u>

"If you seek her as silver, And search for her as for hidden treasures;" Proverbs 2:4
"An excellent wife is the crown of her husband..." Proverbs 12:4

In her book, **For Women Only,** author Shaunti Feldhahn includes a chapter on what women need to know men want. In a survey she designed to learn how men feel about various relational aspects, the final question is "What is the one thing that you wish your wife/significant other knew, but you feel you can't explain it to her?" Out of five choices this response was given almost twice as any other: "I want her to know how much I love her..." (13) Every Godly man who has a Godly wife who loves him, enjoys his company and is a good mother to his children has truly found a treasure. I know because I fell in love with the most beautiful, sweetest, unselfish Godly young lady placed on planet earth. During our college years we found a special but unusual place to sit and talk – an old graveyard wall located on campus. It was there I asked her to be my wife - a forever memory. Give God special thanks and praise for the treasure He had hidden just for you. Tell her often you love her, as Christ loves His church and gave Himself for her.

September 24
<u>Be Authentic</u>

"For I say, through the grace given to me, to everyone who is among you, not to think of himself more highly than he ought to think, but to think soberly, as God has dealt to each one a measure of faith." Romans 12:3

"...For you devour widows' houses, and for a pretense make long prayers. Therefore you shall receive the greater condemnation." Matthew 23:14

Are you authentic? Are you the real thing at all times, at all places, with all people? Jesus confronted hypocrisy numerous times. He deplored those who pretended to be what they were not. You probably feel like Jesus when you observe someone at work, at church and/or an acquaintance who wears a façade in certain places to impress certain people. Certainly, you may "let your hair down" at home or on the river bank or at a football game. But even in those places, your conduct is being watched by our family and others to see if you are the "real McCoy". Your Christian witness can be easily stained and diminished if you are a pretender. Some men pretend by acting super spiritual at church and when the pastor visits, but as soon as the scenery changes they revert back to profaning and other ungodly behavior. A popular cartoon character, *Popeye*, frequently declared, "I am what I am and that's all that I am". Seek to be a genuine and authentic Godly man so that your testimony will be powerful and effective.

September 25
Speak Out

"Then Paul stood in the midst of the Areopagus and said, 'Men of Athens, I perceive that in all things you are very religious; for as I was passing through and considering the objects of your worship, I found an alter wit this inscription: TO THE UNKOWN GOD. Therefore, the One whom you worship without knowing, Him I proclaim to you." Acts 17:22-23

Paul took the opportunity to speak publicly to religious leaders and others who gathered at the Areopagus, or Mars Hill. He began by relating to the religious leaders by referring to their gods and one, in particular, TO THE UNKNOWN GOD. Using this to get their interest, he proclaimed Jesus to them as the Son of God. Paul spoke out. David Limbaugh states: "Christians committed to their faith and to American freedom, I believe, have an unmistakable right, if not a duty, to engage in the political arena and to seek to influence the course of this country." (14) As a Godly man you are to show courage, be strong in the Lord. Take every opportunity while it is available to become involved as an elected official at some level of government. Several of my state's legislators and senators consistently defend religious freedom and vote their convictions. Attend school board meetings, city council meetings, etc. Local political offices are in need of Godly men with unashamed boldness to speak out for Christ and denounce the secularists' attempts to thwart Christian values. Make yourself available for God to give you opportunities in your community to speak out for Godliness and for religious freedom.

September 26
"Thank You for Giving to the Lord"

"The Lord grant to him that he may find mercy from the Lord in that Day—and you know very well how many ways he ministered to me[a] at Ephesus. II Timothy 1:18

"But a certain Samaritan, as he journeyed, came where he was. And when he saw him, he had compassion. So he went to him and bandaged his wounds, pouring on oil and wine; and he set him on his own animal, brought him to an inn, and took care of him." Luke 10:33-34

"Giving to the Lord" takes on many meanings. Typically the first thing that comes to mind is giving tithe and offerings. God expects you to give of your finances. Money, when given to the Kingdom of God, will go far, changing lives, feeding the hungry and supporting local ministries and faithful missionaries who live sacrificial lives. But there are other ways we can give to the Lord. Today's scripture verses offer two examples. Paul was expressing his gratitude for Onesiphorus for his ministering him. The "Good Samaritan" story is an excellent model for Godly men to follow. You give to the Lord every time you help someone in need. Each time you demonstrate Godly "giving to the Lord"; remember to tell those on the receiving end you are doing it for the Lord or that you will be pray for them. This will serve to witness of Jesus and it will give Him the glory. Giving to the Lord is an act of servanthood following the example of our Lord. Pray that God will make you more aware of opportunities to give to Him by giving to others.

September 27
Christian Men: Living Sacrifices

"And I will very gladly spend and be spent for your souls; though the more abundantly I love you, the less I am loved." 2 Corinthians 12:15
"I beseech you therefore, brethren, by the mercies of God, that you present your bodies a living sacrifice, holy, acceptable to God, which is your reasonable service." Romans 12:1

Few Christians are comfortable with the topic of sacrificing. They know it means letting go of something of value to them. The scriptures are replete with God's admonition to give ourselves to Him. Total abandonment of your will is the key to finding God's purpose for your life. Godly men, like non-Christian men, are accustomed to pursuing the American dream. Many Godly men have an addiction to getting more and better material things. Few Godly men are interested in becoming a living sacrifice or abandoning self for Jesus' will for their lives. It may take some shattered dreams for Godly men to recognize that it is only through sacrifice and suffering that they reach fully grasp God's love. I confess my struggle to abandonment. But it is time for authentic Godly you and me to become willing to yield our will and ask God what He would have us do. Let's pray today that the Holy Spirit will lead us to become like clay in the potter's hand. As you pray each day seek God for the more love for Him, a stronger desire and willingness to give up self to be in the center of His will. There you will find peace and joy.

September 28
Life's Spiritual Markers

"Then I remembered the word of the Lord, how He said, 'John indeed baptized with water, but you shall be baptized with the Holy Spirit.' If therefore God gave them the same gift as He gave us when we believed on the Lord Jesus Christ, who was I that I could withstand God?" Acts 11:16-17

"Now it happened, as I journeyed and came near Damascus at about noon, suddenly a great light from heaven shone around me. And I fell to the ground and heard a voice saying to me, 'Saul, Saul, why are you persecuting Me?'" Acts 22:6-7

Every man of God who has lived for Christ very long should have special events and/or experiences which mark significant places along their Christian journey. Do you remember the day when you asked Christ to become your Lord? Do you remember the day you were baptized? Are there spiritual experiences that increased your faith, greatly encouraged you or revealed a calling of God on your life? On our Christian journey God steps in and touches us with His Spirit and power that cannot be confused with simply an emotional experience. These events are like camera still shots imbedded in our hearts and minds. It might be the time when you had reached the end of your rope with some family problem that seemed to be excruciatingly endless. And someone led by the Holy Spirit touched you and prayed a prayer of faith. Or a telephone call came with a message of hope. Spiritual renewals should be cherished. Today, focus on those spiritual markers in your life. Re-live the feelings and the victories which came with the experience. Take time to bask in God's love, His mercy and His grace. Praise Him for His love and grace.

September 29
Known for Your Good Works

"This same Hezekiah also stopped the water outlet of Upper Gihon, and brought the water by tunnel[a] to the west side of the City of David. Hezekiah prospered in all his works." Chronicles 32:30

"And let us consider one another in order to stir up love and good works" Hebrews 10:24

You were not saved by any effort of your own or by good works. The scriptures teach that works should complement our faith. James explains it by saying if you tell a hungry person to go by faith and be filled and not feed him, your faith is empty. So many Godly men fail to recognize the significant witness of a Christian who demonstrates his love of God by doing. Doing good deeds may involve taking a vacation day and working on a Habitat for Humanity house. Doing good works may be that ten-day missionary trip to share your ability, skills and talents. You may be the only "Jesus" others will ever know. Hezekiah did what he did for others and left a legacy for his good works. In the book of Acts, Jesus' disciples saw that there was a need to help tend to widows in the community. Did they simply pray for them? No. They chose seven Godly men to go and provide these widows with food and shelter. Become a model for your children as you give of your time and means to do good for others through the name of Jesus.

September 30
Football and Character

"...knowing that tribulation produces perseverance; perseverance, character and character, hope." Romans 5:4-5

"But you know his proven character, that as a son with his father he served me in the gospel" Philippians 2:22

"Also if anyone competes in athletics, he is not crowned unless he competes according to the rules." II Timothy 2:5

It's now about the half-way point in the season for high school and college football. Winning is important and well it should be. Vince Lombardi once said: "Winning isn't everything, it's the only thing." (15) However, winning with character is the only legitimate win. The lack of character at some level of football is in daily newspapers across the country. Stories of recruitment violations, playing ineligible players, the use of illegal steroids and other drugs, assaults by players, and vile and profane language on the field by coaches are rampant. Recently, I listened to a popular radio talk show hosted by two Christian men. The issue was the language coaches used to motivate a local high school team which was top ranked nationally. One of the hosts excused the bad language of the coach as "it's just part of the game." A lack of character by a role model should not be excused. Real men are men of character. Cheating, profanity and other rule-breaking should not be tolerated. As one college professor said, "If I used that kind of language in class, I would be fired". Godly men, don't participate in or accept this kind of behavior. Character still counts and God's counting on you.

REFERENCE FOR SEPTEMBER

1. Gail Wood, "Alexander the Great", *New Man Magazine,* (Strange Communications, Lake Mary, Floriday) p. 21 - 26
2. Alex Barnett, "The Quotable American" (The Lyons Press, Guilford, Connecticut) p. 317
3. John Heisler, "Quotable Rockne" (TowleHouse Books, Lanham, Maryland), p. 112
4. Ibid.p. 106
5. Eugene H. Peterson, "Leap Over A Wall", (Harper, San Francisco) 1997 p. 189
6. David Limbaugh, "Persecution: How Liberals Are Waging War Against Christianity" (Regnery Publishing, Inc., Washington D.C.) 2003 p. ix
7. Ann Coulter, "Godless: The Church of Liberalism", Crown Publishing, New York) 2006 p. 281
8. Limbaugh, p. 3
9. Larry Crabb, "Shattered Dreams" (Waterbrook Press, Colorado Springs, Colorado) 2001 p. 180
10. Billy Graham, "The Journey" (W. Publishing Company, Nashville, Tennessee) 2006 p. 72
11. Ibid., p. 57
12. Stuart Hamblen, "Until Then" (Hamblin Music Company, 1958, and re-reprinted by permission by Gaither Music Company, Alexandria, Indiana – "Bill Gaither Homecoming Souvenir Songbook) 1993 p. 56
13. Shaunti Feldhahn, "For Women Only" (Multnomah Publishers, Sisters, Oregon) 2004 p. 180
14. Limbaugh, p. 352
15. Alex Barnett, "The Quotable American" (Lyons Press, Guilford, Connecticut) 2002 p. 317

October 1
Love Yourself

"Let no one despise your youth, but be an example to the believers in word, in conduct, in love, in spirit, in faith, in purity." I Timothy 4:12
"If I say, 'Surely the darkness shall fall on me', Even the night shall be light about me;" Psalm 139:11

God is love. He loves you. Unfortunately, there are Christian men loaded down with guilt and shame who despise themselves. When you do so, it is an insult to the God of love who created you in His image. Sure, you will have bad days and bad times in this life. You are not immune from trials, temptations and stumbling. As long as you live, you will struggle with issues - the same issues with which other Godly men struggle. It may appear that your Christian brothers are always victorious and happy. The truth is every Godly man has his strongholds with which he has to battle day in and out. Believing that God has created you as some flaw is to diminish the love and grace of God demonstrated in His Son, Jesus' death on the cross to pay for your sins and mine. He took your sins and nailed them to that cross. And now He is sitting at the right hand of the Father making intercession for you and your sins. So love yourself. God does.

October 2
Putting Life Back Together

"One of the servants of the high priest, a rela-tive of him whose ear Peter cut off, said, 'Did I not see you in the garden with Him?' Peter then denied again; and immediately the rooster crowed" John 18:26-27

"Then Samson called to the LORD, saying, 'O Lord GOD, remember me, I pray! Strengthen me, I pray, just this once, O God, that I may with one blow take vengeance on the Philistines for my two eyes!'" Judges 16:28

Peter and Samson had something in common. They had both failed God miserably and, through sorrow they put their lives back together for God. They did so by turning around and abandoning themselves for God. They paid the ultimate sacrifice for the One whom they had failed. Peter was cruci-fied as was His Lord whom he betrayed. Samson, in the end, obliterated evil men by using his God-given strength to pull down the walls on those who had mocked him. You have failed God and will do so again. Though not all your failures will be as awful as denying Christ or yielding to multiple sexually immoral encounters, some of them may be devas-tating to you and hurt others. "No matter how dark the night or how evil the situation, you must remind yourself that God is not only present with you in those situations, but he also loves you and will provide for you." (1) No matter what you've done, God can restore you and put your life back together. Express your thankfulness and gratitude for God's love and grace. Then give yourself to Him for His purpose.

October 3
<u>Wait Expectantly for God's Answer</u>

"But those who wait on the LORD Shall renew their strength; They shall mount up with wings like eagles, They shall run and not be weary, They shall walk and not faint." Isaiah 40:31
"But if we hope for what we do not see, we eagerly wait for it with perseverance." Romans 8:25

Waiting can be a terrible thing for men. You sit and wait for your physician to see you, you wait in line at the grocery store and you wait late nights for your teenage daughter to get home. Waiting tries our patience. The Psalmist David wrote: "Rest in the Lord and patiently wait for Him". (Psalm 37:7) When I was in Army Basic Training one of the worst daily experiences was to "hurry up and wait". We waited in line to eat, we waited in formation, and we waited eight long weeks to complete our training. In today's scripture in Romans, Paul says to "wait for it with perseverance". Waiting on God to answer your prayers can try your patience. Sometimes you find God answers, but answers "no". However, I strongly believe that if we earnestly pray for something/someone and wait in faith God will come through in His time. After years of praying for my relatives most of them have accepted Jesus. There are many testimonies which affirm the "effective fervent prayer of a righteous man avails much". (James 5:16) Never give up faithfully praying. Wait patiently on God.

October 4
Football: Depending On One Another

"And also if anyone competes in athletics, he is not crowned unless he competes according to the rules." 2 Timothy 2:5
"Only let your conduct be worthy of the gospel of Christ, so that whether I come and see you or am absent, I may hear of your affairs, that you stand fast in one spirit, with one mind striving together for the faith of the gospel," Philippians 1:27

As in athletic team competition the principles of working together, supporting teammates and depending on other teammates are essential to victory. This is especially true in football, basketball, soccer, baseball, volleyball and a relay race. Too many Godly men attempt to be victorious in the game of life without the support of and dependence on their Christian teammates. Unlike women, who seem to more easily find friendships and share their burdens with other women, men tend to be more self-reliant, reluctant to share their inner conflicts and less willing to surround themselves with fellow Christian brothers to get them through tough times. With several months left in football season, especially at the professional level, notice that without the offensive line protecting him, the quarterback would sacked on every play and would be unable to pass or gain yardage. It takes others to support you and help you as the enemy continuously tries to defeat you. The Apostle Paul understood this and admonished the Christians at Philippi to "strive together". Don't isolate yourself and try to win spiritual battles alone. Associate with other Godly men and learn to depend on each other for Godly counsel and gaining victory.

October 5
A Price to Pay

"But I discipline my body and bring it into subjection, lest, when I have preached to others, I myself should become disqualified." I Corinthians 9:27
"Endure hardship as a good soldier of Christ Jesus. No one serving as a soldier gets involved in civilian affairs – he wants to please his commanding officer." II Timothy 2:3-4

Today's verses describe the costs of becoming unfettered for Christ. Paul reminds the Christians at Corinth what it takes to be ready and able to preach Christ Jesus to others. He uses the analogy of the conditioning of an athlete who trains his body to qualify for the athletic competition. In the second verse Paul writes to Timothy and admonishes him to endure the hardships of a soldier. He tells him that a soldier must not be distracted by the things of the world. To be an effective Godly man for Christ, learn to surrender your will to God. Oswald Chambers explains it this way: "The battle is lost or won in the secret places of the will before God… The Spirit of God apprehends me and I am obliged to get alone with God and fight the battle out before Him. That is the great divide in life; from that we either go towards a more…useless type of Christian life, or we become more and more ablaze for the glory of God." (2) Ask God to give you a desire to pay the price. You need not struggle or fret. Simply allow Him to complete the work in you which He began.

October 6
You Cannot Keep the Law

"For what the law could not do in that it was weak through the flesh, God did by sending His own Son in the likeness of sinful flesh, on account of sin: He condemned sin in the flesh," Romans 8:3
"Stand fast therefore in the liberty by which Christ has made us free, and do not be entangled again with a yoke of bondage." Galatians 5:1

Many well-meaning Christians experience disillusionment because they believe they must keep the Old Testament law. It is Christ who suffered and died on the cross to take away the requirement to keep the law. Yet many Christians, perhaps you, struggle to live by "rules". In his book "The Pressure's Off" Larry Crabb states: "When the law works... we become proud. When the law doesn't work, we assume we simply didn't follow it well enough. We become more defeated than trusting. It doesn't occur to us that the law might no longer be in effect." (3) Accept Christ's death and resurrection for the victory over sin and for your salvation. His grace *is* sufficient for you. You may tend to measure the status of your salvation by being "good". "We can't make life work – but the pressure's off. We no longer want life to work as much as we want Him." (4) For most of my life I felt if I could be "good" enough, life would be good. That kind of thinking gives you and me credit for earning a good life. Remember, it is only through Jesus Christ that we are saved throughout eternity. Rest in Him. Trust Him.

October 7
God's Purpose for Your Children

"Train up a child in the way he should go, And when he is old he will not depart from it." Proverbs 22:6

"But when she could no longer hide him, she took an ark of bulrushes for him, daubed it with asphalt and pitch, put the child in it, and laid it in the reeds by the river's bank... And the child grew, and she brought him to Pharaoh's daughter, and he became her son. So she called his name Moses, saying, 'Because I drew him out of the water.'" Exodus 2:3, 10

Jesus encouraged children to come to Him. He taught others to become as little children – innocent, loving, trusting and like clay in the potter's hands. The Old Testament is replete with children borne for a purpose. The Psalmist David was one such child. Later he would write about how God knew him when he was still in his mother's womb. From a baby to a shepherd boy to a giant killer to a king and to patriarch – David was known as a man after God's heart. God had plans for Moses. Despite a decree that could have caused his death, God protected him as a baby and later used him to deliver the Israelites out of Egyptian bondage and to the Promised Land. Time and space are insufficient to tell the stories of Abraham, Joseph, Nehemiah and Jeremiah. Do you have children? Dedicate them to God. Pray over them. Remember what a responsibility God has given you to influence and impact the lives of little children who, some day, will be fulfill the call of God on their lives. Pray for them, show them God's love and teach them in the ways of righteousness through Jesus and in the love of God.

October 8
<u>Self-Loathing</u>

"Casting all your care upon Him because He cares for you." I Peter 5:7
"And we have known and believed the love that God has for us." I John 4

Loathing (dislike with disgust) one's self is living a life of defeat and unbelief. Some men demonstrate the mindset of a loser and a failure. Men who think and act accordingly send the message, "God doesn't care about me and He is unable to help". This man places himself as the "captive of his fate" and reduces God to a mere observer. I recently heard a young Christian man say: "I am a failure as a husband, as a son, as an employee and as a Christian. I am worthless." That is the epitome of self-defeatism. In his book, "The Bondage Breaker", Neil T. Anderson writes: "The father of lies {the devil} can block your effectiveness as a Christian if he can deceive you into believing that you are nothing but a product of your past – prone to failure and controlled by your habits." (5) Do you sometimes feel like a failure and a loser in areas of your life? To do so is an insult to God. Get up out of your self-pity and count your blessings. Thank God for the many ways He has provided for you to touch the lives of others. Others need your spirit-filled optimism and faithful Godly influence.

October 9
<u>Minister with Humility</u>

"And he said to him, 'Well done, good servant; because you were faithful in a very little, have authority over ten cities.'" Luke 19:17
"I would rather be a doorkeeper in the house of my God than to dwell in the tents of wickedness." Psalm 84:10

For fifteen years our family lived in a small, rural college town. It was during those years when our small children grew to be teenagers – one in high school and one in college. We attended, for that area, a relative large church in town. I learned that for many years an aging college professor had mowed the church lawn without pay. He had a gentle spirit, bringing no attention to himself. Few church members knew that he single-handedly mowed the large lawn around the church. Such mundane ministries often go unnoticed and unappreciated. But this brother in Christ did it neither for recognition or reward. He did it for his Lord. Do you serve your church or have a ministry? Are you committed to the selfless giving of your time, money and effort? Or do you expect recognition and reward? Our Lord set the example. When he healed the leper (Matthew 8:4) and later two blind men (Matthew 9:30) He sternly told them to go and tell no one of what He had done. As did Jesus, so do you. There is really no unimportant ministry or service in God's Kingdom. Whatever you do, do it in the name of Jesus.

October 10
<u>Walking With God</u>

"After he begot Methuselah, Enoch walked with God three hundred years, and had sons and daughters." Genesis 5:22
"Finally then, brethren, we urge and exhort in the Lord Jesus that you should abound more and more, just as you received from us how you ought to walk and to please God" 1 Thessalonians 4:1

I remember walking beside my father as a young boy and teenager. I always felt safe even when we were deep in the woods hunting. When I was five years old he took me for a walk about a mile to a small store and back home. As if it were yesterday, I remember the feeling as we walked that cool night toward home. Nearly twenty-five years later, as a father, I would experience those same walks with my son. How memorable are those days! In his book, "Leap Over a Wall", Eugene Peterson tells the story of David's life. He writes: "Everything that David knows about God he experiences...God isn't a doctrine he talks about but a person by whom he's led and cared for. God isn't a remote abstraction...but an intimate presence..." (6) David writes about God as a father, "As a father pities his children, so the Lord pities those who fear Him." (Psalm 103:13) It is a privilege to walk with God. As a Godly man become aware of your walk with your Heavenly Father today. You are very special to Him. He will never let go of your hand.

October 11
<u>The Trap of Materialism</u>

"For we brought nothing into this world, and it is certain we can carry nothing out." I Timothy 6:7

"Let your mind on things above, not on things on the earth." Ephesians 3:3

The Great Depression of the 1930's hit most Americans hard. Banks closed and the economy collapsed leaving folks with nothing. Many who had amassed wealth lost everything. The rate of suicide rose. The middle class was no longer "middle" losing their once prosperous lifestyle. Industries and businesses all over the country turned "belly up" taking millions of jobs. My parents spoke often about those days. They, like many others of that generation, valued their jobs and seemed more content with a simple lifestyle than did the following generations. A look at our nation's national debt, the billions in extended credit and the rising number of those using bankruptcy is telling. Millions are obsessed with material things. This includes Christians. There is a pervasive attitude of getting everything one wants regardless of the cost or the ability to pay. Many have become slaves entrapped in debt. Far too many set their hearts on "things" at the expense of their devotion to their Lord. They are entrapped by the god of this world – money. Seek God with an open heart asking Him to reveal to whom or to what you are you are indebted – to Him or things.

October 12
Do Other Christian Men Struggle?

"Resist him, steadfast in the faith, knowing that the same sufferings are experienced by your brotherhood in the world." 1 Peter 5:9

"Brethren, if a man is overtaken in any trespass, you who are spiritual restore such a one in a spirit of gentleness, considering yourself lest you also be tempted." Galatians 6:1

If you are struggling with some temptation, an addiction or some sin in your life, do not feel as if you're "bad seed" with a twisted mind. Perhaps you feel as if other Christian men are not experiencing such struggles. Remember these words of James: "We all stumble in many ways". (James 3:2) Every Godly man faces his "roaring lions" which circle him, trying to destroy him. As you, they wear façades which masks their inner conflicts. But be sure that underneath the breast bone of every man is a battle raging for his heart and mind. In his book, "Men's Secret Wars" (7), Patrick A. Means shares the story of falling into a sin of immorality following twenty years of ministry. After several years of restoration he now ministers to thousands of Christian laymen and pastors. His survey findings from hundreds of men reveal two-thirds struggle with sexual sin. Twenty-five percent admit having an extra-marital affair as a Christian. Your struggles are those of your Christian brothers and yielding is not an option. Stay in the Word, pray earnestly and find a men's accountability group to encourage each other to stand strong. Ask the Holy Spirit every to be your comforter and guide.

October 13
Real Men Take Risks

"Then the LORD said to Gideon, 'By the three hundred men who lapped I will save you, and deliver the Midianites into your hand. Let all the other people go, every man to his place.'" Judges 7:7
"When the three hundred blew the trumpets, the LORD set every man's sword against his companion throughout the whole camp; and the army fled to Beth Acacia, toward Zererah, as far as the border of Abel Meholah, by Tabbath." Judges 7:22

Are you risk-taker? When you drive your automobile you are at risk for injury or death. When you climb aboard a plane you accept the risk of crashing. When you participate in water or snow skiing, "pick-up" basketball, hunting and running, you're taking risks. With risk comes the possibility of failure. Are you a risk-take like Gideon? Are you a risk-taker in spiritual matters or do you shy away from taking risks because you fear failure? Just as Jesus called for Peter to get out of the boat and walk on raging waters, He needs Godly men as you willing to step out to reach others. Eugene Peterson says: "The life of faith encourages the risk taking that frequently results in failure...When we are in situations where we are untested or unaccustomed, we are sometimes going to fail...These failures, though, are never disasters because they become the means by which we realize new depths of our humanity and new vistas of divine grace." (8) Sure, taking risks can be dangerous. Stephen risked preaching the gospel and was stoned to death. Ask God to give you faith and courage to be a risk-taker when the Spirit leads you to step out.

October 14
<u>Be a Mentor</u>

"This charge I commit to you, son Timothy, according to the prophecies previously made concerning you, that by them you may wage the good warfare, having faith and a good conscience, which some having rejected, concerning the faith have suffered shipwreck" Timothy 1:18-19

"Now when the sons of the prophets who were from Jericho saw him, they said, "The spirit of Elijah rests on Elisha." And they came to meet him, and bowed to the ground before him." II Kings 2:15

Today's scriptures offer two good examples of mentors. Mentoring is a very important ministry for the Godly man who has matured in the Spirit and can serve as a role model for another brother in Christ. You have probably had a mentor sometimes in your lifetime to for guide you and serve as an example for you to follow. Throughout Paul's writing are his instructions and encouragement to Timothy on how he should conduct himself as Godly man. Timothy looked to him as his mentor, thus, becoming a profitable minister. Elisha saw the Spirit of God upon Elijah's life. He saw the power of God flow through the life of Elijah and he yearned to be endowed with that same Spirit. When Elijah was taken up by the Spirit Elisha caught his mantle, a symbol of God's power. Elisha continued the ministry of Elijah allowing the Spirit and power of God to use him mightily. Every man, regardless of age, needs another Godly man as his mentor. This is especially true for young men and men young in their Christian walk. Seek the Lord now asking Him to reveal how and to whom you should mentor.

October 15
Listen to the Holy Spirit

"You stiff-necked and uncircumcised in heart and ears! You always resist the Holy Spirit; as your fathers did, so do you. When they heard these things they were cut to the heart, and they gnashed at him with their teeth." Acts 7:51, 54

"And do not grieve the Holy Spirit of God, by whom you were sealed for the day of redemption." Ephesians 4:20

The Holy Spirit has always existed just as God the Father and God the Son have always existed. Before Jesus was crucified, he told His disciples that when He left that He would send the Holy Spirit to abide with them and guide them. Following the initial endowment of the Holy Spirit on the Day of Pentecost, Peter told the people: "For the promise (Holy Spirit) is to you and to your children, and to all who are afar off, as many as the Lord our God shall call". (Acts 2:39) You receive the Holy Spirit when you accept Jesus as Lord. You have within you God the Holy Spirit who comforts you, enables you to serve and guides you in you every aspect of life. However, you must listen to Him and be obedient to that distinct inner voice. As a sincere Godly man you should spend time in prayer and God's Word, seeking to be filled daily with the Holy Spirit. If you allow Him to rule your heart and mind, His power in your life will make a difference in the lives of others.

October 16
The Benefits of Brokenness

*"Make me hear joy and gladness, that the bones
You have broken may rejoice." Psalm 51:8
"Before I was afflicted I went astray, but now I
keep Your word. You are good, and do good; Teach
me Your statutes". Psalm 119:67-68*

You've heard sermons and Bible study lessons on drawing
nearer to God - getting to the heart of God. As a Godly man,
you have prayed that God will change your heart, increase
your love for Him and bless you. These are worthy prayers
and desires. However, you may feel that you have never
experienced the closeness of Jesus. Though you hope that
you will not suffer loss or experience hurt as God's child that
is exactly what may need to happen to prepare your heart
and mind to reach higher heights and deeper depths with
God. Larry Crabb expresses it this way: "Only when you
discover a desire for Him that is stronger than your desire for
relief from pain will you pay the price necessary to find Him.
You must go through, not around, whatever keeps you from
Him. The process is what spiritual people call brokenness
and repentance." (9) This is not a pleasant thought for the
day. Yet, men struggling with inner spiritual battles will find
God's peace when they totally abandon themselves to the
Lordship of Jesus. Pray to become "crucified to the world"
and "count all things but loss". Then you'll experience that
closeness and peace in Jesus.

October 17
<u>The Blood of Christ</u>

"...knowing that you were not redeemed with corruptible things, like silver or gold, from your aimless conduct received by tradition from your fathers, but with the precious blood of Christ, as of a lamb without blemish and without spot." 1 Peter 1:18-19

"And according to the law almost all things were purified with blood, and without the shedding of blood there is no remission {forgiveness}" Hebrews 9:22

Written by Robert Lowry, the age-old hymn rings as clear today as it did in 1876 – "What can wash away our sins? *Nothing but the blood of Jesus!*" The Old Testament Law required a blood sacrifice for the forgiveness of sins. This had to be done every year. In God's master plan He sent His Son Jesus to live as man on earth and die on a cross where His blood was shed once and for all for our sin. When you believed in Jesus as your Lord and Savior and confessed your sinfulness, His shed blood washed away all your sin... nothing but His blood. You no longer have to pay a price or sacrifice the life of an animal to know that your sins have been washed whiter than snow. Jesus paid the price you could pay for eternal salvation. Seek to fully grasp this unmatched love of God. Never take it for granted. Now offer yourself as a "living sacrifice" to Him. Make yourself available to be used daily through the power of the Holy Spirit. Because of His shed blood you have access to the thrown of God and Jesus is your advocate for any sin you may commit.

October 18
The Obscure Touched by Jesus

"For she said, 'If only I may touch His clothes, I shall be made well.' Immediately the fountain of her blood was dried up, and she felt in her body that she was healed of the affliction." Mark 5:28-29

"And it happened when He was in a certain city, that behold, a man who was full of leprosy saw Jesus; and he fell on his face and implored Him, saying, 'Lord, if You are willing, You can make me clean.' Then He put out His hand and touched him, saying, 'I am willing; be cleansed.' Immediately the leprosy left him." Luke 5:12-13

In today's fast paced life do you ever notice some obscure individual? This person may be in the same location so frequently that he/she goes unnoticed as part of that particular environment. Growing up in a small town there were those obscure folks who were always around, usually at the same place – doing nothing. Some were "permanent fixtures" sitting on a sidewalk bench on Main Street or standing on a street corner day in and day out. A couple of elderly men were on creek bank most days fishing with cane poles. Most folks just walked or drove past them without a word or a glance. They didn't have the amenities as many did but lived on bare necessities. Occasionally I would speak or offer a nod. But rarely did I take time to stop and say or do something kind in the name of Jesus. In our verses today Jesus set the example for us to follow. Take time out of your busy day to notice the obscure and allow the Holy Spirit guide you what to say or do for them in the name of Jesus. And for sure, pray for them.

October 19
Your Personal Testimony

"He answered and said, 'Whether He is a sinner or not, I do not know. One thing I know: that though I was blind, now I see.'" John 9:24-25

"Then they said to the woman, 'Now we believe, not because of what you said, for we ourselves have heard Him and we know that this is indeed the Christ, the Savior of the World'" John 4:42

One of the few memories I hold from early childhood is a vivid and emotional experience sitting beside my mother during church services. There was a visiting evangelist that week who also sang. He was a large brawny man toughened from hard work. I remember as if it was yesterday one of his songs I've seldom heard since. With his teenage daughter accompanying him on the piano, through tears of joy he bellowed the lyrics, *"My God is real; He's real in my soul. My God is real for He has bought and made me whole. His love for me is like pure gold. My God is real for I can feel Him in my soul."* Today's first scripture describes a blind man healed my Jesus being interrogated by Pharisees. After unsuccessful efforts to explain, he proclaimed simply that whereas he was blind now he could see. In our second scripture a Samaritan woman who met Jesus, believed in Him, shared her testimony to the townspeople and led them to Jesus. If you're at a loss for words in a witnessing opportunity you should always boldly give your testimony: "My God is real because He has changed my life!"

October 20
Wilderness Experiences

"And David stayed in strongholds in the wilderness, and remained in the mountains in the Wilderness of Ziph. Saul sought him every day..."
1 Samuel 23:14
"But he himself went a day's journey into the wilderness, and came and sat down under a broom tree. And he prayed that he might die, and said, 'It is enough! Now, LORD, take my life, for I am no better than my fathers!'" 1 Kings 19:4

Every Christian goes through spiritual wilderness experiences. A wilderness is usually not a place you desire to stay for long. Its rough terrain, its thick tangle of dense trees and undergrowth and the sounds from all sorts of wildlife can be frightening. One can learn much about God and His creation. He can learn to scale rocks and cliffs, to deal with harsh conditions and to develop sharper sensory skills. On your spiritual journey you will find yourself in a spiritual wilderness alone. Eugene Peterson says: "When we find ourselves in the wilderness, we do well to be frightened: we also do well to be alert, open eyed. In the wilderness we're plunged into an awareness of danger and death; at the very same moment we're plunged, if we let ourselves be, into an awareness of the great mystery of God and the extraordinary preciousness of life." (10) Whenever you're in a spiritual wilderness, get to know God better and to listen to His voice. When He leads you out, your spiritual compass will help you find the heart of God in a real and new way. Your wilderness experience can give you a deeper appreciation for walking with God in times of blessings.

October 21
Hope for What You Cannot See

"If in this life only we have hope in Christ, we are of all men the most pitiable." 1 Corinthians 15:19
"If we hope for what we do not see, we eagerly wait for it with perseverance." Roman 8:25

There is little need to hope for those things which you know or sure that already exist or for what you can see. Do you hope for a car to drive with one sitting in your garage? Do you hope for God's presence today? You need not hope for a car or for God's presence since you are assured that both are available to you. Real hope is when we hope for someone or something that we cannot see or do not have. You need hope for what you long for or for what you have been promised to receive at some future time. You need hope when circumstances appear to be diametrically opposed to achieving your goal or receiving a promise. Wilferd A. Peterson once wrote: "Hope is a man's shield and buckler against defeat. Hope never sounds retreat. Hope revives ideals, renews dreams, and revitalizes visions. Hope scales the peak, wrestles with the impossible, achieves the highest aim. As long as a man has hope, no situation is hopeless." (11) No matter how dim the future may seem keep your hope in Almighty God who transcends time and distance. Your hope is in Jesus who promised never to leave you or forsake you.

October 22
The World Series Championship:
Keep Pressing Forward

"I stress toward the goal for the prize of the upward call of God in Christ Jesus." Philippians 3:14
"Now they do it to obtain a perishable crown, but we for an imperishable crown." I Corinthians 9: 25

The 2005 Baseball World Series was one of the biggest upsets in professional sports in decades. It had been eight-six years since the Chicago While Sox had won a World Series – 1917. Yet, the franchise remained solvent and with the arrival of each year's baseball season, the Chicago White Sox recruited great players, practiced, prepared for each game to near perfection and played to win, only to be eliminated somewhere during the season or in the playoffs. Life is like that sometimes both in your earthly and spiritual life. You commit yourself to Jesus, you pray and read the Bible, you attend church regularly, read devotionals, set goals, yet some somehow victory seems to elude you. Your victory over sin has already been won by Christ's death and resurrection. God did not necessarily call you to do great things as seen through the eyes of others or as measured by the church's standards. But he did call you to stay in shape, to practice, to prepare for the opponent and get into the game to win. Keep pressing forward every day. Listen to and follow the Holy Spirit's lead. Victory is yours in Christ. Never give up!

October 23
The Traveling Man

"Be sober, be vigilant; because your adversary the devil walks about like a roaring lion, seeking whom he may devour. Resist him, steadfast in the faith, knowing that the same sufferings are experienced by your brotherhood in the world." 1 Peter 5:8-9

"But each one is tempted when he is drawn away by his own desires and enticed." James 1:14

In a recent men's Bible study the topic of life on the road came up. We realized that most men, at times, must travel whether to attend professional conferences or as a requirement of their jobs. There was a truck driver, an entertainment marketing representative and others who traveled occasionally. All expressed the common problems encountered. Truck stops, motels and condos can make for a slippery slope for men who travel alone. Satan's traps are set wherever you travel alone. They range from motel adult movies to women who also travel along to company parties where wine and women can be a poisonous mix. Few men are unaffected by these allurements to include the ordinary Godly man. When traveling alone you become a target for Satan's fiery darts. Today's scriptures are for you when you travel alone. "Be sober, be vigilant...resist him" should be memorized and internalized in your heart and mind before you leave home. It takes a made-up mind and continuous praying for you to insure victory. Plan specific work-related activities, take a Christian-authored book and/or invite a fellow Christian brother to dinner to keep each other accountable. Pray, believe and trust God to keep you. Victory is yours

October 24
When the Alarm Goes Off

"O God, You are my God; Early will I seek You..." Psalm 63:1
"Through the Lord's mercies we are not consumed, Because His compassions fail not. They are new every morning. Great is Your faithfulness."
Lamentations 3:22-23

There is something special about the morning, especially the early morning. Early morning the sun rises, birds seem to sing a bit more lively, a new day dawns and there's a freshness in the air. Abraham rose early in the morning (Genesis 19:27). Jacob rose early in the morning (Genesis 28:18). Moses rose early in the morning (Exodus 24:4). Joshua rose early in the morning (Joshua 3:1). Gideon rose early in the morning (Judges 6:38). Samuel rose early in the morning (I Samuel 15:12). David rose early in the morning (I Samuel 17:20). Jesus went to the temple early in the morning (John 8:2). The early morning seemed to be a special time for the patriarchs and Biblical heroes. They began their days early worshipping God. I believe that it is significant for men to arise early – early enough to spend time communing with God before the hustle and bustle of the day. This does not negate nighttime prayer if you find that a quieter time to focus on God. But try spending time with the Father each morning before your mind becomes cluttered with the day's activities. Ask Him for strength for the day ahead.

October 25
<u>Prepare for Satan's Assaults</u>

"If you have run with the footmen, and they have wearied you, then how can you contend with horses? And if in the land of peace, In which you trusted, they wearied you, Then how will you do in the floodplain[a] of the Jordan?" Jeremiah 12:5

"Put on the whole armor of God, that you may be able to stand against the wiles of the devil" Ephesians 6:11

God told Jeremiah that if he thought his past and present circumstances were difficult, he needed to prepare for worse adversaries and bigger problems. He used an athletic metaphor to describe what it would take to be prepared and in shape to stand against greater opponents. Paul told the Ephesians that they must prepare for battle by putting on the spiritual armor needed for warfare against those people and things that will attack them. He described the essential pieces of spiritual armor: a warrior's belt of truth, a breastplate of righteousness, foot protection, the shield of faith, a helmet of salvation and the sword of the Spirit (the Word of God). This spiritual armor is just as important for you today as when Paul penned these words some 2,000 years ago. As a Godly man who longs to know God better and to be in the center of His will, consider each part of this armor as necessary spiritual protection as you face Satan's daily attacks on your mind, heart, body and your family. Paul also admonished Christians: "Be strong in the Lord" and "Praying always". Defy the Satan's lies. He's a defeated foe – Jesus is your victory.

October 26
Search Me, Oh God

"Search me, O God, and know my heart; Try me, and know my anxieties;" Psalm 139:23
"Now He who searches the hearts knows what the mind of the Spirit is, because He makes intercession for the saints according to the will of God." Romans 8:27

A common problem among many Christians is living a secret life. It's as if some believers think that God doesn't know their thoughts and motives. These are Christians who are living in a lukewarm state and are not seeking to please God. In Psalm 139 David asks God to search him and to know his heart. David wanted more than anything else to please God and have the inner qualities God wants in a man He can use. Paul reminds us that God searches our hearts. He knows your every thought, every ulterior motive, every desire and any lack of love for Him. In his book, "The Man God Uses", Henry and Tom Blackaby share a few conditions of the heart that God is searching for in you: Set your heart to follow God; Yield your heart to God; Cleanse your heart for God; Guard your heart: and Do not harden your heart. (12) Ask God to search the inner recesses of your heart and reveal any areas that need shoring up. Ask Him to shine the light of the Son on your heart. And seek Him diligently to be used for His purpose.

October 27
<u>Live Like You Were Dying</u>

"...whereas you do not know what will happen tomorrow. For what is your life? It is even a vapor that appears for a little time and then vanishes away." James 4:14

"While I live I will praise the LORD; I will sing praises to my God while I have my being." Psalm 146:2

A recent popular county music song describes the important things a man should do as if he were dying. The lyrics grip my heart as they talk about taking time to do the simple things with those most important to us. Few men really expect to die soon. Unfortunately, the obituary column usually announces the deaths of both young men and old. We have no promise for tomorrow. We know not whether we will awake in our bed or in eternity. A thirty-eight year-old man near our home one day, like dozens of others, walked into some familiar woods to hunt and, as usual, climbed to a deer stand built high in a tree. He fell and died instantly. He left a broken-hearted wife and two bright young boys. How quickly life, like a vapor, can vanish. Consider the brevity of life and the very real possibility that you may not see tomorrow's sunrise. Then ask the Lord to remind you of the most important things in life. Ask Him to search your heart and sanctify you for His use. Then slow down and take time for Him and for those most important in your life.

October 28
<u>Turn off the TV</u>

"You shall teach them diligently to your chil-
dren, and shall talk of them when you sit in your
house..." Deuteronomy 6:7
"Your wife shall be like a fruitful vine in the
very heart of your house, Your children like olive
plants all around your table." Psalm 128:3

Men, our secular culture has become increasingly immoral and corrupt. Hollywood's influence through movies and headlines of un-Godly lifestyles are splashed across newspapers and magazines. Society's tolerance of perversion and despicable public behavior has crept into the minds of our children. Profanity in movies, on television and in filthy music lyrics have crept into our schools, our homes and into the minds of our children. As a Godly man you should take a stand against these influences in your community. More importantly, God appointed you ruler of your home and the guardian of your family. You have a God-given responsibility to say as Joshua, "But as for me and my house we will serve the Lord" (Joshua 25:15). Begin immediately by removing any objectionable channels from your T.V. programming. Turn off your T.V. more often in the evenings and have some family time, whether a devotional time or just time listening to your children's activities of the day. Consider removing TV's from the children's bedrooms. Restrict certain internet sites. Take charge of your home and kick Satan's influence out. Your kids will complain, but your Godly stand will be worth well it. And someday your children will be proud of their Godly father.

October 29
<u>On the Game Field of Life</u>

"I press toward the goal for the prize of the upward call of God in Christ Jesus." Philippians 3:14

"And also if anyone competes, he is not crowned unless he competes according to the rules." II Timothy 2:5

Jason Hanson, long-time kicker for the National Football League's Detroit Lyons, experienced kicks which went wide or fell short of the goal posts. While he had many successes as a kicker, he understood life on the game field of football. He persevered and was selected twice to Pro-Bowls (1997 and 1999) – an honor bestowed on few players in a career. Jason Hanson found it impossible to be perfect on the game field of life as well as on the field as an All-Pro kicker with its ups and downs. You are on a game field of life as you press toward your Heavenly goal. Often you seem to experience victory after victory, gaining yards toward the goal line. Other times, perhaps recently, Satan's hard-hitting tackles behind the line of scrimmage, the penalties for not playing by the rules and the missed passes and kicks discourage you. You feel that you can never reach the goal that is set before you. But you will. May God give you assurance that perseverance and hope will keep in the faith and give you courage to win. You have the best coach who's able to keep you from falling.

October 30
<u>Beyond Your Part of the World</u>

"But you shall receive power when the Holy Spirit has come upon you; and you shall be witnesses to Me in Jerusalem, and in all Judea and Samaria, and to the end of the earth." Acts 1:8

"But now I am going to Jerusalem to minister to the saints. For it pleased those from Macedonia and Achaia to make a certain contribution for the poor among the saints who are in Jerusalem." Romans 15:26

This part of the year when the leaves and temperature have fallen, you may be enjoying college and professional sports or the solitude of the woods as hunting season opens. It is one of the most pleasant times of the year when cooler weather is a welcome retreat from the extreme heat where some work year-round. Living in the land of plenty and in a society of prosperity relative to most of the world, those who have accepted God's call to "go to the end of the world" are far from our thoughts. Thousands of God-called, self-sacrificing Christian men and women are in remote parts of the world living among the underprivileged, the infirmed and the dying. Missionaries fulfill Christ's great commission whether full-time or on a short-term mission trip. While you may not have been specifically called to foreign missions, you are called to minister those around the world through offerings, maintaining encouraging communication with one serving abroad or praying daily for those who once proclaimed, "Here I am Lord, send me". Think on these things and ask God what you should be doing to reach those beyond your part of the world.

October 31
When You've Been with Jesus

"Now when they saw the boldness of Peter and John, and perceived that they were uneducated and untrained men, they marveled. And they realized that they had been with Jesus." Acts 4:13

"By this all will know that you are My disciples, if you have love for one another." John 13:35

Do others recognize that you are a Christian? If on trial for being a Godly man, would there be enough evidence to convict you? Truthful answers to these questions may be disturbing. But you should honestly answer them. Every word which comes from your mouth, every response you have to difficult circumstances and temptations, every place you go and every one with whom you associate are reflections of your character and your relationship with Jesus. Through the years on this official date of Halloween (associated with evil); I have answered my front door to see a neighborhood child dressed up like someone else. However, usually I recognized who was behind the mask by his/her voice, by the way he/she walked or with whom accompanied them. Similarly, the real you is recognized by most folks despite how distinguished you dress at work or how holy you appear to be at church. Conversely, when you and I spend time on our knees before the Lord in intercessory prayer and seeking His help for vulnerable areas of our lives, our "walk" will support our talk. Ask God to search your heart. Commit to fervent prayer, Bible study and continuous praise. Be recognized as His child.

REFERENCES FOR OCTOBER

1. Joyce Meyer, "Battlefield of the Mind Devotional" (Warner Faith, Nashville, Tennessee) 2005 p. 179
2. Oswald Chambers, "My Utmost for His Highest" (Barbour Publishing, Uhrichsville, Ohio) 1963 p. 362
3. Larry Crabb, "The Pressure's Off" (Waterbrook Press, Colorado Springs, Colorado) 2002 p. 21
4. Ibid.p. 180
5. Neil T. Anderson, "The Bondage Breaker" (Harvest House Publishers, Eugene, Oregon) 2000 p. 11
6. Eugene H. Peterson, "Leap Over A Wall" (HarperCollins Publishers, Inc., New York, New York) 1997 p. 141
7. Eugene H. Peterson, "Traveling Light", (Helmers and Howard Publishers, Inc., Colorado Springs, Colorado) p. 96-97
8. Patrick A. Means, "Men's Secret Wars", (Fleming H. Revell, Grand Rapids, Michigan) p. 9-10
9. Crab, p. 100-101
10. Peterson, p. 74
11. Bette Bishop (Selected), "I Will Lift Up Mine Eyes" (Hallmark Cards, Inc., Kansas City Missouri) 1968 p. 10-11
12. Henry and Tom Blackaby, "The Man God Uses", (Broadman & Holman Publishers, Nashville, Tennessee) 1999 p. 21 - 23

November 1
God's Magnificent Creation

"You who laid the foundations of the earth, So that it should not be moved forever, He waters the hills from His upper chambers; the earth is satisfied with the fruit of Your works. He causes the grass to grow for the cattle, and vegetation for the service of man, that he may bring forth food from the earth who disdained freedom, He has made everything beautiful in its time..." Ecclesiastes 3:11

A couple of years ago about this time of year I was blessed with the opportunity to take an all day deer hunting trip with my son. While there, I had a rare experience of viewing only a slither of God's magnificent creation. It was during this time of the year. The Appalachian mountain range looked like a tapestry on which God had painted tints of yellow and gold mingled with deep green of southern pines. I stood with awe at the expansive grassy pastures with carpet-like texture that filled the valleys between mountains and the quaint tree-line old leaf-covered dirt road. The beautiful landscape was covered from horizon to horizon with a clear blue sky. Those moments of beholding the grandeur of earth's beauty seemed like a snapshot of life as I experienced the fullness of God's greatness, His goodness and His blessings. If you have not taken time to get away and see some of God's magnificent creation, please plan a day or more to spend viewing, smelling and listening to the great outdoors which was created for you to enjoy. And thank Him for the miracle of creating you.

November 2
<u>The Danger of Presumption</u>

"Uphold my steps in Your paths, That my foot-steps may not slip." Psalm 17:5
"Therefore let him who thinks he stands take heed lest he fall." 1 Corinthians 10:12

As a born-again man you should not worry and fret about your salvation or God's promise of eternal life. However, you should know that God did not promise to make you immune from temptation, suffering and disappointment. You may have been taught since your youth that if you do good God is obligated to bless you, heal you and keep you from sinning. Men are so often presumptuous regarding their own strength to live a victorious and blessed life. That thinking is dangerous. God does have the power to keep you and He will be always be with you. But Jesus made it clear that we would suffer for His sake. Never ever be presumptuous about your own strength. Never presume your "things" and your family will always be there. Remember Job. His prosperity turned to ashes. Bob Barnes writes: "So what will you do when the things of life are taken away from you? What will happen to the inner man? Will you stand strong in Christ? Will the loss purify and strengthen your character or break you?" (1) Keep your trust in Christ, and watch your footsteps. What He promised is His everlasting love, grace and mercy.

November 3
Who Will Go?

"So passing by Mysia, they came down to Troas.
And a vision appeared to Paul in the night. A man
of Macedonia stood and pleaded with him, saying,
"Come over to Macedonia and help us." Acts
16:8-9
"Whom shall I send and who will go for us?"
Isaiah 6:8

Has God called you to a special work or mission? Do you feel that you should be teaching a class, serving at a local homeless shelter or go on a church mission trip to another state or country? Has the Holy Spirit gently urged to witness to a certain individual or visit someone who may have a terminal illness and have not accepted Jesus? I firmly believe that God did not call you to be an ordinary Christian. God called men to be warriors, walking in the Spirit. He called you to take courage and stand strong. Far too many Christian men are content to live a mundane life for Christ. While attending church and Sunday school are important, God has a specific purpose for you in the here and now to "go". Jesus has/is calling you to be His messenger. He is sending you to do something for Him, whether great or small. Dietrich Bonhoefffer wrote: "Neither failure nor hostility can weaken the messenger's conviction that he has been sent by Jesus. For there is no way they have chosen themselves..." (2) Seek the Lord and ask Him to make you willing to accept His assignment to go.

November 4
<u>Surrender Your Will</u>

"Therefore let those who suffer according to the will of God commit their souls to Him in doing good, as to a faithful Creator." 1 Peter 4:19

"For I have come down from heaven, not to do My own will, but the will of Him who sent." Me. John 6:38

Your will is selfish to the core. When you accepted Jesus as your Lord and Master, you your will should have been swallowed up in His will. Every sin has as its root the self-centered will of a man or woman. As a leader, the head of the home, the decision-maker and the courageous seem to call men to have a strong will and a mind of their own. In a sense that may be somewhat acceptable. But a Godly man loses himself and his own will and crucifies it. This makes him a better, stronger leader, a better husband and father, a more prudent decision-maker and anointed with Spirit-filled courage. Oswald Chambers wrote: It is of no value to God to give Him your life for death. He wants you to be a "living sacrifice" to let Him have all your powers that have been saved and sanctified through Jesus." (3) Giving up your will may be the most difficult thing you have endeavored. But until you and I abandon our will and become lost in His will, we will amble along our spiritual journey never fully becoming what God purposed.

November 5
The Greatest Commandment

"Teacher, which is the great commandment in the law? Jesus then said to him, You shall love the Lord with all your heart, with all your soul, and with all your mind." Matthew 22:36-37

"I will love You, O Lord, my strength." Psalm 18:1

Do you have a love problem? I'm convinced that anemic borne again believers lack a deep love for their Lord. You may say, "Well, if they don't love God as they should, they aren't borne again". I believe that not all believers love God at the same degree as do others. Paul wrote to the Christians at Ephesus and prayed that they would be "rooted and grounded in love" and be able "to know the love of Christ". In the Book of Revelations God first commends the church at Ephesus but expresses one concern: "Nevertheless, I have this against you, that you have left your first love." (2:4) Mary clearly loved Jesus with more intensity others. Your love for God is in direct relation to your spiritual proximity to Him. The more prayer time you spend with Him, the more you read His word, the more you worship Him and the more your mind stays on Him your love for Him will grow. If you're not in love with Jesus, seek Him today asking to draw you nearer to Him and increase your love for Him. Remember: "We love Him because He first loved us". (I John 4:19)

November 6
<u>Never Forget From Where He Brought You</u>

"Then beware, lest you forget the LORD who brought you out of the land of Egypt, from the house of bondage." Deuteronomy 6:12
"But now in Christ Jesus you who once were far off have been brought near by the blood of Christ." Ephesians 2:13

Never forget from where Jesus brought you and where you could be. Whether you grew up in church or whether you grew up in sin's darkness or whether you were disadvantage having little hope for a bright future, the ground at the foot of the cross is level and we all come to Christ as sinners. Being saved at an early age does not negate the possibility that had it not been for Christ's love, you could be living in the streets or in prison today. Never forget that you, like the vilest sinner "once were far off" from Jesus. Maybe you had a tough time growing up, became involved in drugs and criminal behavior. You may have been saved as a child but somewhere along the way you strayed from God and decided you didn't need Him. Whatever your former circumstance, ask God to remind you where you could be if it were not for His limitless mercy and grace. Thank Him today that you have the Holy Spirit guiding you and heaven waiting for you. Look at some of your former friends in dire straights and say "But for the grace of God, go I".

November 7
<u>A Man's Word is His Bond</u>

"'Therefore swear now to me by the LORD that you will not cut off my descendants after me and that you will not destroy my name from my father's house'. So David swore to Saul. And Saul went home, but David and his men went up to the strong-hold." 1 Samuel 24:21-22

"My little children, let us not love in word or in tongue, but in deed and in truth. And by this we know that we are of the truth, and shall assure our hearts before Him." 1 John 3:18-19

So often I can hear the words of my Dad: "Son, a man's word should be his bond". Somehow, I had difficulty comprehending the significance of those words back when I was growing up. But as I've grown older, I grasp the integrity and honor which come with men who live by the slogan. A man's word should be something one can count on and place their trust in without hesitation. Yet, hundreds of media stories report corporate fraud by CEO' and leaders in government. A lack of character has been increasingly exposed among those in whom we once trusted including coaches, teachers, ministers, police officers, priests, and judges. Nowadays you cannot assume that a man's word is reliable. If fact, you can't even trust written agreements between two parties. As a Godly man it is absolutely imperative that your word is your bond and anyone who knows you must be assured of your honesty. When you fail to keep your word in any kind of circumstance, you do harm to not only your witness as a Godly man, but you strike a blow to Christ's church in the eyes of others.

November 8
Hard Pressed, but Not Crushed

"We are hard-pressed on every side, yet not crushed; we are perplexed, but not in despair; persecuted, but not forsaken; struck down, but not destroyed." 2 Corinthians 4:8-9

"Therefore we do not lose heart. Even though our outward man is perishing, yet the inward man is being renewed day by day" 2 Corinthians 4:16

Few Christian men escape devastation, despair and disappointment in their lifetime. For many, such experiences paralyze them emotionally and crush them spiritually. When these experiences come your way you may respond with disillusionment, questioning God and asking "why". Paul probably experienced persecution, despair and loneliness few men have for Christ's sake. Yet, his attitude was "do not lose heart". He valued the strength of spiritual character more than he valued a healthy body. Billy Graham, shares his wisdom about such difficult times: "Almost before we realized it, our emotions overwhelm us and we find ourselves swept away in a flood of anger or frustration or despair. That's why the time to prepare for life's disappointment and hurts is in advance, before they come crashing down upon us. Now is the time to build spiritual foundations." (4) Dear Christian brother, no matter what you've been through and no matter what tomorrow brings, remember "not to lose heart" and stay focused on our supreme example, Jesus Christ, "who for the joy set before him endured the cross". Put you faith in Him. You will be victorious if your faith is founded on the Rock of Ages.

November 9
A New Heaven and a New Earth

"Nevertheless we, according to His promise, look for new heavens and a new earth in which righteousness dwells" 2 Peter 3:13
"Now I saw a new heaven and a new earth, for the first heaven and the first earth had passed away. Also there was no more sea." Revelation 21:1

Every one of us sees the unseen with different pictures in our thoughts. For example, when someone says the word "house" each individual hearing that word has a unique picture in their mind's eye. I may imagine a two-story brick home on a one-acre lot surrounded with a white wooden fence. You may recall the house in which they were raised - an old farm house under large oak trees. It's kind of like that with our images of the new heaven and the new earth where God will set up his eternal reign. And with the exception of the New Jerusalem as described in the 21st chapter of The Revelations, we do not know exactly what Heaven and the new earth will look like and be like. What we do know is that "Jesus is preparing a wonderful place to spend eternity with His followers. Although we can feel comfortable and reasonably happy here, we must remember that earth is our temporary home – we're passing through on our way to a much better place. Paul encourages us in Colossians 3:1 – 4 to focus our thoughts and desires on eternal things to maintain a proper perspective." (5)

November 10
<u>Do Not Grumble and Complain</u>

"Do all things without complaining and disputing...These are grumblers, complainers, walking according to their own lusts; and they mouth great swelling words, flattering people to gain advantage." Jude 1:16, 22
"Though now you do not see Him, yet believing, you rejoice with joy inexpressible and full of glory..." I Peter 1:8

Have you ever known grumbling to do any one any good? Has grumbling ever changed your circumstances? I think not. As a Godly man, you should not be a grumbler or a complainer. To do so indicates your lack of gratitude for what God has done and can do. It sends the message that being a Christian man must be miserable. Did Jesus grumble or complain about His destiny? Did Paul grumble and complain because of the beatings he took on his back for the sake of the gospel? He gloried in his persecution and thought it a privilege to suffer for Christ's sake. Christians grumble and complain about their standard of living, their church, their jobs and their struggles. The Apostle Peter could have complained about persecution, about his past failures and about what he expected to endure for the cause of the gospel. Yet, he admonished the early Christians, though they could not see Jesus as he had to rejoice. If you tend to grumble and complain, go to the Lord in prayer today and ask Him to remind you that as His child you "rejoice and be glad in him".

November 11
Be a Man of Courage

"Be of good courage, and let us be strong for our people and for the cities of our God. And may the LORD do what is good in His sight." Romans 12:10

"...as I was with Moses, so I will be with you. I will not leave you nor forsake you. Be strong and of good courage. Only be strong and very courageous..." Joshua 1:5-7

Being a man sets you apart in many different ways than your female counterpart. Not only in obvious physical attributes, but also in other masculine characteristics. Despite modern sociological and psychological theories and the feminist movement, man was created by God to be the dominate sex. Men have always been warriors, fighters, defenders, builders and hunters. This does not exclude women from some traditional male roles. However, generally speaking women who participate in the more grueling kinds of work and sports are the exception. Godly men must possess certain essential characteristics for which God created them to use. One of these is courage. The Bible is replete with Godly men of courage...far too many to list. In fact, most men of God were courageous men. To be a spiritual leader and stand against the evil rulers, Godly men needed spiritual courage. Stu Weber writes: "The true measure of a man is not his physical power, in the skill of his hands, in the quickness of his wit, or in his ability to pile up possessions. True, manly courage is best seen in his willingness to make and keep promises – though all hell should oppose him." (6)

November 12
Let Go of Guilt

"For by grace you have been saved through faith, and that not of yourselves; it is the gift of God" Ephesians 2:8
"There is therefore now no condemnation to those who are in Christ Jesus, who do not walk according to the flesh, but according to the Spirit. For the law of the Spirit of life in Christ Jesus has made me free from the law of sin and death".
Romans 8:1-2

Are you carrying the baggage of guilt? If you have sin in your heart and/or practicing sin, then the Holy Spirit works through your conscience to convict you and lead you to repentance and restoration. However, many men allow guilt for past sins to nag them and pull them down. Search your heart and ask the Holy Spirit to reveal guilt from past sins and failures or guilt which you're carrying because you struggle measuring up or lack of faith in Jesus atonement for your sins. Guilt is debilitating and will sap your joy and victory, keeping you in a perpetual state of condemnation. God does not want you to carry this burden of guilt one more day. Jim Thomas write: "If our conscience is healthy and is working as God designed it to, our sin will weigh us down. God's answer for sin and guilt is not blame-shifting or denial, it is forgiveness." (7) If you have asked God to forgive you, to cleanse you and restore you, sin's guilt has no business burdening your heart. This day claim God's promise: "There is now no condemnation to those who walk in Christ Jesus."

November 13
The Unjust Know No Shame

"For many walk, of whom I have told you often, and now tell you even weeping, that they are the enemies of the cross of Christ: whose end is destruction, whose god is their belly, and whose glory is in their shame—who set their mind on earthly things".
Philippians 3:18-19
"The LORD is righteous in her midst, he will do no unrighteousness. Every morning He brings His justice to light; he never fails, but the unjust knows no shame." Zephaniah 3:5

Unbelievers have one distinguishing trait from borne again Christians. It is not always their conduct, but it is their blindness to spiritual matters. Paul explains it this way: "having their understanding darkened, being alienated from the life of God, because of the ignorance that is in them, because of the blindness of their heart." (Ephesians 4:18) Unbelievers are carnally minded. As a Godly man you have become enlightened as to God's ways and have the Holy Spirit to guide you. They don't and, consequently, they cannot understand the shame of their sinful behavior. They are the "enemies of the cross of Christ". Politicians, government officials and media pundits cannot grasp or explain why evil rulers war against our nation. They fail to see the "elephant in the living room". These Godless infidels have no shame in their evildoings. They persecute and murder Christians in foreign lands and on American soil. American secularists also have their understanding blinded. They strive to remove God from schools and to extinguish any expression of Christianity. It behooves you, a Godly man and the

head of your home, to know this and prepare your heart and
your family to stand strong in the faith.

November 14
<u>An Encounter with Jesus</u>

"The woman then left her water pot, went her way into the city, and said to the men; "Come, see a Man who told me all things that I ever did. Could this be the Christ?" John 4:28-29

"As he journeyed he came near Damascus, and suddenly a light shone around him from heaven. Then he fell to the ground, and heard a voice saying to him, 'Saul, Saul, why are you persecuting Me?' And he said, 'Who are You, Lord?' Then the Lord said, 'I am Jesus, whom you are persecuting.'." Acts 9:3-5

The woman at the well, the blind man who received his sight, Peter, the father of the sick daughter, Nicodemus, Paul and others who came into contact with Jesus were never the same again. Once you've met Jesus in authentic way you will be a different man. One cannot meet Jesus and ever be the same again. He is life-changing. He is peace of mind and heart. He is love. He is truth. He is Lord of lords and King of kings. He is he the Prince of Peace. He is joy. He is hope. He is who every Godly man should worship continuously. It is Jesus who, through the power of His Holy Spirit who can keep your mind, your soul and you heart through the raging storms of life which threaten your faith. It is He who will be with you when you're the one closest to you dies and you question "why?" You should long for Him and become like David, a man after God's own heart. Today pray that your relationship with Jesus will be refreshed as if it were the first time you met him. Desire to introduce Jesus to others.

November 15
Dealing with Retirement or Unemployment

"Not that I speak in regard to need, for I have learned in whatever state I am, to be content." **Philippians 4:11**
"For we know that all things work together for good to those who love God, to those who are the called according to His purpose." Romans 8:28

Lost your job or retired? Losing your job - your primary source of income, the place you went five days a week, that which gave you a title and status and the where you had friends and colleagues – can be devastating to a man's dignity. Retirement can have similar outcomes. You lose the identity and status which was associated with your job. As a "baby boomer" I know have many men who have been fired, lost their jobs due to downsizing, and retired as soon as they became eligible. You may feel you've lost that from which you derived your masculine identity. You may feel un-needed. After a few months of enjoying your new-found freedom, reality smacks you in the face. You think, "Hey, I'm still young and vibrant enough to contribute my knowledge and skills." If you're unemployed finding a job may be difficult. You struggle with feelings of inadequacy. But God has a plan for your life. And what seems hopeless may be God revealing a new opportunity. You may not understand why. But pray and trust God for "all things to work together for good..." Then rest in Him waiting to see what He has planned.

November 16
<u>Your Children Need Your Approval</u>

"Paul, an apostle of Jesus Christ by the will of God, according to the promise of life which is in Christ Jesus, To Timothy, a beloved son: Grace, mercy, and peace from God the Father and Christ Jesus our Lord...when I call to remembrance the genuine faith that is in you, which dwelt first in your grandmother Lois and your mother Eunice, and I am persuaded is in you also." II Timothy 1:1, 2, 5-6

If you are a father or plan to become one, it is of utmost importance that your children know that you love them, are devoted to them and will always be there for them. It is important that, whenever possible, that they know they have your approval. I grasped this concept after several years of fatherhood. Some fathers tend to discourage their children with frequent criticism of their efforts, who ignore their interests and fail to express their love and confidence them. Every young girl and boy has a deep-seated need to hear their father say, "well done" and "I love you". This is not intended to diminish the influence of a mother. Her presence and love is extremely important along with her nurturing and encouragement. But far too often there is an absence from the father in the home or the father who is in the home abdicates his responsibilities to the mother. What does this mean for you? Be there and be your child's biggest supporter. Be there to encourage and offer fatherly wisdom which will be with them for a lifetime. Do not underestimate your influence on the live of your son or daughter.

November 17
<u>A Day with Your Son or Daughter</u>

"No it came to pass after these things that Joseph was told, 'Indeed your father is sick'; and he took with him his two sons, Manasseh and Ephraim. And Jacob was told, 'Look, your son Joseph is coming to you'; and Israel strengthened himself and sat up on the bed". Genesis 48:1-2

There is no more inspiring story than that of Joseph. Sold into slavery by his brothers as a lad, he was blessed by God. Many years passed and Joseph found himself in a prominent position in the House of Potepher. During a drought people came to Egypt for food. Joseph was responsible for the distribution of food. When his brothers came to Egypt to get their allotment of food and grain, Joseph recognized them but they didn't recognize him. He asked about their father who was very old. He forgave his brothers and restored joy to his elderly father who had grieved for many years thinking Joseph was dead. As a Godly man you love your children. When they grow into young adults and leave the nest of home, special times with them are often those in your memories. But you can continue to build good memories. Consider a day excursion or a visit with your daughter or son. Make it a pleasant experience, giving yourselves time to talk and to strengthen your relationship. They still need to know that you are their rock, protector and security. Thank God this day for each of your children and pray for them.

November 18
In Football and in Life There are Bad Calls

"Then Moses lifted his hand and struck the rock twice with his rod; and water came out abundantly, and the congregation and their animals drank." Numbers 20:11

"So Pilate, wanting to gratify the crowd, released Barabbas to them; and he delivered Jesus, after he had scourged Him, to be crucified." Mark 15:15

As college football nears the end of its season, some fans become increasingly intense about their team's success. By now critical games have been won or lost because of one bad call. One bad call, one missed interference or one missed face mask call can make the difference in winning and losing. One bad clipping call or one bad placement of the ball for the scrimmage line can result in a missed touchdown by inches. One bad call by Moses resulted in his eligibility to enter the Promised Land. One bad call by Pontius Pilate set a criminal free and gave Jesus the penalty of death. Living a Godly life is tough. You should be assured of your eternal salvation. Yet decisions still result in consequences. One bad call to engage in a sexual affair can result in losing your family. One bad call to commit fraud at work can result in jail time. You will stumble. But the Holy Spirit serves to warn you and to guide you when making the big calls of the game of life. That's why it so important that you consistently stay in spiritual condition. Ask God to help you make the right calls.

November 19
"This Nation, Under God": The Gettysburg Address

Righteousness exalts a nation, but sin is a reproach to any people." Proverbs 14:34
"Blessed is the "nation whose God is the LORD, the people He has chosen as His own inheritance." Psalm 33:12.

America is founded on the principles of Almighty God. Despite U.S. Supreme Court decisions and lower courts' interpretations over the years, our founding fathers never intended to leave God out of public life nor deprive citizens the right to worship as they pleased. The Declaration of Independence of 1776 made it clear by adding the phrase, "with firm reliance on the protection of divine Providence". Then just over eight-seven years later amid the devastation of a Civil War, President Abraham Lincoln delivered the Gettysburg Address at the battlefield where thousand of both Union and Confederate soldiers had died. In only a two minute speech, President Lincoln gave what has to be one of the most profoundly unifying presentations in the history of our country. Lincoln affirmed this nation's reliance of God in this excerpt: "...that we here highly resolve that these dead shall not have died in vain, that this nation, under God, shall have a new birth of freedom..." (8) Never be led astray by the secular humanists in our country who declare that this country was never intended to acknowledge God. And as a Godly man, be prepared to take a stand where the opportunity arises.

November 20
Legalism vs. Freedom in Christ

"For the law of the Spirit of life in Christ Jesus has made me free from the law of sin and death." Romans 8:2
"But that no one is justified by the law in the sight of God is evident, for 'the just shall live by faith.'" Galatians 3:11

Do you continue to have the legalistic mind set about your salvation? Do you believe in a "condition-response" relationship with Jesus? This is the old way. Under the old way God's people had a set of rules, the Law, which, if followed, resulted in blessings. Man could not be good enough to keep the Law. This mindsct "is rooted in linearity, the bondage of control: do this and that will happen. The former arrangement of doing good to secure God's blessings has been replaced by...the Law of Liberty." (9) Now we serve God because we love Him and we have a better hope in Him, not a better life. (10) Yet, many Christians have not broken free from an inner bondage and belief that God's love for them is based their degree of goodness. Neil Anderson offers a few truths which He believes must be and lived by: "I renounce the lie that I am rejected, unloved, dirty or shameful because in Christ I am completely accepted. I renounce the lie that I am guilty, unprotected, alone or abandoned because in Christ I am totally secure. And...by the grace of God I am what I am." (11)

November 21
Winter's Coming On, But Stay in the Race

"And it may be that I will remain, or even spend the winter with you, that you may send me on my journey, wherever I go." 1 Corinthians 16:6

"...that the older men be sober, reverent, temperate, sound in faith, in love, in patience;" Titus 2:2

"They shall still bear fruit in old age; They shall be fresh and flourishing," Psalm 92:14

As the winter of life approaches for some, it's time to contemplate where you've been, what God means to and where you are in your spiritual growth.

In almost a month from today it will be the first day of winter. Will you stay focused on the goal of the high calling of Christ? Will you stay in the race of which the Apostle Paul spoke? In your spiritual race there's no finish line. You must adapt and stay spiritually viable. There is no spiritual retirement. In an essay in Men's Health's "Best Life", Charles Gaines writes: "Just as there's time in a man's life for the full and unapologetic enjoyment of physical strength and beauty, there is a time to leave those things behind and journey toward completeness." (12) Note that he uses the verb "journey". You're still in the race. Perhaps you've been focusing on yourself. That must change. "You don't get there from here by rubbing testosterone on your wrists. You get there by taking your licks of wrinkles and sags and scars and by praying that those licks turn you outward, away from self..." (13) Look forward to winter – it could be your best season.

November 22
Anointing with Oil

"Is anyone among you sick? Let him call for the elders of the church, and let them pray over him, anointing him with oil in the name of the Lord." James 5:14

"And when Jesus was in Bethany at the house of Simon the leper, a woman came to Him having an alabaster flask of very costly fragrant oil, and she poured it on His head as He sat at the table." Matthew 26:6-7

The use of oil in anointing is seen throughout the New Testament. Jesus sent His twelve disciples out (Mark 6:13) and they "anointed with oil many who were sick and healed them." Practically, it offered healing to wounds as mentioned in Isaiah 1:6 and in the story of the Good Samaritan. Regarding today's verse found in James, J.A. Motyer writes: "James is very likely relying on this apostolic example and tacit dominical approval. Both these aspects of the use of oil, the medicinal and the spiritual, would be in the minds of the elders and of their sick brother." (14) Mary anointed the head of Jesus with fragrant oil. In Jesus' parable of the ten virgins, oil in their lamps typifies the Holy Spirit. Oil was usually related to a more significant issue, i.e. the Holy Spirit, prayer and healing and a reflection of deep devotion. Today, churches of many denominations use oil as a spiritual anointing for healing or other sacramental purposes. I believe that when you, as elders of the church, use oil to anoint the forehead of one sick or near death, you do it in the same spirit and custom of the New Testament.

November 23
<u>Dealing with Regrets</u>

"This I also did in Jerusalem, and many of the saints I shut up in prison, having received authority from the chief priests; and when they were put to death, I cast my vote against them . And I punished them often in every synagogue and compelled them to blaspheme; and being exceedingly enraged against them, I persecuted them even to foreign cities." Acts 26:10-11

Today's scripture passage regards Paul's recalling his evil days before his encounter with Jesus on the road to Damascus. Though he uses his past to emphasize what change God had made in his life, he must have regretted the punishments and the deaths which he reveled in at the time. Though he had had one of the most miraculous and dramatic conversions in the New Testament, he still remembered the wrong-doing of his past. You and I have many regrets in our lives. Some men wallow in their regrets and allow those past sins to remain like a heavy ball and chain. Other men cannot break through these regrets and experience their freedom in Christ. Often the consequences of your past still exist, thus serving as memories with regret. If you are struggling with regrets whether they be decisions you made, people you offended, children you neglected or sins you committed, ask Jesus now to release you from this bondage of Satan. Those things are under the blood of Christ. You carry them needlessly. Then rebuke Satan's attacks on your mind, claiming your forgiveness and freedom in Jesus. Then your joy and peace will be restored.

November 24
<u>God is Great, God is Good</u>

*"But God, who is rich in mercy, because of His
great love with which He loved us," Ephesians 2:4
"Bless the LORD, O my soul! O LORD my God,
You are very great: You are clothed with honor and
majesty," Psalm 104:1*

Perhaps as a child you were taught to pray the blessing
over your meals. A common children's prayer included
these words: "God is Great, God is God let us thank Him
for our food." I prayed that simple prayer as a child and
taught it to my children. "Simple" is not a good adjective
for that prayer. The foundational truth of the words, "God is
Great, God is Good", is profound. George Beverly Shea, the
veteran soloist for Billy Graham's crusades often sang the
hymn "How Great Thou Art". The first verse only partially
describes God's grandeur: "O Lord my God when I in
awesome wonder consider all the worlds Thy hands have
made, I see the stars, I hear the rolling thunder, Thy pow'r
thro'-out the universe displayed." (15) Signs and wonders
which God created continue to be discovered today by scien-
tists. Man has only miniscule knowledge of God's creation.
Though God is so great to have created the universe, He is
so good to love you and me. It's impossible for our minds
to grasp just how big, powerful our God really is. Make
your best effort today to worship Him for His greatness and
goodness.

November 25
<u>Oh Give Thanks Unto God!</u>

"I will bless the LORD at all times; his praise shall continually be in my mouth." Psalm 34:1
"Now thanks be to God who always leads us in triumph in Christ, and through us diffuses the fragrance of His knowledge in every place." 2 Corinthians 2:14

How often do you really give thanks to the Lord and praise Him? There are many Christians who seldom take time to praise God. Some may mummer or sing praise to Almighty God only during a church worship service. Perhaps you praise Him in your devotional or quiet time with Him each day. This is good. But is it enough? You simply cannot praise God too much or too often. In Psalm 34, David says, "I will bless the Lord at all times; His praise shall continually be in my mouth." Read that again and meditate on it. Psalm 119:164 reads, "Seven times a day I praise You." God wants you to praise Him and delights in your praise. When you praise Him and thank Him for His goodness, you benefit by being lifted in the Spirit and experiencing the joy of the Lord. Praise Him while you're stuck in traffic. Praise Him while sitting at your desk. Praise Him while laboring at work. Praise Him while you're fishing or hunting. Play a Christian tape or CD with praise songs when in your truck or car. He is worthy of your praise. Let your praise be almost continuous each day.

November 26
Commercializing Christmas Begins With a Frenzy

"And she brought forth her firstborn Son, and wrapped Him in swaddling cloths, and laid Him in a manger, because there was no room for them in the inn. Now there were in the same country shepherds living out in the fields, keeping watch over their flock by night. And behold, an angel of the Lord stood before them, and the glory of the Lord shone around them, and they were greatly afraid."
Luke 2:7-9

The day after Thanksgiving is traditionally been the "official" day to begin Christmas shopping. Billions of dollars are spent, or charged, between today and the day before Christmas. This is one of those rare occasions when unbelievers, secularists, atheists, Jews and Christians all pack the malls with their cash and credit cards to purchase gifts. And for those who don't believe in God or in His Son as Savior, there is Santa Clause as the common icon who brings everyone together to celebrate in spending and in partying for what is supposed to be the recognition of the birth of our Savior Jesus Christ, God's Son. But hold on. In recent years secular nonbelievers have targeted the "Christ" in Christmas. Any semblance of Christ is increasingly being removed from the public view. In his book, *Persecution*, David Limbaugh shares but a few stories from among hundreds where Christian symbols are found objectionable and removed. He writes: "Truly one of the hot button issues involving Christian presence on government property concerns Christian celebrations and displays." (16) As Godly men, let us stand in the gap. De-emphasize commercializing

Christmas and guide your family as you reverently celebrate His birth.

November 27
Evil Men Will Grow Worse

"But evil men and impostors will grow worse and worse, deceiving and being deceived." 2 Timothy 3:13
"knowing this first: that scoffers will come in the last days, walking according to their own lusts" 2 Peter 3:3

Though Christians in every generation since Christ's resurrection believed they lived in the last days, the increased number of fulfilled prophesies, the existence of destructive weapons and global changes are more convincing than ever before that we live in the last days. Read the newspapers and watch your T.V. news cast. World-wide violence has proliferated and touched nations which have historically been at peace for centuries. Not only is the Middle East a powder keg, revolutions are rampant in South America, suicide bomb blasts occur throughout Europe and tension among Asian countries include threats of military action. The news media around the world publish the despicable slaughter of innocent people. We are seeing increasing world-wide conflicts unparallel in history. American society tolerates far too much violence in our streets, in our schools and in our movies. Evil is found in the highest offices of our government. Illicit, perverted sex is rampant and drug trafficking has outpaced law enforcement's efforts. In urban neighborhoods, neighbors live in fear of their lives. Innocent children are being murdered and molested. What can you do? Pray and keep yourself and your family safe and prepared for the only hope we have – Christ's return.

November 28
The Potter and the Clay

"Arise and go down to the potter's house, and there I will cause you to hear My words. 'O House of Israel, can I not do to you as this potter does?' declares the Lord. 'Like clay in the hand of the potter, so are you in My hand, O House of Israel"
Jeremiah 18:2, 6
"The precious sons of Zion, valuable as fine gold, how they are regarded as clay pots, the work of the hands of the potter!" Lamentations 4:2

As a child I heard my mother sing often as she did the dishes or mopped the floors. Though she had several favorites which she sang frequently, there was one which when she sang it she seemed to be in a spirit of worship. "Have Thine Own Way", written in the early 1900's by Adelaide Addison Pollard, rings so clear today and causes my heart worship the Lord. *"Have Thine own way Lord! Have Thine own way! Thou are the potter; I am the clay. Mold me and make me after Thy will, while I am waiting yielded and still."* Today's scriptures along with the words of this ageless hymn pretty much say it all. Are you clay in the Master Potter's hand? Are you yielded and still? Only when we become pliable like clay and allow God to shape us into His image and His purpose will we ever know real peace and the real love of God. Worship and praise Him for His grace and love and peace.

November 29
Basketball: Be a Winner Despite the Odds

"Then all this assembly shall know that the LORD does not save with sword and spear; for the battle is the Lord's, and He will give you into our hands." Then David put his hand in his bag and took out a stone; and he slung it and struck the Philistine in his forehead, so that the stone sank into his forehead, and he fell on his face to the earth." 1 Samuel 17:47, 49

It's time for basketball! If you are a basketball enthusiast this year has plenty of excitement ahead. As in any sport, every player and team wants to win. If you've never watched the movie, "Hoosiers" you must. It's about a small high school team who ultimately defeats the best team in Indiana. Perhaps the most exciting college game I watched was in Tuscaloosa, Alabama where Division II Samford University, a small Baptist University in Birmingham, traveled to take on the Division I Crimson Tide. Of course, the outcome seemed inevitable. But like David and Goliath, despite the odds the Samford Bulldogs defeated the Tide and went on that year to play in the NCAA Tournament. What a thrill! You are a winner too. Though you may consider yourself an ordinary Christian man struggling to stay in the game, Jesus sealed your victory on the cross, He has given you the right gear to put on and He's sent the Holy Spirit to be your coach. Yes, you will stumble. You may fall behind. But by faith, be strong in the Lord. You will defeat your adversary the devil and win time and time again and prevail in the end.

November 30
A Vessel of Honor

"...that each of you should know how to possess his own vessel in sanctification and honor" 1 Thessalonians 4:4

"Therefore if anyone cleanses himself from the latter, he will be a vessel for honor, sanctified and useful for the Master, prepared for every good work." 2 Timothy 2:21

Honor. Webster defines it as a "good name or public esteem; merited respect". Honor was once held in high regard in our country, in our communities and among folks. But somewhere along the way with integrity, respect, kindness and honesty, honor lost its significance. The military and the Boy Scouts have struggled to maintain the true meaning and evidence of honor. Honor is not a thing which can be seen or touched. It is not something which can be easily taught. Rather honor is that characteristic inside a man or woman which is instilled through intense, disciplined training and/or through the power of the Holy Spirit as He sanctifies one from the rudiments of carnality. Read the scripture again: "...if anyone cleanses himself...he will be a vessel for honor..." No greater word can be used in describing a Godly man than "honor". It's not something you can conjure up. You become a man of honor as you keep your heart's eyes on Jesus Christ and seek daily to walk in the Spirit. Ask God to sanctify you as you sanctify yourself from sinful practices and unclean thoughts. Let your epitaph read: "He was a man of honor".

REFERENCES FOR NOVEMBER

1. Bob Barnes, "15 Minutes alone with God for Men" (Harvest House Publishers, Eugene Oregon) 1995 p.13
2. 2. Dietrich Bonhoeffer, "The Cost of Discipleship", (A Touchtone Book, Simon and Schuster, New York, New York) 1959 p. 213, 21
3. Oswald Chambers, "My Utmost for His Highest" (Barbour and Company Inc. Uhrichsville, Ohio) p. 8
4. Billy Graham, The Journey (W Publishing Company, Nashville, Tennessee) 2006 p. 200
5. Stu Weber, "The Heart of a Tender Warrior" (Multnomah Publishers, Sisters, Oregon) 2002 p. 33
6. Tyndale House Publishers, "Living Waters for those who thirst" (Tyndal House Publishers, Wheaton, Illinois) 2000 p. 90
7. Jim Thomas, "Answering the Big Questions About God" (Harvest House Publishers, Eugene Oregon) 2001, p. 188
8. Toby Mac and Michael Tait, "Under God" (Bethany House, Minneapolis, Minnesota) 2004 p.171
9. Larry Crabb, "The Pressure's Off" (WaterBrook Press, Colorado Springs, Colorado) 2002 p.26
10. Ibid.p.27
11. Neil T. Anderson, "The Bondage Breaker" (Harvest House, Publishers, Eugene, Oregon) 2000 p. 248-250
12. Charles Gaines, "How to Grow Up" (Men's Health, The Best Life, Winter 2004, Rodale, Inc. Emmaus, PA.) p. 52
13. Ibid.p. 55
14. J.A. Motyer, "The Message of James", (Inter-Varsity Press, Downers Grove, Illinois) 1985 p. 195
15. "The Hymnal for Worship and Celebration", (Word Music, Waco, Texas) 1986 p. 4

16. David Limbaugh, "Persecution" (Regnery Publishing, Inc., An Eagle Publishing Company, Washington D.C.) 2003 p. 160

December 1
Behind the Facade

"Woe to you, scribes and Pharisees, hypocrites!
For you cleanse the outside of the cup and dish,
but inside they are full of extortion and self-indul-
gence." Matthew 23:25
He who says, 'I know Him'" and does not keep
His commandments, is a liar, and the truth is not in
him." 1 John 2:4

Every man has a façade wrapped around his inner self.
You, I and all other men have a dark side, a stronghold or a
secret sin which is often well hidden from those around us.
Recently a highly respected minister who pastured a mega-
church of 14,000 and head of a national evangelical group
lost his façade when his inner darkness was exposed. He
had been having illicit sexual encounters with another man.
He not only lost his façade, but his church and good name.
You like most every man is under some type of pressure
to measure up to expected standards. Yet, deep within you
war rages. In his book, "Men's Secret Wars", Patrick Means
writes: "Men from all walks of life are under unprecedented
pressure. The suicide rate for men is two and one-half higher
than that of women." (1) Many men appear to be spiritual,
self-confident and at peace but inside they're suffering pres-
sures of family strife, financial loss and/or an adulterous
affair. The time is now to take steps to deal with that which
torments your mind. Ask Jesus to cleanse, heal and rescue.
Prayer, Christian counseling and confronting your struggle
begins healing what's behind the façade.

December 2
Be Faithful in Small Things:
God's Preparing You for Greater

"And Potiphar, an officer of Pharaoh, captain of the guard, an Egyptian, bought him {Joseph} from the Ishmaelites who had taken him {as a slave} down there. The Lord was with Joseph, and he was a successful man:" Genesis 39:1 & 2 "And Pharaoh said {to Joseph} 'See, I have set you over all the land of Egypt'." Genesis 41:41
"He who is faithful in what is least is faithful also in much;" Luke 16:10

There are many men, believers and non-believers, who have their hearts set on positions of prominence, high salaries and power. They are not content to accept or linger long in ground level positions and prove themselves. These types of men often have a bad attitude. Consequently, their quality of work may suffer. The same holds true of Christian men, whether they serve God in a lay ministry role or in full-time ministry. The story of Joseph offers the perfect illustration of a man who is satisfied to be obedient where God puts him and does his job as unto the Lord. Joseph went from a slave to second only to the Pharaoh of Egypt. Jesus recognized that before one would be faithful with much responsibility, they must have proven themselves responsible in meager jobs with little responsibility. "God has placed us in situations according to His will and purposes. In other words, we don't wait to see our employee treats us before deciding how hard to work." (2) Wherever you are in life and whatever your responsibilities, live and work to the best of your ability so that you will be found worthy of greater responsibilities. God honors faithfulness.

December 3
Becoming Good Leaders

"And Moses said to the people, 'Do not be afraid. Stand still, and see the salvation of the LORD, which He will accomplish for you today. For the Egyptians whom you see today, you shall see again no more forever.'" Exodus 14:13

"Only be strong and very courageous, that you may observe to do according to all the law which Moses, my servant commanded you: do not turn from it to the right hand or to the left that you may prosper wherever you go." Joshua 1:7

As a Godly man you are a leader and will be called to lead in future circumstances. Remember, you are a spiritual warrior. A warrior must have character and courage to lead. In today's scriptures, we focus on two great leaders – Moses and Joshua. Not only were they organizational leaders and strategists, but they were military leaders who conquered many mighty armies with God on their side. God told Joshua to be "strong and very courageous" and to observe the law which Moses had delivered. Winston Churchill once said: "Courage is rightly esteemed the first of human qualities… because it is the quality which guarantees all others." (3) In whatever leadership role you find yourself you must follow God's will for you and for those whom you lead, whether family, a company or church. John Maxwell, a former pastor and now a prolific author and speaker on leadership, goes to the heart of being a leader: "If you can become the leader you want to be on the inside, you will be the leader you want to be on the outside. People will want to follow you." (4) Ask God to develop you to be a leader with courage and character.

December 4
Draw Nearer to God

"Draw near to God and He will draw near to you. Cleanse your hands, you sinners; and purify your hearts, you double-minded." James 4:8
"And you will seek Me and find Me, when you search for Me with all your heart." Jeremiah 29:13

There is no greater need among Christians men than to move closer to God. So many Godly men have drifted so far from the Lord that they no longer hear His voice. Instead of accepting the role of a courageous warrior for Christ, some men have waved the white flag of surrender, becoming spiritual sissies. Few new converts are made because few intercessory prayers are prayed. Consequently, Christianity in your community and in the nation is losing ground to a valueless, secular belief system. There is but one answer – "Draw near to God". When you, as a Godly man, fervently seek the Lord you will be baptized in the Spirit and change will occur in your home, in your church and in your spheres of influence. The third verse of an old hymn, "I Am Thine, O Lord" so eloquently goes to the heart of this need: "O, the pure delight of a single hour that before Thy throne I spend, when I kneel in prayer, and to Thee, my God, I commune as friend with friend. {Refrain} Draw me nearer, nearer blessed Lord to the cross where Thou hast died..." (5) Begin today to draw nearer to your Heavenly Father.

December 5
God is for You, Not against You

"The LORD is on my side; I will not fear. What can man do to me?" Psalm 118:6
"Yet in all these things we are more than conquerors through Him who loved us." Romans 8:37

Do you ever feel as if God is against you? Do you find your circumstances have sapped your joy and peace? Where is God, you may be asking? You may have been led to believe that your joy and good feelings come when God makes life good for you. When you are blindsided by some crisis you may ask, "Where is God?" Bad things do happen to good people and you are no exception. The problem lies in the fact that Christians most often equate God's love with how they feel and in how God responds to their predicaments. You will never understand why God seems far away when you need Him. Larry Grabb writes: "We should enjoy God's blessing; the good things of life should generate good feelings. But I am coming to see something wrong that before I thought was spiritual gratitude: Those good feelings have become my basis for joy. I claim them as my right. I pray they will continue. It praying from that mindset that makes God seem so unresponsive." (6) Despite your expectation that He make everything right, you matter to Him. He loves you. He cares about you...no matter how you feel.

December 6
Celebrate His First Coming

"So it was, when the angels had gone away from them into heaven, that the shepherds said to one another, 'Let us now go to Bethlehem and see this thing that has come to pass, which the Lord has made known to us.'" Luke 2:15

"Then the shepherds returned, glorifying and praising God for all the things that they had heard and seen, as it was told them." Luke 2:20

What an exciting time for Christians all over the world! The miracle birth of Jesus Christ our Savior is to be reverenced. It marked the fulfillment of Old Testament prophesies. It was God's greatest act of love – to send His son in the form of man to live among men and to be the once and for all sacrifice for sin. The shepherds were led to the scene of Christ's birth and became witnesses of this literal "earth-shaking" event. Today you are a witness of that event. You have been reconciled to God through Jesus' death and resurrection. The shepherds glorified and praised God for what they had seen. You too should be glorifying and praising God for what He did for you and for all those who will come to Him. This is a season of celebration and praise, not for creating more debt and stress. Begin today to thank God every day from now until Christmas day for His divine love which He has for you. This year begin a new Christian tradition of making the entire month of December a celebration and praise for you and your family.

December 7
Pearl Harbor: An Attack on Our Nation

"Now it happened, when David and his men came to Ziklag, on the third day, that the Amalekites had invaded the South and Ziklag, attacked Ziklag and burned it with fire," 1 Samuel 30:1

"So David inquired of the LORD, saying, 'Shall I pursue this troop? Shall I overtake them?' And He answered him, 'Pursue, for you shall surely overtake them and without fail recover all.'" 1 Samuel 30:8

On this day in 1941 America was attacked at Pearl Harbor in Oahu, Hawaii by the Japanese air force. This tragic event was a surprise to the men and women living and working in Pcarl Harbor where over 2,400 people were killed, most of them U.S. military personnel. December 7 has been officially recognized to commemorate that attack on American soil and those who lost their lives defending our personnel and ships. This dastardly event resulted in the United States entering World War II and fighting against he evil forces of Hitler's Nazi Germany and Italy's Fascist Government. David faced similar circumstances when the Amalekites had invaded Ziglag and plundered and burned that city. With God's approval David pursued the enemy and obeying God to "recover all". A nation founded on religious freedom and a belief in Almighty God as our creator, America responds when attacked by godless nations. As Godly men of honor, thank God today that your country has responded to attacks like that of Pearl Harbor so that you and your children's freedom to worship Jesus may continue. Take time today to acknowledge the lives of those sacrificed for you.

December 8
<u>Care for the Less Fortunate</u>

"They desired only that we should remember the poor, the very thing which I also was eager to do". Galatians 2:10
"So when Jesus heard these things, He said to him, "You still lack one thing. Sell all that you have and distribute to the poor, and you will have treasure in heaven; and come, follow Me." Luke 18:22

During this Christmas season there will be Christian and charitable groups ready and willing to gather food, clothing, toys and necessities for living to give to those less fortunate. The Salvation Army has a strong campaign to raise money, food and items for families who cannot afford any "extras" for their families. Cities throughout the country have homeless shelters where those with no family and no home can enjoy a kind greeting, a warm meal and, perhaps, a Christ-centered devotion. Churches and their Sunday school classes, universities, businesses and other groups collect food, clothing and toys for struggling families. There is legitimate cynicism about some of those on the receiving end. There are those who take advantage of others' giving. But your focus should be on the giving and on others during this season and all year. What have you personally done this year and during this season to help others who are in real need? We find in the sixth chapter of The Acts church leaders set up a committee of seven to see that widows' needs were met. Seek ways in which you can bless others by your sacrificial giving. And do so in the name of Jesus.

December 9
Attacks on Christianity

"We are hard-pressed on every side, yet not crushed; we are perplexed, but not in despair; persecuted, but not forsaken;" II Corinthians 4:8-9

"Yes, and all who desire to live godly in Christ Jesus will suffer persecution. But evil men and impostors will grow worse and worse, deceiving and being deceived." 2 Timothy 3:12-13

It is particularly sad that Christianity is under attack over Christmas symbols under the guise of the term "Separation of Church and State" which is not even mentioned in either the U.S. Constitution or the Bill of Rights. Just forty short years ago it would have been unthinkable to believe that the nativity scene, a Star of David or even the word Christmas would ever be removed by government officials for being offensive. But believe it. It is happening all over the country. It is happening daily in every aspect of American life. "Anti-Christian discrimination in our society is getting more blatant and more widespread every day. The cultural assumptions of our society influence changes in the law..." (7) In her book, "Godless", Ann Coulter writes: "This is a country in which taxpayers are forced to subsidize "artistic" exhibits of aborted fetuses, crucifixes in urine, and gay pornography. Meanwhile, it's unconstitutional to display a Nativity scene at Christmas or the Ten Commandments on government property if the purpose is to promote monotheistic religion." (8) Men, it's time to fall to your knees and say as Joshua, "But for me and my house, we will serve the Lord." (Joshua 24:15)

December 10
The New Jerusalem

"Then I, John, saw the holy city, New Jerusalem, coming down out of heaven from God, prepared as a bride adorned for her husband." Revelation 21:2
"And he carried me away in the Spirit to a great and high mountain, and showed me the great city, the holy Jerusalem, descending out of heaven from God, having the glory of God. Her light was like a most precious stone, like a jasper stone, clear as crystal." Revelation 21:10-11

Christmas and the birth of Christ are about expectancy. God's promise of a better way to salvation was fulfilled when the baby Jesus was borne to the virgin Mary. On that long-awaited fulfillment of that promise on which men and women had their hopes was made real in the form of a Savior. He came, lived, he was crucified resurrected and sits at the right hand of God. Similarly, God has, through John on the Isle of Patmos, made another promise to which we should look forward with excitement. Following Jesus' promised second coming and a new heaven and new earth, the new City Jerusalem, will come down out of heaven to earth. Its description found in the twenty-first chapter of Revelations is breathtaking. I have assurance through faith that I will see that new City Jerusalem coming down out of Heaven and walk on the streets of pure gold. What a thrill! It will happen just as Jesus' birth and resurrection happened. If you to waiver and doubt God's promises, ask Him for a renewed hope for what He has indeed promised. Look forward with excitement and peace to what Jesus is preparing for you.

December 11
<u>A Man's Reputation</u>

"A good name is better than precious ointment,
And the day of death than the day of one's birth."
Ecclesiastes 7: 1
"...in all things showing yourself to be a pattern
of good works; in doctrine showing integrity, rever-
ence, incorruptibility..." Titus 2:7

As a Godly man it is imperative that you have a good reputation before the church and the world. Not to do so has significantly detrimental affects on fellow Christians and unbelievers. Growing up in a small country church it was preached that it was not important what people said about me, because as a Christian I would not be respected nor liked. I understand now that as a Christian I will experience persecution. But it should be for Jesus' sake, not because I am a dishonest, untrustworthy fellow. "A good name" is seldom recognized or valued as it used to be. But you should have a good name which flows from your character or who you are when no one is looking. "...showing yourself a pattern if good works" is not something you can pretend to do over a lifetime. It will be difficult to maintain a façade of goodness for very long. It is that "pattern" that demonstrates your integrity. Are you a genuinely Godly man who lives a life of "incorruptibility"? As you pray, ask God to cleanse your heart and mind so that your will display on the outside what is on the inside.

December 12
<u>Your Wife's Role</u>

"Your wife shall be like a fruitful vine In the very heart of your house, Your children like olive plants All around your table." Psalm 128:3 "Now to the married I command, yet not I but the Lord: A wife is not to depart from her husband. But even if she does depart, let her remain unmarried or be reconciled to her husband. And a husband is not to divorce his wife." I Corinthians 7:10-11

To write about the role of wives can put a man on a slippery slope! But God's written word offers sound principles to follow. Though our culture outside and inside of the church has moved away from the strict instructions given my Paul in Ephesians and in I Corinthians, the scriptures clearly command wives to submit to their husband's authority and to respect him. Paul taught husbands to love their wives as Christ loves the Church and gave Himself for it. Peter exhorted wives to win their unbelieving husbands by their chaste conduct and to let their "adornment...be the hidden person of the heart, with incorruptible beauty of a gentle and quiet spirit, which is very special in the sight of God." (I Peter 3:1, 3 & 4) Paul teaches wives to give "due affection" to her husband and not to deprive each other from sexual intimacy except under special circumstances. (I Corinthians 7:5) In the Old Testament wives were expected be like "a fruitful vine" and bear children. I believe a husband must love, show respect and offer intimacy to his wife and the wife should respond and by showing him respect and lavishing him with her love.

December 13
Helping Victims of Disasters

"For You have been a strength to the poor, A strength to the needy in his distress, a refuge from the storm, a shade from the heat; for the blast of the terrible ones is as a storm against the wall." Isaiah 25:4

"Blessed be the God and Father of our Lord Jesus Christ, the Father of mercies and God of all comfort, who comforts us in all our tribulation, that we may be able to comfort those who are in any trouble, with the comfort with which we ourselves are comforted by God." 2 Corinthians 1:3-4

The aerial attacks on several locations on September 11, 2001 and the flooding of New Orleans when Hurricane Katrina's waters broke through the levies in 2005 were among the worst disasters faced by our nation. Following both disasters, Americans were quick to come to the aid of those in need. Congregations all over the nation offered prayers of mercy, deliverance and help for the thousands of victims and their families. Truck loads of food, clothing, medical supplies, blankets and care packages drove into New York City and into New Orleans as soon as the debris was cleared enough. In both cases, public safety personnel from other states voluntarily went into these areas of devastation to protect and assist victims. Perhaps you were among those who went to help or sent necessities for the victims. Remember the 5,000 hungry folks who had followed Jesus as he went about preaching? He had compassion on them and fed them. You may have opportunities to help in disaster close to home. Ask God to give you a heart for others and demonstrate the love of Christ.

December 14
A Few Good Men

"Then the LORD said to Gideon, 'By the three hundred men who lapped I will save you, and deliver the Midianites into your hand. Let all the other people go, every man to his place.' "Judges 7:7

"Finally, my brethren, be strong in the Lord and in the power of His might." Ephesians 6:10

Not many years ago the United States Marine Corp used the slogan "A Few Good Men" to attract recruits into their ranks. The idea was to challenges young men to become part of an elite, masculine organization. What the church and the world needs today are a few good men who have crucified their will, their confidence in themselves and have become dependent on God for their masculinity. Brave men of the Bible were always reliant on God for their strength, for their leadership and for their victories. To be in the company of a few good men you need not have tattoos on your forearms, ride a Harley or talk like John Wayne. But you must be strong, courageous and decisive. Real Godly men are empowered with those traits by allowing God to be their source of power. Gordon Dalbey writes: "Our modern temples of humanly defined manhood must fall. Everything on which we base our manhood, besides God, must be taken from us;" (9) Will you become among the elite few good men of God? Are you willing to yield your strong-headed will to God's will and allow His strength to make you a real Godly man?

December 15
When Your Child Has Cancer

"Lord, have mercy on my son, for he is an epileptic and suffers severely; for he often falls into the fire and often into the water. So I brought him to Your disciples, but they could not cure him." Matthew 17:15-16

"Now therefore, let not my lord the king take the thing to his heart, to think that all the king's sons are dead. For only Amnon is dead." 2 Samuel 13:33

Perhaps you have had a son or daughter who was diagnosed with cancer. Maybe you've lost a child to this disease. Your mind becomes a roller coaster of emotions…one day angry, another day doubting and some days believing God will intervene. I have a brother in Christ with whom I served with each Sunday as a worship greeter. Shock and questions raced through his mind when the physicians advised him and his wife that their 13-year old son, John, had cancer and it was serious. On my few visits John seemed upbeat. But I could see the worry and stress on Mom and Dad. I asked my Godly brother to share some thoughts and feelings that he experienced in those early days. He writes: "I stayed numb for a few weeks, didn't eat much or if any. Didn't sleep, thought it was all a nightmare and I would wake up and realize it was all a bad dream." He used the terms "confused" and "frustrated". He asked "why?" and blamed himself for some past failure. Despite these usual feelings he had this to say: "We believed that God had plan for John and us. We also believed God's promises…"

December 16
Jesus Often Withdrew Himself

"So He Himself often withdrew into the wilderness and prayed." Luke 5:16
"Coming out, He went to the Mount of Olives, as He was accustomed, and His disciples also followed Him." Luke 22:39
And He was withdrawn from them about a stone's throw, and He knelt down and prayed, Luke 22:41

Though He was the Son of God, He became "flesh and dwelt among us". Jesus was tempted, He became weary and He bled… like you. Jesus required communications with the Father and needed God's strength to stay the course. Jesus walked a lot sharing the gospel and meeting the needs of as many people as possible. The sand, the wind and the harsh elements must have taken a toll on Him. He needed an occasionally retreat from the crowds and the harsh climate and get alone with the Father. He prayed. John Eldredge writes: "…a man needs to get away from the noise and the distraction of his daily life for time with his own soul." (10) No matter your age, you should be growing and learning. You should delve into God's word and listen to the Holy Spirit as He leads you into deeper truths. You can't do so on the run. "Our whole journey into authentic masculinity centers around those cool-of-the-day talks with God. Ask Him, "What are You teaching me here, God? What are you asking me to do…or let go of?" (11) Set aside a regular time to be alone with God…and pray.

December 17
Be Vigilant

"Be sober, be vigilant; because your adversary the devil walks about like a roaring lion, seeking whom he may devour." 1 Peter 5:8
"For indeed, when we came to Macedonia, our bodies had no rest, but we were troubled on every side. Outside were conflicts, inside were fears." 2 Corinthians 7:5

I believe many Christian men whose lives are filled with work, family, activities and stress often forget that they are in a spiritual warfare. We have talked about spiritual warfare throughout this year. But do you find yourself so focused on the natural world and your obsession of the things of this world that you drift along without noticing how far from the shore you've gone? the conditions of the spiritual waters and weather encroaching in on you? Do you live day after day in the business of surviving and keeping afloat in this natural world that you become unaware that you are still in a spiritual warfare and your enemy is strategically laying traps for you? I believe we all become complacent, thus giving Satan opportunities to set us up for defeat. To make matters worse these days and weeks before Christmas can cause us to retreat from the battle to do "Christmas things". Stop! Be reminded that your enemy is creeping about sizing you up and seeking how he might devour you, neutralizing you for his advantage. Be sober, be vigilant! Spend more time alone and allow the Holy Spirit to awaken your spiritual sight so that you will not be caught off guard.

December 18
<u>Beside Still Waters</u>

"Then He arose and rebuked the wind, and said to the sea, 'Peace, be still!' And the wind ceased and there was a great calm." Mark 4:39
"He leads me beside the still waters" Psalm 23:2

Still waters conjure different pictures in our minds. Contemplate yours. I see waters close to the shore where the water is still, separated from the stream's rush or rippling. The long branches of the weeping willow hang over the still water creating a shady cool spot. In the twenty-third Psalm David speaks of the still waters. Perhaps as a shepherd boy he led his sheep there so they could drink the cool still water. Do you need still waters? Do you need a refrain from your hectic days and late nights? God provides still waters for you…a time of refreshing for you if only you will come and relax in His presence. This might be a literal place familiar to you where you find quietness and reassurance. This might be a spiritual place and time where you stop your fast-paced living and allow the Holy Spirit to calm your heart and mind. It may be at night before sleep comes that you experience God's still waters of refreshing. In *Psalm 121:3 & 4* the Psalmist writes: "He who keeps you will not slumber. Behold, He who keeps Israel shall neither slumber nor sleep." Ask Him for still waters.

December 19
<u>The Fruit of the Spirit in Your Life</u>

"But the fruit of the Spirit is love, joy, peace, long-suffering, kindness, goodness, faithfulness, gentleness, self-control. Against such there is no law."
Galatians 5:22-23

Paul lay out explicitly the "fruit" of the Spirit which followed his list of the "works" of the flesh. He said that these 'are contrary to one another and you cannot do the things what you wish." {Please read the fifth chapter of Galatians.} The nine attributes of the "fruit" are those which are produced and are evident in the life of a believer when he is walking in and are led by the Holy Spirit. While every believer receives the Holy Spirit when he accepts Jesus Christ as his Lord and Savior, not every believer continues to be filled with the Spirit. Some believers permit carnality to seep into their lives, thus some "works" of the flesh is produced in their lives. A believer should seek to stay filled with the Holy Spirit. Charles Stanley writes: "Do you have desire today to love God and to love others more {the first of the "fruit" listed}, with a purer heart and mind, and with greater compassion and expression of generosity? Ask the Holy Spirit to help you reach your full potential to love" The fruit of the Spirit in your life is evidence that you are a Spirit-filled believer.

December 20
Keep Your Family Focused
on the Reason for the Season

"Therefore let all the house of Israel know assur-
edly that God has made this Jesus, whom you cruci-
fied, both Lord and Christ." "For this promise is to
you and to your children, and to all who are afar
off, as many as the Lord our God will call." (Acts:
2:36, 39)

Unfortunately, the true meaning and spiritual celebration
of the birth of Jesus has been overshadowed by commer-
cialism of this Holy Day. For some reason, most everyone
knows this, but most everyone still "shops 'till they drop"
and billions of dollars are spent in our country. Even among
Christians, the authentic meaning of Christmas seems to
pale and be diminished in favor of Santa Clause, purchasing
gifts and social events having nothing to do with Jesus. What
about you? What are you teaching and modeling for your
family? Does your Christmas celebration include the Advent
during each of the four weekends before Christmas? Do you
attend special church Christmas programs where your children can gain a deeper appreciation for the season? Does
your family have prayer on Christmas morning? As the
man in your family or as a young man living with parents,
it is important that you seriously focus the attention on your
family on what Christmas is really all about. You will be
passing on to another generation traditions that will keep
Christ the central meaning of Christmas.

December 21
Seasons of a Man's Life: Winter

"I have been young, and now am old; yet I have not seen the righteous forsaken, nor his descendants begging bread." Psalm 37:25 "Thus David the son of Jesse reigned over all Israel. And the period that he reigned over Israel was forty years; seven years he reigned in Hebron, and thirty-three years he reigned in Jerusalem. So he died in a good old age, full of days and riches and honor; and Solomon his son reigned in his place." 1 Chronicles 29:26-28

Today, give or take a day, marks the first day of winter. In most part of North America cold temperatures have begun to creep into the South with a few moderately cold days and light freezing. Snow covers much of the Northeast and West. There's an old saying, "It may be white on the roof, but there's still fire in the stove". In her book, *"Understanding Men's Passages"*, Anthropologist Gail Sheehy writes: "The sixties used to mark the beginning of a slow fade to retirement and hobbies and a creeping sense of uselessness. But the new story for an American man who reaches age 65 today…is a life expectancy that has advanced to 81." (13) One chapter is entitled, "Passage to the Age of Integrity". In it she makes an interesting, but a significant statement about men in their later years. She writes: "Most men want to feel before they die that they have made a difference …And the years after retirement from one's primary career offer a great opportunity to leave things a little better than you found them." (14) To the man of God: He has not retired you. He has a meaningful purpose for you. Embrace it.

December 22
Gifts of Christmas

"For by grace have you been saved through faith, and that not of yourselves; it is the gift of God." Ephesians 2:8
"Therefore He says: 'When He ascended on high, He led captivity captive, and gave gifts to men'." Ephesians 4:8

You know that Jesus is the real Gift of Christmas sent from God to become our Savior. However, as a result of this Gift of God, you are blessed with other gifts from Him through His Holy Spirit. In the twelfth chapter of I Corinthians, Paul clarifies the various gifts which come from the Holy Spirit. They include wisdom, knowledge, healings, prophesy, discernment, different kinds of tongues, and the interpretation of tongues. Not every individual has all the gifts, but as a body, one part serves one function and another part serves another function in the body of Christ, the church. In Romans, Chapter 12, Paul lists others spiritual gifts such as ministry, encouragement, giving, leading, and mercy. In I Corinthians, the thirteenth Chapter Paul adds faith, hope, and love. But he is very clear that the greatest of these is love. As a Christian man, you are "graced" with one or more spiritual gifts and God wants you to use them for His glory and honor. Many men are already serving as leaders, as encouragers, as wise counselors, and with others gifts of the Spirit. As you pray today, ask Him to show you your spiritual giftedness.

December 23
It Will Come to Pass: Jesus' First Coming Foretold

"For unto us a Child is born, Unto us a Son is given; And the government will be upon His shoulder. And His name will be called Wonderful, Counselor. Everlasting Father, Prince of Peace." Isaiah 9: 6

As we and our families prepare to celebrate the birth of our Lord, it will be good to remember that God did not decide at the last minute to send His Son as a sacrifice for sin. We know that His plan for man was botched with the sin of Adam and Eve. It was then in Genesis 3:15 that God first predicted the birth and crucifixion of Christ. For thousands of years God dealt with mankind with the sin and disobedience to His law. Time and time again man rejected God. Despite his attempts, man simply could not pay the penalty of sin and become free of its enslavement. We also know that about 800 years before Christ's birth the prophet Isaiah foretold of the only way man could be set free from sin – through God's sacrificing His only Son's life on the cross. Not only should you be grateful for God's plan for salvation, you should try to fathom the almighty omniscience of your God who had a plan for you long, long ago. As you pray, praise Him for His greatness and His awesome love that He has demonstrated for you.

December 24
It Came to Pass: Mary's Faith

"Then the angel said to her, 'Do not be afraid, Mary, for you have found favor with God and bring forth a Son, and shall call His name Jesus. He will be great, and will be called the Son of the Highest';" Luke 1:31-32

In today's scripture is a description of the event in which an angel appeared to Mary and announced that she would conceive a Son. Obviously, Mary was more than a little confused and questioned the angel how this could be since she was still a virgin. The angel answered her and said, "The Holy Spirit will come upon you, and the power of the Highest will overshadow you; therefore that Holy One which is to be born will be called the Son of God." (Luke 1:35) As did Sarah thousands of years earlier, Mary accepted God's word by faith. At the ripe old age of ninety Sarah was told by God that she would bear a son: "By faith Sarah herself also received strength to conceive seed, and she bore a child when she was past the age, because she judged Him faithful who had promised." (Hebrews 11:11) Mary's faith carried her through public speculation and ridicule that she had conceived out of wedlock. Mary's faith fulfilled Isaiah's prophesy. Mary's faith kept her close to her Son, even to His crucifixion. Pray today that when God speaks, you will not question Him despite the odds.

December 25
Great Joy, Our Savior is Born!

"And she brought forth her first-born Son, and wrapped Him is swaddling cloths, and laid Him in a manger..." Luke 2:7
"Then the angle of the Lord said to them, 'Do not be afraid, for behold, I bring you good tidings of great joy which will be to all people. For there is born to you this day in the city of David a Savior, who is Christ the Lord'." Luke 2:10-11

Great joy... As part of God's plan since the beginning of time and exactly on His eternal time table this was the event that the prophets of old foretold. It was the event that fulfilled God's plan to send His only Son who would ultimately pay the price for our sins. This day is a day of "Great Joy" for you and Christians around the world. As a man of God, a husband, a father or a son, take time to gather together with friends and family and thank God for sending His Son, for His earthly life and His ultimate sacrifice. If you man alone as a soldier, an employee at work, a prisoner, a missionary, or living alone, rejoice with great joy that Jesus was born for you. Though you may be blessed with gifts under a tree, remember the greatest Gift of all is Jesus.

December 26
Loneliness

"But Peter said, 'Man, I do not know what you are saying!' Immediately, while he was speaking, the rooster crowed. And the Lord turned and looked at Peter." Luke 22:60-61
"...for Demas has forsaken me, having loved this present world, and has departed for Thessalonica – Crescens for Galatia, Titus for Dalmatia. Only Luke is with me." II Timothy 4:10-11

Loneliness can be one of the most painful emotions a person can experience. You have, no doubt, experienced loneliness to some degree. Real loneliness is a feeling of rejection and ostracism. Loneliness can be experienced in a crowd. That can be emotionally crippling as you see others caring and loving one another. Jesus experienced loneliness. Following his arrest, all of his disciples scattered and his loved ones kept their distance. In our first verse we find Jesus in the High Priest's house under arrest. Though Jesus predicted that Peter would deny Him, He surely felt the pain of betrayal and loneliness when Peter vehemently denied knowing Him. After having "finished the course" Paul was in a cold, damp prison alone awaiting his execution. Though Luke was near, Paul no doubt felt the depths of loneliness as former friends left him in prison. Underneath Jesus' and Paul's loneliness was the antidote – hope. Some ten years earlier Paul declared, "Now hope does not disappoint." (Romans 5:5) If you find yourself in the quagmire of loneliness "lay hold of the hope" set before you. Your hope is in the love God has for you and His promise never to forsake you.

December 27
<u>Your Stronghold</u>

"For the weapons of our warfare are not carnal but mighty in God for pulling down strongholds," 2 Corinthians 10:4
"For this is the will of God, your sanctification: that you should abstain from sexual immorality; that each of you should know how to possess his own vessel in sanctification and honor," 1 Thessalonians 4:3-4

What almost continuously tempts you, torments you, inflicts anxiety or attacks your mind? There is something with which you have struggled for most of your life. I believe that every Godly man has a stronghold in his life. Some call them giants or beasts. It may be an addiction to alcohol, gambling, drugs, pornography, lust, homosexuality, child abuse, pedophilia, spousal abuse or any number of fetishes. Perhaps your stronghold does not keep you from serving the Lord, but hinders your freedom and joy in Christ. You may you appear to everyone as perfectly fine and happy. Yet, deep inside you a battle rages. In his book, *"Facing Giants"*, Max Lucado writes: "Where does Satan have a stronghold within you? Ahh, there is the fitting word – *stronghold:* a fortress, citadel, thick walls, tall gates. It's as if the devil staked a claim on one weakness and constructed a rampart around it. Strongholds: old, difficult, discouraging challenges." (15) What do you do? Attack your stronghold! Begin with fervent prayer - daily. Keep your mind on God. Change your music, your friends or anything which distracts you from God. Seek an accountability partner. Go to a Christian counselor. And never, never give up!

December 28
Reflections On This Year

"Remember His marvelous works which He has done, His wonders, and the judgments of His mouth..." I Chronicles 16:12
"You have hedged me behind and before, and laid Your hand upon me. Such knowledge is too wonderful for me: it is high, I cannot attain it." Psalm 139:4, 6

As the next year approaches in just a few days, you will probably be anticipating a New Year's celebration, making a New Year's resolution and, perhaps, seeking how you can become a more dedicated man of God. As this year nears its end, it is important to reflect on your life and what good things God has provided. If you're reading this it is an indication that you are an authentic Godly man who is interested in spiritual truths. Today, focus your thoughts on all of the blessings of this year. Though, it would be impossible to recall everything "good and perfect gift". But consider some highlights along your Christian journey. Has God sustained your health this year? Has He provided for you and your family? Has the Holy Spirit helped you grow in the Lord? Have you influenced someone else by living a Godly lifestyle or by ministering to a need? Has God intervened when you felt no hope and brought joy and peace? Has your wife, children and/or fellow Christians expressed their love for you? Has God strengthened your faith through some difficult personal circumstance? Has He kept you from harm? Hasn't God been good?

December 29
God's Strength is Sufficient

"But the Lord stood with me and strengthened me, so that the message might be preached fully through me, and that all the Gentiles might hear. Also I was delivered out of the mouth of the lion." 2 Timothy 4:17

"...that He would grant you, according to the riches of His glory, to be strengthened with might through His Spirit in the inner man," Ephesians 3:16

God's strength will continue to sustain you and uphold you through whatever comes at you in life. Yes, you will face adversity, illness, loss, hopelessness and death. But your God and Savior Jesus Christ will be with you through it all. Never worry about the future. As a believer in the Almighty Creator, the Savior of all mankind, you must know beyond a shadow of doubt that you belong to Him and He cares about you. In Isaiah 60:2 God asks this rhetorical question to Israel: "Is my hand shortened that I cannot redeem? Or have I no power to deliver?" Then in Isaiah 59:19 Isaiah declares to the people of Israel: "When the enemy comes in like a flood, the Spirit of the Lord will lift up a standard against him." Never allow fear to make you doubt God's strength. God is sufficient for you in whatever your circumstance you may face. No matter what you have done, no matter what a mess you're in and no matter who is your adversary, God is your strength! He will never leave you or forsake you. Trust Him with a heart full of assurance and a mind at peace.

December 30
<u>Time to Go Up to the Mountain</u>

"And Elijah went up to the top of Carmel;...and he said to his servant 'Go up now, look toward the sea'. So he went up and looked and said 'There is nothing'...the seventh time, that he said, 'there is a cloud, as small as a man's hand rising out of the sea!' So he {Elijah} said 'Go up, say to Ahab, 'Prepare your chariot, and go down before the rain stops you.'" I Kings 19:43-44

Have you experienced a mountain-top experience with God lately? We talk about the valleys we go through, the wilderness and the strongholds. But God desires that we have mountain-top experiences - times when the Holy Spirit anoints you with Himself so that you experience His awe-inspiring presence. God has blessed me with a few my life. They were times that God enveloped in His Spirit and gave me an extra-ordinary anointed blessing. They're difficult to describe and difficult to explain the "why". But following these spiritual encounters with God your faith is strengthened. You're overflowing with the joy of the Lord. These times of blessings have always "charged my battery" and refreshed my soul, heart and mind. Elijah had that mountain-top experience both literally and spiritually when he prayed for rain and God had it on its way. Moses was on a mountain where God allowed him to see the Promised Land. You will come down from the mountain, but refreshed with the Spirit of God. Continue to draw nearer to God and walk in the Spirit. I pray you will the mountain-top blessing.

December 31
<u>Prepare for the New Year</u>

"Search me, O God, and know my heart; try me, and know my anxieties. Psalm 139:23
"...but, speaking the truth in love, may grow up in all things into Him who is the head-Christ."
Ephesians 4:15

Tomorrow will mark the beginning of a new calendar year. Your spiritual race continues. No doubt you've been through some difficult times this year. You will face tough times in the coming year. It seems fitting before you wake tomorrow morning to ask God to search your heart and mind and to prepare you spiritually to face all the tomorrows which you will live, whether you're in the springtime of life or winter. In Psalm 139 David begins it with, "O Lord, you have searched me and known me." In verse 23 David asks God, "Search me and know my heart..." David, "a man after God's own heart" describes in great detail how intricately God knows him, yet he seeks God to search his heart for "any wicked way" in him. There is a timeless hymn, "Cleanse Me", which includes these words: "Lord, take my life, and make it wholly Thine; Fill my poor spirit with Thy great love divine; Take all my will, my passion, self and pride; I now surrender, Lord, in me abide." (16) Today, ask God to examine your heart and your thoughts and make you wholly His throughout the new year.

REFERENCES NOTES FOR DECEMBER

1. Patrick A. Means, "Men's Secret Wars" (Fleming H. Revell, A Division of Baker Book House, Grand Rapids, Michigan) 1999, p.14
2. Henry and Tom Blackaby, "The Man God Uses" (Broadman & Holman Publishers, Nashville, Tennessee) 1999, p. 18
3. Winston Churchill, "The Wit & Wisdom of Winston Churchill" (Harper Perennial, A Division of HarperCollins Publishers, New York, New York) 1994 p. 23
4. John C. Maxwell, "The 21 Indispensable Qualities of A Leader" (Thomas Nelson Publishers, Nashville, Tennessee) 1999 p. xi
5. Fanny J. Crosby, "I Am Thine, O Lord" (Word Music, Waco Texas) 1986 p. 358
6. Larry Crabb, "Shattered Dreams" (Water Brook Press, Colorado Springs, Colorado) 2001, p. 143
7. David Limbaugh, "Persecution" (Regnery Publishing, Inc., An Eagle Publishing Company, Washington, D.C.) 2003 p. x
8. Ann Coulter, "Godless" (Crown Publishing Group, New York) 2006 p. 2
9. Gordon Dalbey, "Healing the Masculine Soul" (W Publishing Group, a Division of Thomas Nelson, Nashville, Tennessee) 2000 p. 10
10. John Eldredge, "Wild at Heart" (Thomas Nelson Publishers, Nashville, Tennessee) 2001 p. 207
11. Ibid.p. 215 & 216
12. Charles F. Stanley, "Living in the Power of the Holy Spirit" (Nelson Books, a division of Thomas Nelson Publishers, Nashville, Tennessee) 2005 p. 42
13. Gail Sheehy, "Understanding Men's Passages" (Random House, New York) 1998 p. 215

14. Ibid, p. 221
15. Max Lucado, "Facing Your Giants" (W Publishing Company, A Division of Thomas Nelson, Nashville, Tennessee) 2006 p. 102 & 103
16. J. Edwin Orr, "Cleanse Me" (Pathway Press, Cleveland, Tennessee) p. 277

CPSIA information can be obtained at www.ICGtesting.com
Printed in the USA
LVOW06s2213161213

365646LV00001B/76/A

9 781602 669048